Percival Goodman

architect · planner · teacher · painter

Percival Goodman
architect · planner · teacher · painter

Edited by Kimberly J. Elman and Angela Giral

Miriam and Ira D. Wallach Art Gallery

Columbia University in the City of New York

2001

This publication is issued in conjunction with the exhibition
Percival Goodman: Architect · Planner · Teacher · Painter
held at the Miriam and Ira D. Wallach Art Gallery, Columbia University
in the City of New York, 14 February to 31 March 2001.
Unless otherwise specified, all works are from the collection of
the Avery Architectural and Fine Arts Library, Columbia University.

The exhibition and publication have been made possible, in part, with the
support of Furthermore. . . a publication project of the J. M. Kaplan Fund,
the Graham Foundation, the National Endowment for the Arts,
and an endowment established by Miriam and Ira D. Wallach.

The articles by Percival and Paul Goodman (pp. 62–71) are reprinted from
Commentary, June 1947, January 1949, by permission; all rights reserved.

Published by the Miriam and Ira D. Wallach Art Gallery, Columbia University in
the City of New York

Copyright ©2000 The Trustees of Columbia University in the City of New York
All rights reserved. No part of this publication may be reproduced or transmitted in any form or by any means, electronic or mechanical, including photocopying, recording, or information storage or retrieval system, without permission in writing from the publisher.

Library of Congress Control Number: 00-136691

ISBN 1-884919-09-X

Distributed by Princeton Architectural Press, New York

Frontispiece: Goodman with a cigarette at drawing board, circa 1945 (cat. 56)

Contents

Preface *Angela Giral*   vii

The Early Years Kenneth Frampton   1

The Goodman Brothers and *Communitas* Taylor Stoehr   17

Synagogue Architecture

• The Quest for Community: Percival Goodman and the Design of the
    Modern American Synagogue *Kimberly J. Elman*   53
• Articles from *Commentary* by Percival and Paul Goodman   62
• Portfolio of Synagogues   72
• A Client's Perspective *Rabbi Martin Freedman*   107

Utopian Freedom: Percival Goodman's Social Thought Robert Fishman   111

The Teacher: Recollections by Former Students and Colleagues
Compiled and edited by Raymond Lifchez and Chiu-Hwa Wang

• Introduction   127
• An Original Mind and a Generous Heart *Chiu-Hwa Wang*   130
• Percival Goodman as Teacher *Romaldo Giurgola*   131
• Planter of Doubts, Seeker of Truth *Val Michelson*   134
• A Tribute to the Man, the Artist, and the Teacher *Costa N. Decavalla*   135
• Teacher, Colleague, Friend *Raymond Lifchez*   137
• Reminiscences of Percival Goodman *Rudolf Guyer*   139
• Percival Goodman *Peter Eisenman*   141
• A Halcyon Year, *N. Michael McKinnell*   142
• A Pivotal Mentor *Joshua Jih Pan*   143
• Goodman and Utopia *Suzanne O'Keefe*   146
• A Symbol of Urban Design *Patrick Ping-tze Too*   147

A Memoir Naomi Goodman   153

List of Projects, 1925–1989   183

Contributors   193

Checklist of the Exhibition   197

Preface

The late nineteen sixties were a time of social unrest throughout the land. Architecture was drifting from the fine arts to the social sciences, and there was a rush to rename institutions in order to reflect these new concerns. At Princeton University, the School of Architecture petitioned the library administration for its own departmental library, troubled by the reluctance of the Fine Arts Library to purchase books on sociology, economics, psychology, and visual perception. My eagerness to jump into this situation helped to create the Urban and Environmental Studies Library and launched my career as an architectural librarian. The name of the library was carefully chosen, following the lead of the University of California at Berkeley, which had turned its architecture school into the College of Environmental Design. With renewed interest in architecture, a field I had been dissuaded from pursuing in adolescence, I audited many courses and read everything that was put on reserve. *Communitas,* though written in 1947, was much in demand, and it opened my eyes, along with those of younger students, to the social role of architecture, deepening my understanding of the direction into which both the school and the discipline were moving.

Many years later, shortly after my arrival at Avery Library, I read a piece in the *New York Times* by Paul Goldberger in honor of Percival Goodman's eightieth birthday. It was there that I learned that he had been a professor at Columbia University for more than twenty-five years. That same day I looked him up in the telephone directory and called him at his home to ask if he had thought about the disposition of his papers. He told me that he had already given his professional papers to the University of Wyoming, in response to a letter of request at the time he closed the office. "But wait," he said, "my wife [whose voice could be heard in the background] tells me I am leaving you my architectural library in my will." The conversation resulted in an invitation to dinner which in turn led to a warm friendship with Percy and his wife, Naomi. Percy showed me the delightful drawings that he had been doing since retirement and I expressed my wish that they would come to Avery.

"After teaching a course on utopias for many years," he said, "and asking my students to turn their readings into actual designs, I thought it was only fair that I should try my hand at it." He showed me the drawings for "An Illustrated Guide to Utopias: An Architect's Diary," a book that has never been published. I also saw then his Postmodern series, his illustrations for the *Herodium* according to Josephus, and other drawings displaying his boundless imagination and his extraordinary skills with pen and pencil.

Underneath the panache that helped him to win the Paris Prize, Percy was always concerned with social justice; he firmly believed in the power of design to improve human living conditions. While he was designing stylish apartments and store interiors for wealthy clients, he was also working on proposals for new forms of living and housing in New York City; and he brought to his synagogue designs concerns over how architecture could both represent and shape the tenets and aspirations of the Jewish faith in the postwar years. Yet there is always a delightfully sardonic edge to his most earnest proposals. I remember my pleasure in reading his irreverent critiques of the iconic texts that shared space with *Communitas* on course reading lists. The library that he bequeathed to Avery included now-rare first editions of the works of Frank Lloyd Wright and Le Corbusier, as well as a signed copy of Buckminster Fuller's *Nine Chains to the Moon*.

When the time came to prepare this book and exhibition, I turned to the professor on whose reading list I first encountered *Communitas*, Kenneth Frampton. As luck would have it, one of his outstanding graduate students, Kimberly Elman, grew up in Massachusetts and attended Temple Beth-El, designed by Percy. It is thanks to Kim's enthusiasm and hard work that the project has come to fruition. She spent many hours in the archive making intelligent and sensitive selections that Ken Frampton and I merely had to vet. She rightly deserves the lion's share of the credit.

The organization of both this book and the exhibition is chronological as well as thematic, in accord with the course of Percy's career which has several distinctive periods. As the project list makes patently clear, his early modernist practice precedes the collaboration with his brother Paul which culminates in *Communitas*. This collaboration in turn leads to the brothers' thinking about the community aspects of Jewish life and the practice of Judaism that informs the prolific building of synagogues that follows. Thus Frampton's analysis of Percy's leftist, art deco period precedes Stoehr's consummate description of the brother's intellectual collaboration. Kimberly Elman introduces a portfolio of selected synagogue designs, her text complementing the two essays by Percival and Paul Goodman that we have chosen to reprint. Rabbi Freedman closes this period with a client's perspective.

Thirty years after the publication of *Communitas*, Percy reviews and updates its reasoning in *The Double E,* maintaining the commitment to both freedom and planning that, as Robert Fishman tells us in his own updating of Goodman's utopian predictions, is the defining essence of his social thought. Ray Lifchez and Chiu-Hwa Wang have assembled a representative gathering of tributes to the multifaceted teacher Percy was, in or out of the studio and classroom; and Naomi provides a poignant memoir of the man from the perspective of his closest partner, in work and thought as well as in life.

Some overlap and duplication is inevitable in a book like this, and we made a conscious decision not to avoid it when commissioning the individual chapters. As a result, while the same events may be mentioned in two or more of the contributions, there is in each case a different context and a different perspective, adding secondary sparkles to each facet and thus making for a more luminous whole.

Upon Percy's death I learned that in addition to his book collection he was leaving his personal papers to Avery Library. As we prepared to transfer them, Naomi thought it would be a good idea to incorporate a complete list of the professional drawings and papers that he had previously donated to the University of Wyoming. Gene M. Gressley, the director of the Archive of Contemporary History at the University of Wyoming, thought that the complete archive should be in one place and, in view of Percy's last will, offered us the drawings that they had inventoried and cared for in the intervening years. We are grateful for his wisdom and generosity.

With the support of Naomi Goodman, and under the guidance of Janet Parks, the curator of Drawings and Archives at Avery Library, Joy Kestenbaum, currently the art and architecture librarian at Pratt Institute, organized the archive and produced a detailed finding aid for the combined collection. We owe her a vote of thanks for the thoroughness of the effort. In addition to Janet Parks's diligent attention to preparing materials for the exhibition, the gracious help of her assistant, Jim Epstein, and the photographer, Dwight Primiano, is acknowledged with gratitude.

The Wallach Art Gallery in general, and this project in particular, have benefited greatly from the competent and thoughtful direction of Sarah Elliston Weiner. She in turn is supported by an expert staff composed of Jeannette Silverthorne, Lillian Vargas, and the ever-cheerful and resourceful Larry Soucy. All of them contributed in no small measure to carry both book and exhibition to a successful completion.

We are especially indebted to Miriam and Ira Wallach for their enlightened support of a gallery in which students can practice – in the best sense of the word – their skills in assembling and staging, exhibitions, and for establishing a publication fund that allows for the creation of a permanent record of these endeavors. Additional support for various stages of the project was gratefully received from the Graham Foundation, from Furthermore...a publication project of the J.M. Kaplan Fund, and from the National Endowment for the Arts.

Finally it is due to Naomi Goodman's unstinting support and gentle perseverance that the combined project of book and exhibition was kept on my radar screen and, after many years and a few false starts, has been brought to completion.

Angela Giral
Director, Avery Architectural and Fine Arts Library

Percival Goodman

architect · planner · teacher · painter

Fig. 1 Emil Schwarzhaupt apartment in the Pierre Hotel, New York, 1930s: chaise longue (cat. 3a)

Kenneth Frampton

The Early Years

Leaving home at the age of thirteen to work as an errand boy in the office of his architect uncle, Percival Goodman was perhaps more affected by circumstance than the average architectural aspirant of his generation. Yet despite his disadvantaged background and the trials of his youth, Goodman was a figure of prodigious talent and drive. It was just such innate attributes that enabled him to overcome his early handicaps and arrive at the threshold of a promising career when he returned to New York at the age of twenty-five after studying for four years at the École des Beaux-Arts in Paris.

It is not within the scope of this essay to account for the way Goodman transformed himself in the space of eight years from being his uncle's office boy to winning the much coveted Paris Prize that took him to France. Suffice it to state that at his uncle's instigation he entered the atelier of George Licht in New York's Beaux-Arts Institute of Design where he acquired the necessary skills and sophistication to compete for the prize which, after one failed attempt, he succeeded in winning, in part through additional part-time tutelage that he received from Jean Carlu of M.I.T.

Goodman came back to New York in 1929 to open an office with his American roommate in Paris, Franklin Whitman, who had returned to the city in the previous year. During the brief three years of their partnership, as the '29 crash evolved into the Depression, Whitman and Goodman were able to perfect an art deco manner which, despite Goodman's subsequent contempt for the style, was a mode in which he proved to be fairly adept. Whitman and Goodman's Sak's Fifth Avenue interior of 1930 was an accomplished up-to-the-minute exercise in deco syntax, as we may judge from the exotic furnishings and subtly contrasting light fittings deployed throughout, ranging from back-lit frosted glass screens to full-height incandescent tubes set within the re-

Fig. 2 Whitman and Goodman. Salon Moderne at Saks & Co., New York, 1930 (cat. 2b)

Fig. 3 Whitman and Goodman. Salon Moderne at Saks & Co., New York, 1930 (cat. 2a)

Fig. 4 Whitman and Goodman. Bonwit Teller, Palm Beach, 1931: shop interior

Fig. 5 Whitman and Goodman. Bacardi Bar for the Schenley Distillery Co., New York, 1930s

Fig. 6 Emil Schwarzhaupt apartment in the Pierre Hotel, New York, 1930s: bedroom (cat. 3b)

veals of richly veneered columns (figs. 2–3). To this lush mise-en-scène were added blocky armchairs in textured fabric, Ruhlmannesque side tables, polychromed rugs, circular wall mirrors, cantilevered tubular stair chairs with Delaunay-like upholstery, and even cubistic episodes vaguely reminiscent of the work of Rob Mallet-Stevens. This exercise would be repeated in a more modest key in their interior of the Bonwit Teller shop in Palm Beach of 1931 (fig. 4), when Goodman once again demonstrated his penchant for devising geometrically ingenious light fittings in the jazz moderne manner.

All in all this became Goodman's "commercial" lingua franca when he left Whitman to set up on his own account in 1933. There followed a number of elaborate deco interiors including the so-called Bacardi Bar in Schenley's Distillery (fig. 5) and the Schwarzhaupt apartment in the Pierre Hotel with its elegant, monumental, built-in, double bed veneered in exotic wood and bar with its safari wall murals (figs. 6–7). But the high point of such exercises in style, and the one that gained him both a faithful client and a colleague, was the apartment interior that he designed for Edith and Jack Straus featuring a Steinway grand piano with bespoke cabinetry by Goodman, a stylish piece of furniture that was again finished in exotic veneers (fig. 8). Velvet was the apotheosis of luxury in this period and never more so than in this apartment with its two-tone fitted carpet and full-height velvet drapes filling an entire wall. We may think of this as Goodman's "mood indigo" manner, at variance with his equally accomplished ability as an avant-garde architect during the same period.

With regard to the latter, I have in mind amongst other works the lavish modernist house that he designed for the Strauses in Mount Kisco, New York in 1933, an unrealized work for which, unfortunately, only one floor plan remains in the Goodman archive (pl. III). Equally brilliant modernist pieces would issue from his hand over the next six years, between the Straus house proposal and Goodman's second-prize-winning design for the illustrious Smithsonian Gallery competition of 1939 (figs. 9–10). The thirties in general saw Goodman in his modernist prime, designing neocubistic suburban residences for the Fox Meadows Estate in Westchester County between 1930 and 1933, a series of middle-class model houses (pls. I–II) which, had they been built, would have rivaled similar neocubistic houses then being realized by Howe and Lescaze in the States and by André Lurçat in France.

Something similar may be claimed for his Community Service Homes of 1932 where, with their ergonomic, modular floor plans (figs. 11–12), the provenance was Germany rather than

Fig. 7 Emil Schwarzhaupt apartment in the Pierre Hotel, New York, 1930s: bar (cat. 3c)

France. The perspectival renderings that survive in the archives (see figs. 13–15), one tinted in gray, red, pink, and white (pl. IV), remind one of the Dessau Bauhaus rather than the School of Paris. It is clear that the model in this instance was not only the Zeilenbau housing of the Weimar Republic but also the welfare state, "master households" as posited in Walter Gropius's book *The New Architecture and City Planning* of 1937. Thus in Goodman's accompanying description of the project we may read:

> Building A-B provides accommodations for bachelors . . . and young couples without children. . . . This building is 12 storeys high, the basement contains space for storage, heating and mechanical plants, etc. The first storey devoted to stores, entrances, managers office, laundry and service. The second storey provides restaurant . . . kitchen facilities and dining and lounging terraces. . . . On the roof; locker room, showers, etc., solarium, for men and women and a gymnasium.

Fig. 8 Edith and Jack Straus apartment, New York, 1932: velvet curtain wall behind Steinway grand piano with custom cabinetry designed by Goodman (cat. 10)

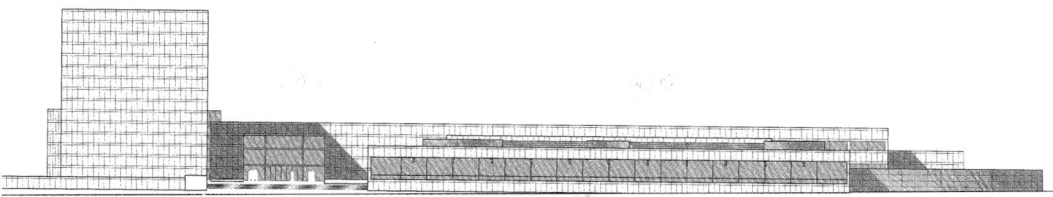

Fig. 9 Smithsonian Gallery of Art Competition, 1939: elevation (cat. 17b)

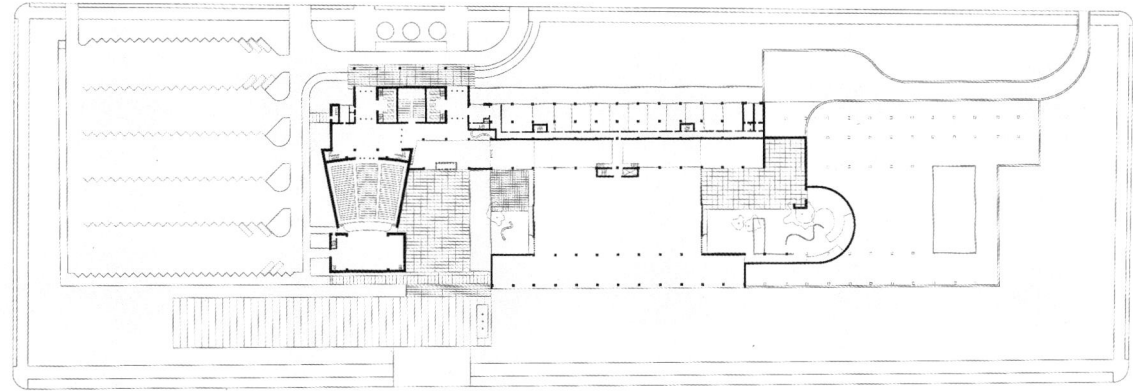

Fig. 10 Smithsonian Gallery of Art Competition, 1939: plan (cat. 17a)

> The two buildings C accommodate families of three or four persons. These are the "walk-up" type of apartment building. Each set of stairs accommodates eight families. In the stair-well a dumb-waiter is provided for the use of cleaners. . . . Each apartment is cross-ventilated; has two bedrooms with closets, bath, small hall with linen closet, living room with open terrace. A small kitchenette is provided for light cooking
>
> The Nursery building provides accommodation for 60 children. The first floor contains a large kindergarten room, dining room and kitchen, doctors and nurses office, record room, dining room and leads to the second floor which contains a solarium for infants, preparation kitchen, etc., and open terrace. In front of the building is an enclosed playground with play apparatus and wading pool.[1]

We should not underestimate the deeply felt protofeminist aspirations of this socialist program, deriving in no small measure surely from Goodman's having had a dysfunctional home life, turning in his case as in others on the exploitation of women.

It is no accident given his strong political commitments of the moment that Goodman's finest work as a modernist architect would appear in the two designs that he projected for the Soviet Union, his 1930 entry for the Palace of the Soviets competition, in which he gained fourth place, and his equally neo-Corbusian design for the Moscow Philharmonic of 1932, a concert hall combined with a hotel, of which only a pencil-and-charcoal perspective remains (fig. 16). According to the project list in the archive, this was commissioned by Albert Coates who was then serving as the conductor of the orchestra.

These Soviet proposals are remarkably tantalizing works. We know very little about their detailed organization since virtually no drawings remain save for two axonometrics and a site plan in the case of the Palace of the Soviets (fig. 17) and a single perspective of the main frontage for the Moscow Philharmonic. What does remain in the case of the former, however, is an extensive description that had been required as part of the competition submission. It is worth quoting certain salient excerpts from this since they shed light on the internal organization of the whole.

7

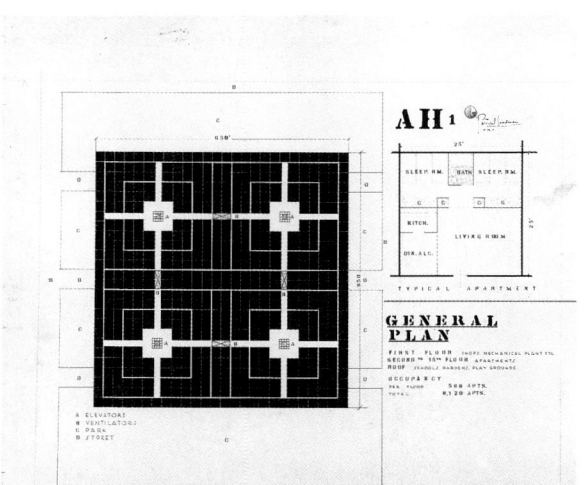

Fig. 11 Community Service Homes, 1932: general plan and typical apartment (cat. 9b)

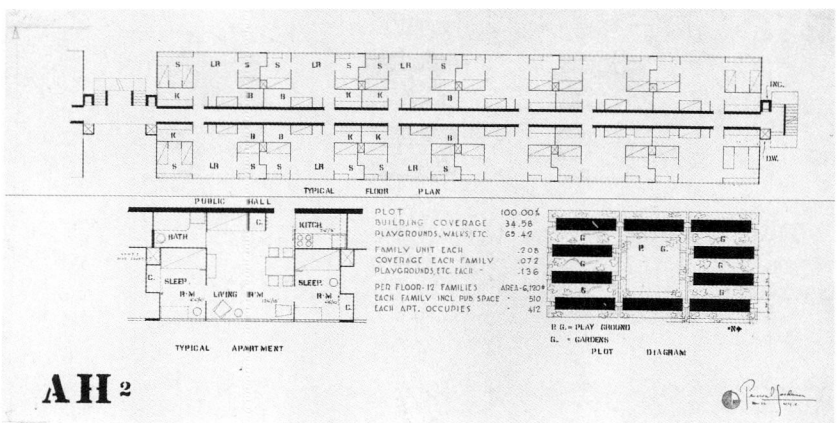

Fig. 12 Community Service Homes, 1932: typical floor plan, typical apartment, plot diagram (cat. 9c)

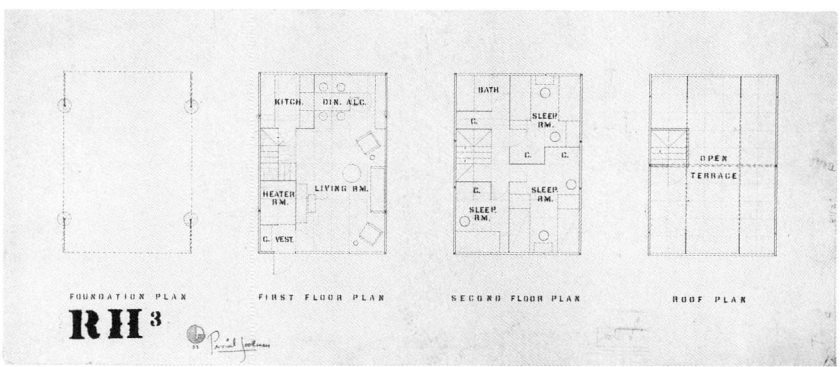

Fig. 13 Community Service Homes, 1932: foundation plan, first-floor plan, second-floor plan, roof plan (cat. 9e)

Fig. 14 Community Service Homes, 1932: perspective of row houses (cat. 9f)

Fig. 15 Apartment house (?), labeled "Shelter—Salvation Army," 1932 (cat. 11)

Fig. 16 Moscow Philharmonic Concert Hall and Hotel (unbuilt), 1932: exterior perspective (cat. 13)

> The general construction is of reinforced concrete. Steel trusses vault the two large theatres. The external aspect shows three materials: rough white concrete, polished pink granite, and glass. The pink granite, which we have been informed is an available material, contrasts with the concrete. Two whole walls of the Convention Hall and the roofs of both this and the Main Hall are of glass. There need be no artificial lighting. The Library book-tower, 73 meters high, offers a splendid observation over the City of Moscow. It is built of glass in two of its walls, of stone in the other two. The whole group, with these three bright materials alternating, will be beautiful to see from the River, from the Kremlin, or from any place.
>
> In this plan, the Palace of the Soviets has its main court opening symmetrically on the group formed by the Fine Arts Museum, the University, and the Marx Engels Institute; its library on the other side, overlooks the Moskva River, the government buildings opposite with an allowance for indoor and outdoor art-exhibitions likewise overlooking the River. The Great Hall of 15,000 people is so situated as to be accessible to traffic via three broad thorofares.[2]

He then discusses in detail the chosen shape for the auditorium . . .

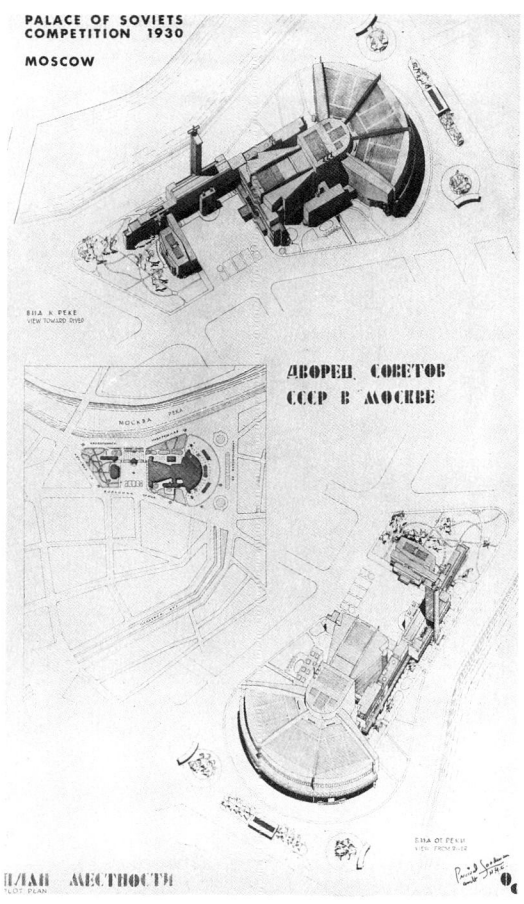

Fig. 17 Palace of the Soviets, Moscow (competition), 1930 (cat. 5a)

The most compact shape for a Hall is an oval or circle, with seats in a series of balconies and with the stage in the center. But this will not allow a lecturer to face his whole audience, and will not allow his words to be generally heard by the audience. The next most compact shape is the broad fan-shape herein adopted. Acoustically according to both Badenal and Wood, and W. Sabine the fan-shape is the most efficient. The maximum distance of any spectator from the stage is 66 meters. The volume of the Hall is 397,150 cu meters, 26.47 cu meters for each person, or well within the acoustical limit. The ceiling is designed to provide the maximum reflecting mirror. A public address, that is, can be heard in any part of the Auditorium without apparatus.

There is no balcony. This is, of course, a great acoustical advantage, since there are no "sound shadows." But most important is the grand and impressive sweep of the single bank of audience, from the stage to the roof. The sight of 15,000 people in a broad band, a sight than [sic] can be seen from any seat, is in itself more inspiring than any pageant.

The massive and pageant-like effect of the whole is augmented by the broad ramps extending upward and outward at either end of the stage and embracing the auditorium. This gives an enormous stretch of stage, immediately accessible to the audience, and along which delegations, etc., can parade. In the rear, further, these ramps, extending under the bank of seats, connect and form one continuous runway.

There is no possible shape to allow 15,000 persons to observe motion pictures on a single screen. The maximum angle of motion picture vision is from 60 to 75 degrees. In this plan, provision is made for partitioning the auditorium virtually into three motion picture theatres, with the excellent angle of 45 deg. by speedily lowering mechanically-drawn curtains at two stated intervals. These are to obviate the distraction of looking at more than one screen.[3]

... and ends with a description of the functioning of the stage.

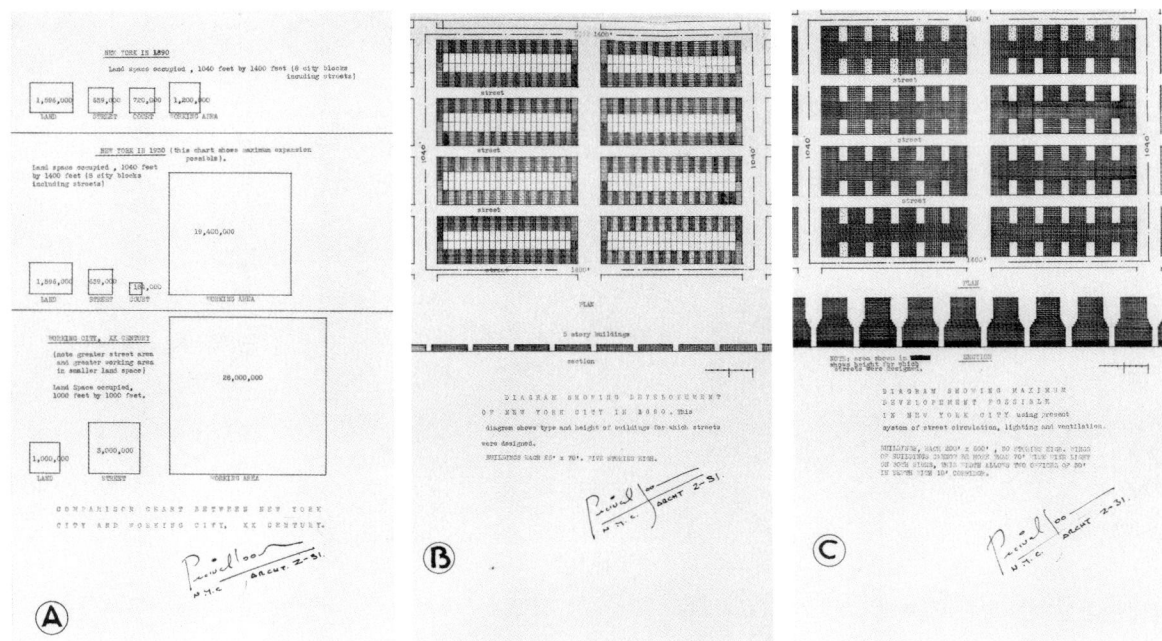

Fig. 18 Working City, comparison chart between New York City in 1890, 1930, and Working City, XX Century, 1931 (cat. 8a)

Fig. 19 Working City, diagram showing development of New York City in 1890, 1931 (cat. 8b)

Fig. 20 Working City, diagram showing maximum development possible in New York City, 1931 (cat. 8c)

> A very important feature of the submitted plan is the juxtaposition and interrelation of the two large auditoriums (of Groups A and B). There is an enormous stage in common. Obvious advantages accrue from this arrangement. The whole stage can be utilized for auditorium A, or for auditorium B. Subdivided by a soundproof wall dropped from the fly-gallery part can be used for A and part for B. Or it can serve both A and B at the same time, allowing an audience of 21,000 persons to participate in a single event. The proscenium arch in either side is 15 meters high, which is considerably beyond the average.[4]

Goodman's tactical provision of a central stage and fly tower between the two main auditoria required by the brief was matched in terms of its economic functionality by the logic that governed his organization of the seventy-eight-meter-high library book-tower. Modeled after the Sterling Library at Yale University, the tower, divided into multiple levels of varying heights according to the bibliographic classification, was served by dumb waiters bringing the books down into the reading room.

One finds Goodman's solution to the Palace of the Soviets program particularly intriguing since it compares very favorably with most of the other projects submitted for the same competition, including the renowned entry from Le Corbusier and Pierre Jeanneret. Apart from the play with countervailing axes, as evident here as in the elementarist quasi-neoclassical entry submitted by Auguste Perret, the outstanding merit of Goodman's design — and possibly the single feature that recommended it to the jurors at the time — was its dimensional modesty and its articulation of the respective elements required by the brief, achieved without diminishing the monumentality of the whole. Surprisingly enough given his affinities at the time, Goodman's all-too-objective project descriptions singularly omit any explicit reference to the May Day parade, although this event is surely provided for by raising the library on pilotis and thus allowing for the penetration of large processions and mass demonstrations into the library forefront.

More than sixty years later, we are left to surmise that the conviction of Goodman's designs for the Soviet Union derived in some measure from the passionate revolutionary views that he held at the time. This was his most leftist period, when he was close to the left wing circle The New Day, surrounding the Marxist art historian Meyer Schapiro. This is also the period when he began to have intimate intellectual discussions with his writer-brother Paul Goodman, who had recently earned his doctorate from the University of Chicago.

Whether through the influence of his brother, who had already adopted an altogether more complex sociopolitical stance, or through the harsh realities of his own experience as an architect in the Depression, one senses that in the second half of the thirties Goodman began to be disillusioned, not only with the historical promise of the Russian Revolution but also with the manifest destiny of the machine age. While he continued to practice as a modernist, his work began to lose something of its earlier conviction. This seems to be confirmed by the general lines of his second-prize entry for the Smithsonian Gallery of Art of 1939 which, while it was a rigorous modern solution, featuring large areas of uninterrupted plate glass, lacked the compositional flair and conviction of his Palace of the Soviets design. This becomes all the more evident when we compare Goodman's entry for the Smithsonian to that of the winning scheme by Eliel Saarinen, which in terms of mass patently achieves a more dynamically resolved assembly of the different components.

In his hypothetical thirty-story Working City project for New York of 1932 (figs. 18–20), Goodman's mode of beholding took a marked logistical turn, one that would color his thinking henceforth. Subject to the challenging intellectual influence of his brother with whom he renewed acquaintance in 1932, the logic of Goodman's Working City proposal seems to have derived in part from Le Corbusier's megalomanical rationalism and in part from the Yankee tinker, pragmatic promise of Buckminster Fuller's Dymaxion civilization dating from the late twenties. Goodman's eight-city-block Working City was, in effect, a gigantic multistoried factory-cum-office development, with all floors being artificially lit and ventilated.

Goodman would return to this theme in *Communitas*, written with his brother and first published in 1947. In this book the 1931 Working City project is reformulated as a twenty-story, air-conditioned cylinder projected as the center of an ideal radioconcentric city (figs. 21–22). Served by a perimeter of city streets at grade, and by truck ramps beneath together with large elevators ostensibly capable of raising vehicles through the full height of the building, this megastructure was envisaged as having an optimum productive efficiency, with freight being distributed throughout the building via elevated roadways running across the section at every sixth floor. Goodman's descriptions of this project amplify the rather schematic section and plan that were published in *Communitas*:

> The center, then, is the container of the work, the public pleasures, and the market. Its population, at the busy hours, is about two and a half-million. It is zoned as follows: The materials and products of light manufacturing come and go via the freight routes in the basement or the cargo planes that

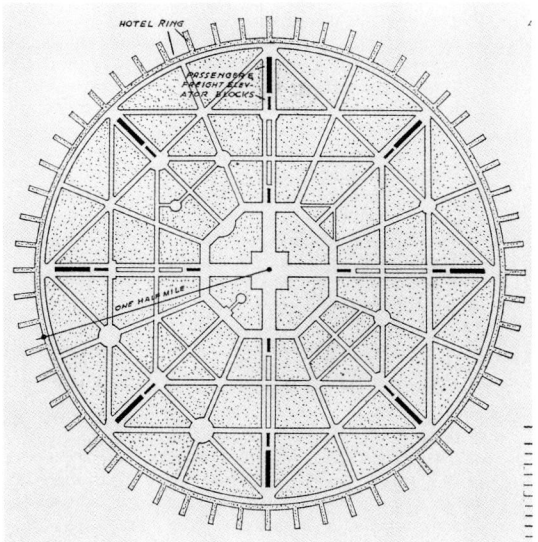

Fig. 21 Drawing from *Communitas* (1947). "Street floor in the air conditioned cylinder: one mile in diameter, air-conditioned, brightly lit, flexible space; transportation vertical, horizontal, and diagonal; continuous interior show window; the perimeter is for hotels and restaurants, air-conditioned but naturally lighted."

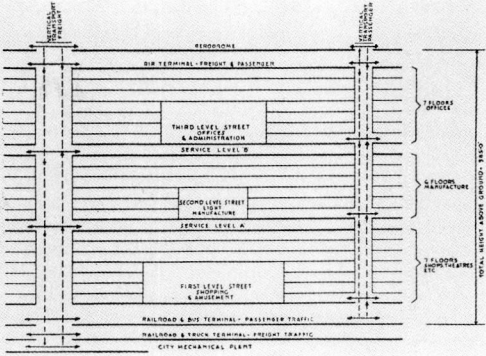

Fig. 22 Drawing from *Communitas* (1947). "A section through the air-conditioned cylinder: twenty stories of continuous rentable area without courts or yards; four stories of passenger terminals for air, railroad, and bus; one story for terminals for light manufacture, with deliveries direct to vertical transportation; the lowest level contains the cylinder service (heat, cold, etc.)."

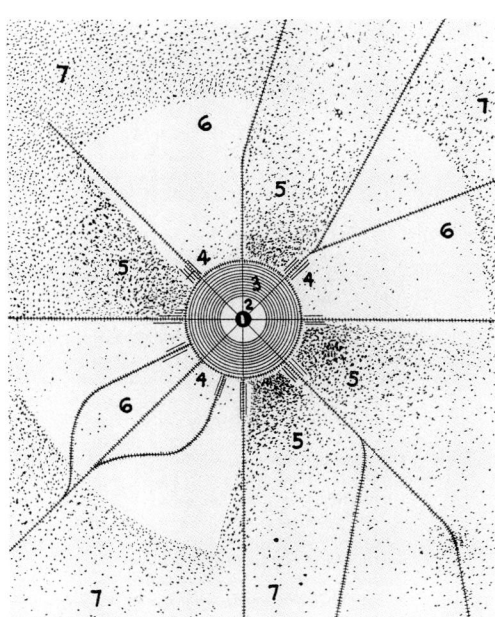

Fig. 23 Drawing from *Communitas* (1947) "Regional plan: 1, market, light industry, offices, entertainment, hotels; 2, culture, universities, museums; 3, residences, schools, hospitals; 4, heavy industry, freight airports, and terminals; 5, forest preserves; 6, agriculture; 7, vacationland."

alight on the roof; and the heart of industry is therefore about in the middle of the whole. Business and administrative offices are in the upper and outer regions. The lower stories — most immediately available to the city folk who come by bus or by car — house the stores and popular entertainments and whatever belongs to them. In the outer envelope and in projecting spokes, with natural light and a good natural view, are hotels and restaurants, opening out, on the ground floor, into the park of the university. Convenient to all is the roof airport and the basement levels of parking and transit.[5]

One cannot help being reminded by this description of the megastructural inventions then being proposed by the pioneer industrial designer Norman Bel Geddes: his mid-Atlantic floating air terminal or his rotating aerial restaurant, miraculously cantilevering out from a single column.

Apart from his commercial practice, Goodman's interest in urban design in relation to the socioeconomic organization of society came to be an ever more consuming passion throughout the late thirties and the early forties, and it is this that finally comes to fruition in the writing of *Communitas*. While Percival Goodman was certainly responsible for all the graphic illustrations in this book, it is equally clear from his independent essays written over the same period that he was responsible for most of the ideas in the text.

At one level, *Communitas* may be read as a critical assessment of the various urban planning models advanced through the latter half of the nineteenth and the first quarter of the twentieth centuries, although the appraisal is selective and certain paradigms are given much greater attention than others. Thus, Camillo Sitte's remedial strategy posited as a block-by-block infill of Vienna's orthogonal, open-ended Ringstrasse is favorably received as is Arturo Soria y Mata's *Ciudad Lineal* of virtually the same date (1888). In *Communitas*, this last, posited as a chain of suburban villas on either side of a tram line linking peripheral villages on the outskirts of Madrid, is clearly preferred to Ebenezer Howard's parallel formulation of the Anglo-Saxon garden city. Howard's corollary of the satellite city, however, is accepted by the Goodmans, particularly as this had been reinterpreted by the British Thomas Sharp in his book *Town Planning* of 1940. Although both Le Corbusier's Radiant City and Frank Lloyd Wright's Broadacre City, dating from the mid-thirties, are admired for their conceptual brilliance, they are rejected for their incapacity to create dense urban spatial episodes comparable to those of Sitte. At the same time, presumably for the application at the regional level, the Soviet version of Soria y Mata's linear city is favorably received but without acknowledging the name of its inventor, N. A. Miliutin. Similarly, without mentioning Le Corbusier's name the Goodmans consider in passing his adaptation of the linear paradigm to the triangulated road network of Europe offered as a potential alternative to the orthogonal transcontinental grid of the United States.

Understandably perhaps, nothing is so unequivocally recommended as Goodman's own proposal for a generic satellite city, circular in plan, where one of the main aims was to keep both forest and agricultural land within a range of five to twenty-five miles from the urban center (fig. 23). This model, which I have already alluded to in discussing Goodman's transformation of the Working City idea into an urban core, would consist of a series of concentric urban rings emanating from the center as follows: (1) the central cylinder seven miles across comprising shopping, light industry, offices, entertainment, and tourism, (2) a cultural ring consisting of the university quarter, together with museums, zoos, etc., (3) a residential ring, simultaneously accommodating schools and hospitals, and finally (4) an industrial ring, plus terminals and long distance airports. Immediately beyond these concentric rings lay the forest and agricultural reserves arranged in quasi-fan formation. Goodman is once again dependent on Le Corbusier for his detailed development of the city, particularly in his treatment of the residential zone that is obviously derived from the *redent* apartment blocks and elevated autoroutes of the Ville Radieuse (see fig. 129).

Communitas is at its critical best in those passages that are ultimately Kropotkinian and where, as was the case with both Wright and Howard, Kropotkin's *Fields, Factories, and Workshops* of 1898 is the ultimate referent, although Kropotkin is never cited by name. Thus renouncing his technocratic preoccupation with the Working City as a multistoried factory-cum-commercial concentration, Goodman opts in *Communitas* for small-scale productive units integrated into everyday life, where the welfare of the labor force is conceived as an end rather than a means and where the workers get to play a role not only in shaping the means of production but also in determining what is produced.

What the Goodmans had in mind was the reorganization of democracy on the basis of cooperative residential settlements integrated with composite units of agricultural production. Their aim was to assure the relative self-sufficiency and political autonomy of each cooperative, so that while each unit would contribute to the governance of the society as a whole, no single settlement could dominate any other settlement by virtue of having a monopoly over a particular economic sector. Percival Goodman would later augment this societal model by an ecological postscript added to the 1960 edition of *Communitas* and by his further elaboration of this thesis in his last book, *The Double E* of 1977, devoted to the symbiotic interplay between ecology and economics.

As the modern project under Stalin degenerated into state socialism and as the worldwide Depression helped to induce the tragedy of the Spanish Civil War, which in turn led to the Second World War and to the genocide perpetuated by the Third Reich, Percival Goodman became, however imperceptibly, more of a societal and urban critic than a socially committed architect. While he practiced more extensively than ever before, building more than fifty synagogues over the next thirty years, these works were not designed with the socialist social conviction that had informed his prewar projects in the brief decade of hope between the Crash of '29 and the outbreak of the Second World War.

Notes

1. Unpublished typescript, "Community Service Homes," 3. Department of Drawings and Archives, Avery Architectural and Fine Arts Library.

2. Unpublished typescript, "Palace of the Soviets,"1. Department of Drawings and Archives, Avery Architectural and Fine Arts Library.

3. Ibid., 3.

4. Ibid., 6.

5. Percival and Paul Goodman, *Communita*s: *Means of Livelihood and Ways of Life* (Chicago: University of Chicago Press, 1947) 72.

Fig. 24 Paul and Percival Goodman in Percy's apartment, circa 1950 (cat. 64)

Taylor Stoehr

The Goodman Brothers and *Communitas*

Born in utterly different circumstances, the Goodman brothers Paul and Percy went down divergent paths for many years, each of them mastering his own art in his own way. It was all the more fruitful a meeting of hearts and minds when the time came for them to collaborate on work that neither could have done alone.

Percival Goodman was born into a prosperous family, and for his first seven years he was pampered and indulged. His father owned an auction house and apparently reveled in material life and worldly pleasures. Dinner plates were edged in gold, and according to their cousins "they lived like kings." Percy's most vivid childhood memory was watching his father prepare a Roquefort salad dressing at their antique sideboard, not exactly royal cuisine but ceremony without a doubt.

Although less infatuated with wealth and style than her husband, who had spent some years in an orphanage, Augusta Goodman had grown up in a solid German-Jewish family that had been settled in New York City for an entire century, long enough to become thoroughly Americanized and comfortably bourgeois. Percy was her second child, born in 1904; the first was Alice, two years older. A third, Arnold, died of meningitis when he was seven — but that was later, after other traumas. In these halcyon days the children were no burden. There was money to hire domestic help, and Augusta sometimes kept shop at her husband's auction rooms, freeing him to travel and purchase estate goods for his inventory.

Everything seemed fine until 1911, the tenth year of their marriage, when her husband acquired a mistress. Augusta confronted him, with results that sound like pulp fiction: private detectives, shots in the night, divorce, abandonment. The antique dealer and his lady friend sailed

Fig. 25 Uncle Benny and Percy at the beach, 1917 (cat. 59)

for Buenos Aires, leaving Augusta with nothing but her four children, the youngest born in the midst of all this. Her parents were dead, but she had three sisters who would take care of the new baby, Paul, and her other children while she went to work. The expensive apartment was given up, the antique furniture sold, and the family slid into poverty and imagined disgrace.

The disaster fell with unequal weight on the two brothers. Suddenly bereft of father and family stability, Percy watched all the comforts of home evaporate. Paul, however, had no such happiness to lose. Born into an atmosphere of loss and bitterness, his world sometimes seemed bleak but was not filled with longing for some golden age. He grew up making do with what little there was.

Although Percy was so devastated by his loss that his memory of childhood was almost totally obliterated, ironically enough he never gave up the values that his father had modeled for him. If his ideal of life could be summed up in a word, that word might be style — high style. For him, life itself was an art, full of beauty and delight. Drawn to architecture and planning even more than painting, he was less interested in creating beautiful objects than in making beautiful living possible. And cutting across these values, his own experience of being declassed laid the groundwork for an enduring utopian zeal, imagining a beautiful world for everyone. In self-critical moments he called himself a parlor communist, and sometimes a revolutionary snob, but neither snobbishness nor politics ever got the better of his bohemian gaiety and art. One might think of him as a latter-day Louis Sullivan.

For Paul, everything was different. Although he grew up in relative poverty, he was surrounded by nurturers: his mother and his aunts, and especially his older sister, Alice, who doted on him. All this attention built a self-confidence that in later life was unshakable, except when threatened by "total institutions" like hospitals, the army, or jail — for he never learned to live with faceless authority. The missing ingredient was his father, whom he never saw, not even a photograph, and whose name no one pronounced. When he was disobedient, his aunts would threaten him with the orphanage. He consoled himself with a mysterious royal lineage; already

Fig. 26 Percy at twenty-one, in proper artistic attire. This photograph was published in the *New York Times* in 1925, when he received the Paris Prize. (cat. 61)

a storyteller, he pretended that he had been stolen away by gypsies. In any case, the prospect of being locked up by the authorities terrified him. This helps to explain why the utopian state appealed to his adult imagination so little, though he considered himself a champion of the young and dispossessed.

Because the Goodmans were poor, they did live like gypsies, constantly on the move to cheaper quarters; and as a result the boys did not make childhood friends. Paul had no doorstep community until age eight, when the family finally settled down in one spot for a few years. By this time Arnold had died, Percy had moved out, and their mother had given up her job in a department store and gone on the road as a traveling saleswoman. The aunts were now married, so Alice quit high school to take over as homemaker and, before long, breadwinner.

Paul's world went topsy-turvy. Suddenly he was a latchkey child, left with no one in the empty apartment until suppertime when Alice returned. Yet he was newly rich in friends the moment he stepped out the door, clever classmates at school and boisterous pals playing stickball in the street. He thrived on this combination and tried to recreate it the rest of his days. If the utopian state frightened and repelled him, a rough-and-tumble life of the mind, lived in bohemian comradeship, was his heart's desire. You could think of him as a modern François Villon.

Circumstances had already pushed Percy in other directions. He hated school, where he felt

Fig. 27 Rear façade of the Florida Tropical Home, Century of Progress International Exposition, Chicago, 1933 (cat. 15e)

Fig. 28 Chaise longue for the Florida Tropical Home, Century of Progress International Exposition, Chicago, 1933 (cat. 15c)

Fig. 29 Chair for the Florida Tropical Home, Century of Progress International Exposition, Chicago, 1933 (cat. 15a)

humiliated and incompetent. His hoity-toity name and spindly physique put him at the mercy of playground bullies. At home, Aunt Frances, the last to marry, was a disciplinarian who sometimes beat the children with an old bedroom slipper and once hit his big sister with fireplace tongs. Percy hated Aunt Frances even more than he hated school. By the beginning of seventh grade he had had enough. He refused to go to school, and he refused to stay home with Aunt Frances.

The impasse was solved by his uncle Benjamin Levitan, a successful architect who had bestowed jobs on various nephews and nieces. When Percy came asking for work, Uncle Ben made him an office boy, arranged for drafting lessons at Cooper Union, and promised Augusta to keep an eye on him. The stiff-necked adolescent did not live with the Levitans, who had a new baby of their own, but moved into a rooming house, paying for food and rent out of his wages of six dollars a week (fig. 25).

Half a century later when they were both famous, Paul used to brag about Percy: "My brother quit school at the seventh grade," he told the rebel students at Berkeley during the free-speech movement:

> He's now a very distinguished architect. If he had had to go to school he would *never* have become an architect. It would have ruined him. And he's a very bright guy — and a great teacher as a mat-

Fig. 30 Armchair for the Florida Tropical Home, Century of Progress International Exposition, Chicago, 1933 (cat. 15b)

Fig. 31 Interior for the Florida Tropical Home, Century of Progress International Exposition, Chicago, 1933 (cat. 15d)

ter of fact. . . . But he was just not bookish or scholarly. He would have hated it. He would have turned out to be a juvenile delinquent, and that's for sure, if he had had to go to school.

Paul's own story was completely different. "I'm a scholarly type myself," he continued. "I was a crackerjack student, a test-passer type."[1] From the beginning he had been treated as a little rabbi in the making and sent to the very best schools of the city, which in those days happened to be public and free. He raced through them on fast tracks, entering the City College of New York when he was barely sixteen.

Meanwhile, Percy had been advancing just as rapidly on his own astounding path, educating himself in a series of leaps and bounds: Uncle Ben, Cooper Union, an atelier, a drawing master who took him into his house and taught him French, a drafting table in a new and bigger architectural firm, summers at the architecture school in Fontainebleau. At sixteen he was already a "designer," making perspective drawings for a forty-story building. At twenty-one his picture (complete with comic props: smock, beret, and garret) was in the *New York Times* as winner of American architecture's most prestigious scholarship, to the École des Beaux-Arts in Paris (fig. 26).

Obviously, there were schools and teachers in his career, but Percy kept the reins in his own hands. After three months at Cooper Union he had learned what he wanted to know. A year or two with Uncle Ben was enough, and before long he had worked in three other offices. After winning the Beaux-Arts prize in 1925, Percy lived a bohemian life in Paris, soaking up modernist art and culture while acquiring old-fashioned beaux-arts facility in his new atelier.

Percy's younger brother also began to read French, in class and out, and to discover Parisian modernism at the public library. While Percy was absorbing Le Corbusier and Picasso, Paul was devouring Gide and Cocteau, *transition* magazine and its avant-garde poets. Although he scarcely knew his older brother, he was eager to claim the man-of-the-world who had never spent a day in high school.

Developing a Collaborative Method

When Percy came back to New York in 1929, he brought with him the International Style before it even had a name. He immediately found lucrative work designing interiors for department stores like Saks Fifth Avenue and I. Magnin, which gave him a temporary base for his larger ambition. Although it was the year of the stock market crash, Percy had high hopes for a career as America's Le Corbusier.

Percival Goodman's earliest houses did enjoy a certain succès d'estime: in 1931 he designed a stunning International Style residence in Long Beach, New York; in 1933 he had a model home in the Chicago Exposition (figs. 27–31); and in 1935 another showpiece was built in Hempstead, New York . All three were featured in the architectural journals, but little came of it. Credit for

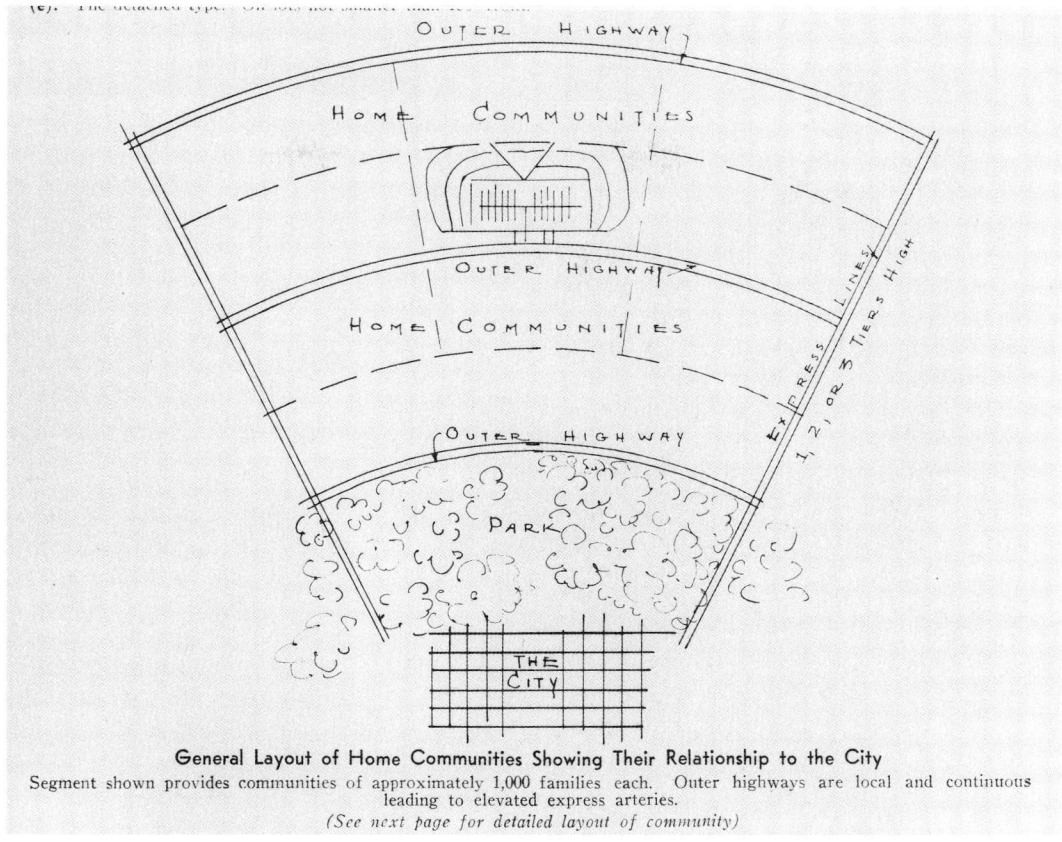

Fig. 32 Drawing for *Architectural Progress* (February 1932) (cat. 32)

the Century of Progress house went to the promoters; and the Hempstead house, a prototype for "modernity's first subdivision," had to be torn down when it was discovered that the builder had cut corners by leaving the reinforcing steel out of the concrete!

During the Depression years, famous architects without commissions turned their imaginations loose on the perfect society. Frank Lloyd Wright unveiled his Broadacre City in 1935, the same year Le Corbusier promulgated the Ville Radieuse. Percival Goodman had similar ambitions to revolutionize the world through architecture. A vigorous and combative writer, he was welcome in journals like *Architectural Progress,* where he published two essays in the early thirties, a foretaste of a book on the ideal city promised "within six months" (fig. 32).[2] He had other manuscripts in the works, "Civic Planning" and "The City Problem in the Twentieth Century." In 1934 he became the architectural editor for the avant-garde magazine *Trend;* but it folded the following year, and his literary projects were soon abandoned (pl. V). He never wrote his promised book on community planning, though many of the drawings for it were complete. Evidently he was an architect more than a writer or a publicist.[3]

Nonetheless, his ideas found their way into print by another route, for his brother *was* a writer. Their collaborations began not many months after Percy's return from Paris. Paul was still an undergraduate at City College, taking his one and only course in creative writing. As his final project, part story and part essay, Paul narrated a portentous conversation that took place in his brother's penthouse offices: pointing down at the chaotic streets below, Percy explained to him how Le Corbusier's Voisin plan for Paris could transform Manhattan. Paul responded enthusiastically and vowed to renounce forever the beaux-arts manner in which his own early fiction had

Figs. 33a–b Drawings given to Paul on his twenty-first birthday, 1932

been floundering. "Lesson" was both a true story and a first step in their lifelong collaboration. Impulse and ideas came from Percy, analysis and final formulation from Paul (fig. 33a–b).

Over the next few years Paul made himself familiar with his brother's subject matter while working to make his own art less labored and pretentious. One might say that Paul was learning both to think and to write in the International Style. In 1931, again with Percy's help, the twenty-year-old author published his first professional writing, a review of Wright's *Modern Architecture,* in a cultural quarterly of considerable prestige. Six months after that — in the wake of the Museum of Modern Art show that gave the International Style its name — he produced America's first "philosophical" critique of Le Corbusier. Soon Percy arranged for him to contribute to *trend:* "A Note on the Materials of Architecture," which began by comparing Percy to Le Corbusier and ended with Paul quoting himself as an authority. These young men were not shy.

As Paul's literary confidence grew, Percy came to rely on him to refine his own views. Each of them continued to write separately during the thirties, but their manuscripts reveal that Percy tossed off letters to the press, speeches, and manifestos for special occasions, while Paul focused on literary magazines and scholarly journals. Although the brothers did not sign anything jointly, they collaborated on six or eight essays and sketches during this period, most of them never published. Typically, Percy would set forth problems and Paul would ask searching questions; then Paul would formulate their position and Percy would critique it. Between them the brothers were inventing the method they described in *Communitas* a decade later:

> Every point was developed independently by each of the authors; and very often, when they came to compare notes, there was a radical disagreement. Then, out of the argument that followed, there arose a completely different position, new to them and superior (we believe) to the original idea of either.[4]

Le Corbusier and Wright

In his earliest thoughts on planning, Percy had accepted a premise of both Le Corbusier and Wright, who for opposite reasons agreed that industry and commerce were to be strictly cordoned off from the rest of life. "People should not live in cities," Percy wrote in 1932, "cities are for work." He imitated Le Corbusier's high-density urban skyscrapers, but he also saw virtues in Wright's Garden City suburbs: "Work should be centralized — living quarters should be decentralized. This means a greater density of buildings used for business purposes and garden cities for living."[5]

At first it seemed to Percy that a synthesis could be derived from the separate insights of the two great planners. Le Corbusier had shown that centralized planning "could make safety, comfort, and sanitation possible, and simplicity and mass-production could make it cheap."[6] He was, however, notoriously enamored of state and corporate power, and his unpeopled vistas of towers and speedways seemed serenely unconcerned with human beings or human scale. Contrarily, Wright's stunning family homes, designed as unique art works for wealthy clients, tempted the Goodmans to call him the first architect to attend to "real human wants."[7] The price tags, however, suggested that the libertarian politics that he espoused were rooted in his own artist's prerogatives rather than serious democratic ideals.

Thinking such contradictions through, the brothers gradually distanced themselves from both Broadacres and the Ville Contemporaine in order to develop a position of their own. The problems of the modern city might be framed in terms set by the rivalry of Le Corbusier and Wright, but the answers would have to transcend their debate. This dialectical potential was dramatized in 1934 when Percy invited them, along with Buckminster Fuller and a few others, to respond to a series of leading questions in four successive issues of *trend*:

For Le Corbusier: Under what economic system will architecture prosper most?

For Fuller: If the future of architecture is the Dymaxion, what will be the fate of cities? Of centralized industries?

For Wright: What objection do you have to the works called "International Style," especially those of Le Corbusier?[8]

The lions roared at one another on cue; but the magazine closed down before Percy could sum up their contentions, and Le Corbusier testily withdrew his contribution when he discovered he would not be paid for it. Nonetheless, the point was made: none of the contributors had all the answers.

Practitioners like Buckminster Fuller, or the homestead advocate Ralph Borsodi, helped the Goodmans analyze Le Corbusier and Wright by taking them to their logical extremes. Fuller's Dymaxion House, completely detached from *any* site, could be regarded as the ultimate extension of Le Corbusier's faceless machines-for-living, whereas Borsodi's ill-fated homesteads in Dayton, Ohio, demonstrated how individual cottagers in a decentralized community like Broadacres, without economic leverage to match their autonomy, might also end up at the mercy of state and corporate power. Rich or poor, the rugged individualist needed a community organized around work, not just a fence around his property, in order to be truly free and independent.

Pushed to their limits by Fuller and Borsodi, the Goodmans found it easier to see through visionary plans to underlying economic and political issues — and in some ways the radical solu-

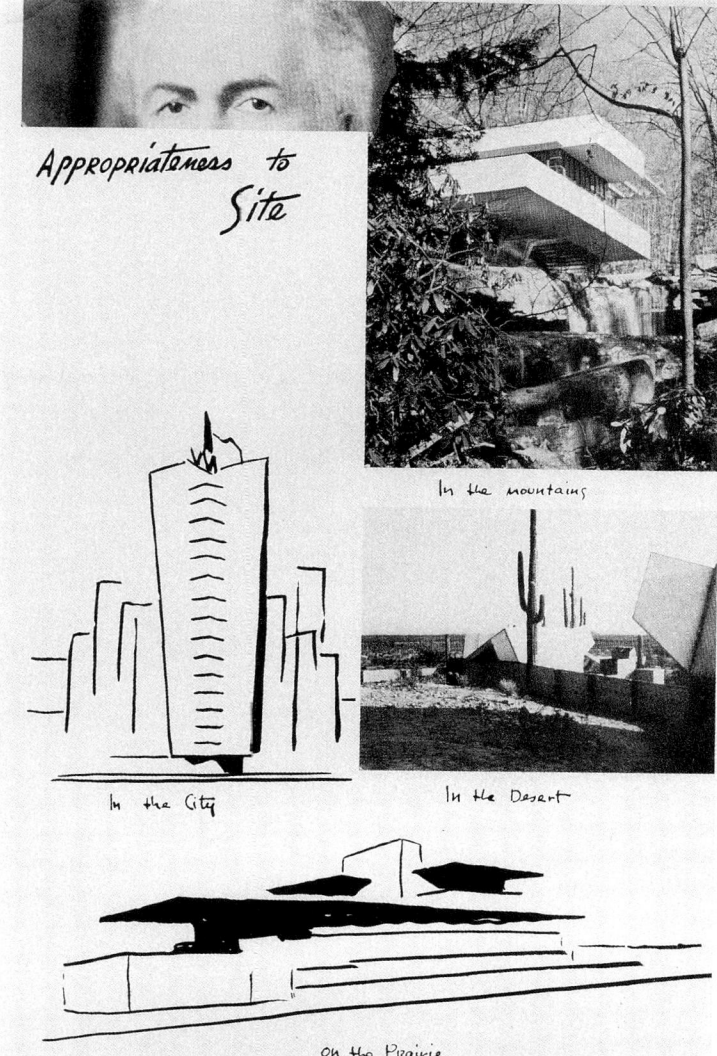

Fig. 34 Drawings by Percival Goodman for the article on Frank Lloyd Wright and Le Corbusier in *Kenyon Review,* (1942) (cat. 34)

tions proposed by the technocrat engineer and the Thoreauvian home economist appealed to them more than the architectural utopias of Wright and Le Corbusier. The Goodmans considered the implications in a long essay written in the summer of 1941, presumably occasioned by the Wright retrospective at the Museum of Modern Art. After considering the alternatives for ten years, Paul and Percy were in full agreement on their own views, as indicated by the fact that for the first time they signed both their names to a collaboration. They seem to have been positioning themselves to lead community planning in a new direction.

Published in the *Kenyon Review* with illustrations by Percy (fig. 34), their essay accused both Wright and Le Corbusier of being "political messiahs" whose true purpose was "to preserve the political status quo and prevent revolution."[9]

> Though both are authoritarian, Wright is so in a more negative way, because what he wants ultimately to defend is the liberty of each inhabitant . . . and the authoritarianism, when it crops up, takes the form of his individual caprice dominating every other life. Le Corbusier is affirmative; he realizes that vast enterprises require strong measures; and the meaningful enterprises for him are especially the vast ones. the steamships and skyscrapers. . . . [Thus he] attempts to rationalize just what we have at its most intense.[10]

In the Goodmans' view, "even adding Wright and Le Corbusier together we do not get an adequate philosophy."[11]

What *would* an adequate philosophy of planning entail? Here are some of the desiderata that can be seen arising out of their critique:

- planning for mass society without standardization and conformity in the lives of its inhabitants
- protecting local initiative against centralized power
- promoting both urban and rural virtues: civic pride, high culture, self-sufficiency, and the habit of freedom
- safeguarding against imprudent technology, consumerism, and a false standard of living
- leaving as much as possible open and unplanned, for people to decide for themselves.

A Philosophy of Planning

In the fall of 1941 the Goodmans decided to write a history of modern planning from their own point of view. Shortly after finishing their survey of Wright and Le Corbusier, they presented a study project to the Guggenheim Foundation: "To evaluate, criticize, and work toward a synthesis of the major architectural theories."[12]

This was just before Pearl Harbor. Military conscription had already begun, and the war that the United States was about to enter was a key factor in their Guggenheim application — for it was apparent that after the inevitable mass destruction,

> one way or another, there [would] be an enormous world-wide post-war expansion in building. . . . [Responsible planning would require] analysis of the writings and works of the modern masters. And all of this must be presented and illustrated in such a way that the *public* can lend its understanding and its voice to the problems.[13]

When their grant did not materialize, the Goodmans reconsidered their approach and decided on a crucial addition. The first half of their book would contain the proposed "Manual of Modern Plans"; the second half would present three paradigms of their own invention, illustrating how different political and economic premises would express themselves if allowed full scope to play themselves out in the utopian imagination.

The brothers already had their paradigms in mind. Although the labels changed from one draft to the next, between themselves they called them the Department Store City, the New Commune, and the Dual Economy. Since these three schemes led to the most surprising and memorable sections of *Communitas,* it is worth looking closely at how the Goodmans came to invent them.

The Department Store City

The first paradigm originated in Percy's unwritten book of the early thirties. As with Le Corbusier, Percy's early "Notes on Community Planning" presumed centralized work and commerce, a key factor of which would be transportation, not just bringing workers and materials in and out of the hub but also "vertical transport," the technology that allowed piling multistoried buildings one on top of another for greater density. But he had taken Le Corbusier one step further. With air-conditioning and electric light, Percy conjectured, "I don't need windows for air and I don't need windows for light. Therefore, I can put everything into a box. . . . The interior would be just a bare structural shell with levels in it, but anything else would be open and high enough so that you could do anything you pleased inside it."[14]

In its original form he called this the Windowless City. A few of the many plans and elevations that Percy drew for it were published in the articles of 1931 and 1932. In the late thirties he got them out again for a new project, a giant cutaway model that he invited the Otis Elevator Corporation to build as a pavilion in the New York World's Fair, along with a movie in the H. G. Wells/Orson Welles manner, to show how people would live in the Windowless City.

Although turned down by Otis (it would have cost millions), Percy's model city had advanced a crucial step from its earliest conception. A world's fair was a marketplace after all, goods on display. Raymond Loewy, who had done for the Chrysler Corporation what Percy wanted to do for Otis, characterized the entire Flushing Meadows site as "a huge department store."[15] What was new in 1939 was the emphasis on commerce and commodities rather than business and industry — and this was true for Percy's model city as well as the fair itself.

The Otis project pulled a lot of the past together for Percy. Unlike Loewy or Norman Bel Geddes, the more famous showmen of the fair, Percy was a practicing architect; even so, most of his remunerative career had been like theirs, as a designer of department store interiors and of products that might be found in such stores, from furniture and silverware to wristwatches and bathrooms. Over the years he had written on industrial design, interior decoration, kitchen gadgetry, home furnishings, and women's fashions. Following in his father's footsteps, he had become a connoisseur of commodities and their marketing.

As a Bauhaus-type functionalist, however, Percy was primarily concerned with quality and utility. He was contemptuous of industrial designers like Geddes and Loewy, who merely "streamlined" everything from grocery scales to locomotives. Percy scorned these empty packages. His own style of living, in elegance but without attachment to things, put him at odds with the consumer society that America had become even in the midst of the Depression. These contradictions guaranteed that his Department Store City, designed for the glorification of goods, would express a deep ambivalence. Percy had a passionate vision of the ideal metropolis, every object and proportion designed according to reason and taste. But what if the perfected utopia served only crass and pernicious values?

Paul no less than Percy was fascinated by the idea of the modern emporium, probably for similar reasons of family history. He remembered his mother working as a saleswoman in department stores. One plot strand of *The Empire City,* his most ambitious novel, centered on a capitalist father-figure whose very home was an auction house in which everything, including his son, was for sale. In the early thirties Paul's first plays had featured strikes and boycotts of department stores like the famous Klein's, and several pieces of fiction written at the end of the decade also took place in stores and inquired into the psychosocial nature of commodities. His attitude may be suggested by quoting one of these, "The Mean, the Maximum, and the Minimum," composed at the very time that Percy was promoting his world's fair project. Among his characters was "an urban Thoreau,"

> disgusted and weary with the continual consumption of goods in which he and everyone else were consuming their lives, and not without a little envy of the rich. . . . Henry founded the National Industrial Boycott, an organization to destroy the bourgeois structure of society . . . by buy[ing] and consum[ing] as little as possible.[16]

This same story also celebrated the modern department store as "an earthly paradise":

> Everything is in the great Department Store! to be got by the infinite power of money, which is exchangeable for all things and proportioned to the infinite appetite.[17]

Spelling out his story's title, the department store represented "the Maximum" and the boycott of the store "the Minimum," whereas the "Mean" was altogether outside the dynamic of material goods.

With these complicated feelings of fascination and revulsion, the Goodman brothers invented the City of Efficient Consumption in *Communitas*. Part of their impulse was to give the society they actually lived in its due: "The problem is how to get a little splendor out of the increasing possibility of luxury."[18] From a utopian point of view, their scheme was a twentieth-century version of the tenth chapter in Edward Bellamy's *Looking Backward* (1888). More ironically, in socioeconomic terms it was "Veblen upside down"[19] — conspicuous consumption as cornerstone of the commonwealth.

But they found it impossible to portray consumer society — especially its utopian apotheosis — with a straight face. The ideal parodied its own soulless magnificence, and "what started as sober description . . . turned into satire."[20] Having noted, for example, that the enormous wartime expenditure brought the Depression to an end, they suggested sardonically that perhaps "even in peacetime, men can be as efficiently wasteful as possible."[21] In order to achieve the equivalent waste, they reasoned, the city "must be throughout . . . a vast department store. Everywhere — as at a permanent fair — are on display the products that make it worthwhile to get up in the morning to go to work."[22] And to guarantee the process, the Goodmans proposed

Fig. 35 Drawing illustrating Carnival, from *Communitas* (1947)

a season of carnival, when waste might become not only efficient but also sacramental (fig. 35). In an orgy of consumption the shelves would be cleared, debts forgiven, and people would rid themselves of superfluity in preparation for a round of new fashions and new models. More than Veblen, Bellamy, or even Aldous Huxley, their absurdist glorification of the Department Store City was indebted to Charlie Chaplin's *Modern Times*.

The result was bound to perplex some readers, who would wonder why so much creative planning had been invested in a satirical proposal. Why take folly so seriously? Ah, but the same question could be asked about the actual Manhattan or Paris! "The spectacle of a society using its riches to its deterioration contains an irony and sarcasm that is not invented into it by authors."[23]

The Dual Economy

Another paradigm that also went back to the early thirties in its initial conception, the Dual Economy in essence simply added a subsistence economy to the luxury economy of the Department Store City. Working one year out of seven, a citizen could produce enough to subsist on the Minimum, Percy calculated. Anyone who chose to aspire to the Maximum might enter the luxury economy too, but everyone would be guaranteed basic necessities in exchange for what amounted to an hour or so of labor each day, or perhaps a decade of one's youth.

Percy considered this scheme a solution to the paradox of industrial capitalism in the early thirties, which had to run at full blast for its workers to buy bread. He believed that every citizen had a right to basic subsistence, not as charity or emergency dole but in exchange for a proportionate amount of labor, rationally determined and minimized through social policy.

Although it appealed to Paul as much as it did Percy, the Dual Economy meant something different to them. Paul himself had always lived frugally — he once calculated his average income as that of a sharecropper in the Deep South. To him the paradigm was a way of reminding people how to enjoy the Minimum. If the Department Store City turned Veblen upside down, the Dual Economy stood the welfare state on its head. Paul did not advocate subsistence living as an economic safety net or as an austerity plan, though he welcomed its check on consumerism. His concern was the freedom to pursue one's own interests without bosses or time clocks, the way he had always lived.

The brothers would undoubtedly have chosen different paths in the Dual Economy, but there was no ambivalence or satire in their attitudes. It was not a utopian conception; and while in many ways a compromise, it was the plan that they thought most worth trying of their three models, because it gave people breathing space, a respite from planning itself — as they meant to suggest in finally titling it "Planned Security with Minimum Regulation." Especially for "undeveloped regions" and "dense, poverty-stricken communities" (they borrowed the current clichés of postwar decolonization), such a plan would "give the people an interim of partial freedom to determine their own community forms and not have them altogether imposed from outside, repeating the old mistakes — but now not even native mistakes."[24]

The New Commune

In Percy's recollection, their third paradigm originated at dinner one evening when Paul said, "I've been thinking about those schemes and I think we can do a book. . . . Has there been any book written which deals with the history of planning but not from a technical point of view, rather a social point of view?" And then he said, "We've got to have a third scheme."[25]

At work on this new approach, they sometimes referred to it as "the middle scheme" because of where they placed it in their book, between the Department Store City and the Dual Economy. The New Commune was their direct and immediate answer to the values of capitalist consumer society, whereas the Dual Economy was an alternative, interim plan, weaning people away from their addiction to commodities. In this sense, too, the New Commune was in the middle, for it envisaged a golden mean of life in modern society: an urban/rural balance reconciling Borsodi's homestead and Camillo Sitte's city square, along with a mixed economy sustained by anarcho-syndicalist principles of work-democracy derived from Peter Kropotkin and William Morris.

It was primarily Paul who brought the politics into their commune — again a middle way between the libertarian anarchism of Thoreau and various collectives in the socialist tradition. Percy's own left-wing orientation had been shifting during the thirties. As they had for many communists, the Moscow trials, the betrayals in Spain, and the pact with the Nazis in 1940 had given Percy qualms; and meanwhile his anarchist brother kept pointing out that the state, with its centralized planning and top-down administration, undermined the initiative and inventiveness that were essential to any community of free citizens, especially the ideal that they had in mind as the New Commune. By 1942 Percy was ready to go along with a communitarian anarchism like that of Kropotkin, though he himself did not read *Fields, Factories, and Workshops* (1898) or *Mutual Aid* (1902) until later.

The meeting ground on which the New Commune was actually built in the Goodmans' imagination was William Morris: "we looked at each other and I said, *News from Nowhere.*" Percy recalled their collaboration on the second paradigm as starting with "the notion of work as being creative. . . . You know, these are Morris's kind of ideas. What Paul pumped into it was a lot of Kropotkin . . . the whole notion of mutual aid. . . . Then I began to sketch the town. And then that generated other discussions."[26]

Fig. 36 "Piazza in the town: a busy square," from *Communitas* (1947)

What emerged was a modest mixture of dwellings, shops, and workplaces side by side, never far from fields and open country but gathered round generous piazzas (fig. 36). Schools would be integrated with workshops, apprentice-style, and the public square was not for public buildings so much as public life — people on their way somewhere, meeting, or simply taking their ease — gossip and debate, ethics and politics, all the business of the commonweal in the same convivial rhythm.

William Morris and Peter Kropotkin might supply key ideas about guild socialism or the syndicalist workshop, but for the Goodmans the New Commune was not merely a matter of social invention. That kind of thinking certainly did appeal to them, for both brothers were inveterate problem solvers. But beyond that, their conversations had taught them that the task was not to come up with final solutions but rather to foster an attitude toward life and work that gave scope for inventiveness itself. Although they felt the New Commune promised more human satisfaction than the Department Store City or the Dual Economy, these were not programs like Broadacres or the Ville Radieuse, utopias demanding to be built. Indeed, part of their aim was to show that the power of planning to choreograph how people live had a dystopian aspect. Since culture and society are living things, evolving over time, every locality and every generation must continually rethink its needs and reconstruct its planned world. A truly utopian spirit would therefore refrain from imposing "perfection" so that responsible citizens might exercise initiative and profit from their own mistakes.

In his short story about Maximums and Minimums Paul had framed his antidote to the cycles of appetite and disgust in spiritual terms: "The Golden Mean is to have just so much there as a person is adequate to, to turn to it his full attention.... To know where one is, proportioning the self and the objects of desire, is prayer. Measure is the same as saying Grace."[27] In their New Commune the brothers translated this vision of spiritual health in language that emphasized its social import:

> [T]he regional and syndicalist method is . . . more efficient in the end, when invention, for instance, is not inhibited and the job is its own incentive. But most important of all, it must be remembered that we are here aiming at the highest and nearest ideals of external life: liberty; personal concern, responsibility, and expertness; and a say in what a man lends his hands to.[28]

No single plan or politics would guarantee these ideals, and so the New Commune was less a program than an invocation. In writing *Communitas* the Goodmans hoped to inspire their readers with an attitude toward planning that was utopian in its ideals, pragmatic in its means, and open to spontaneous invention — and resistance! — from those whose lives were determined by it.

Getting into Print

The writing began in September 1942. Paul had no job, his new novel was not selling, and his anarchist opposition to the war had gotten him blacklisted at several magazines. He needed work, and Percy advanced him a few dollars now and then, as recompense for his labor and in anticipation of royalties on their book.

Not opposed to the war himself, Percy had volunteered for the Air Force. After failing the physical, he had formed a camouflage company to do his bit against Hitler, and he was now traveling back and forth to Washington frequently. He worked at the book on the train:

> I would jot down ideas and I'd do some reading and I'd jot down some ideas. And then Paul came out with a chapter.... So I pointed out that the chapter had a lot of things that weren't quite right in it. We had a lot of arguments about it. Paul said, "Well, I don't care what's written, this is the way it really is." But he agreed that he'd better take a look at some of the stuff.
> So it gradually began to form itself.[29]

Sometimes Percy would produce the first version of a chapter; for example, he probably composed the section dealing with Soviet experiments — an early typescript has corrections in his hand. He later estimated that he drafted perhaps a fifth of the pages. But "ultimately Paul rewrote everything."

By Christmastime the first half was finished, and in May they were ready to send the book to publishers. At first they hoped to reach the general public; but after four months of knocking on editorial doors, they gave up on the commercial houses and approached their contacts in the universities. Percy had recently joined the faculty at Columbia, and his dean put in a word for him at the Columbia University Press.

The publications committee liked the manuscript, and so did colleagues consulted in the architectural school. The editor of *Harper's* magazine said he would print an excerpt if the book were published, and in November the press reported that things looked good for acceptance.

While financial negotiations were going forward, the brothers initiated their own promotional campaign through articles in the national press. Paul had connections at the *New Republic,* and by December 1943 the first of these efforts, "Architecture in Wartime," appeared there, with author notes announcing their forthcoming book. But behind the scenes the smooth sailing had run into trouble.

Although reactions from architectural experts had been entirely positive, someone at the press suddenly got cold feet and decided to consult a sociologist, just to be sure there was nothing out of line in the Goodmans' analysis of society. The satirical attitude toward the American standard of living would certainly puzzle some readers, and the positing of some sort of socialism as essential for large-scale planning would distress others. Worried about unfavorable reviews, the press was looking for academic authority to put a stamp of approval on the book's "utopianism."

Unfortunately the choice fell on one of the foremost promoters of the standard of living as an index of American progress, who not surprisingly found *Communitas* a farrago of sociological impertinence. He saw no hope of revising it to meet the criteria of his discipline. This put the press in an awkward spot since the book had been virtually accepted, though there was no contract yet. In March 1944 the manuscript was turned back to the authors for rectification of its sociological content. It needed repackaging.

Although disappointed, the brothers thought they might outface or outmaneuver the expert whose identity could only be guessed. When attacked in the press, the Goodmans had always taken it as a challenge to answer their critics irrefutably. But in this case they did not know precisely what bothered the anonymous gatekeeper, aside from their lack of the proper academic password. What exactly would "answer" such a critic? Strengthening their position might well be fatal to their chances for publication.

The task of revision fell to Paul. Most of the social analysis originated with him, and his author's vanity was piqued. The main changes came in the long introduction spelling out aims and premises. Never before had he done such elaborate restructuring: cutting whole pages, moving large sections around, trimming and smoothing the prose. The result was rhetorically stronger but not substantially changed. Paul made no attempt to mouth sociological jargon or to bow in the direction of professionals. References to authorities aside from planners remained offhand, almost flip: no footnotes and rarely a book title, just Veblen or Marx — and never a Mead, Merton, or Lynd.

Back in the hands of the press, the book was judged greatly improved, but the editors must have realized that its attitude toward society was unchanged. To speak of "social control" instead of "socialism" made very little difference. The manuscript now went to an even more prestigious scholar, who returned it within a week in complete agreement with his colleague's earlier dismissal. The embarrassed press informed Percy that there would be no need to pay any production costs after all, as Percy was prepared to do, for their book had been rejected.

The Goodmans fumed, but they did not give up. Now it was Paul's turn to see what his contacts could do for them. He sent the manuscript to his friend and mentor Richard P. McKeon, a professor of philosophy and the dean of humanities at the University of Chicago:

> Dear Dick,
>   After having "accepted" this book for over a year, Columbia U. Press now welches on it because we won't make changes conforming to their notions of sociological terminology (and — er — thought?)

Fig. 37 "Bibliography for three ways of life today," frontispiece of *Communitas* (1947)

> Will U. of C. do it? On what terms? We can meet anything moderate (we have a little grant). Please get us some quick action one way or the other, for I'm kind of fed up.[31]

On 1 September 1944, McKeon passed it along with his strong recommendation — especially of its "philosophy and sociology" — and by January 1945 it was accepted. The only changes stipulated were matters of presentation. For example, the Chicago press did not like their original title, "Ways of Life and Means of Livelihood" — fine for a subtitle but not jazzy enough for the dust jacket of a trade book. Paul came up with *Communitas*.

The Chicago press *did* see it as a trade book, convinced by Percy's layout in coffee-table size and format. From the beginning the brothers had regarded illustrations as integral to their argument, and Percy had collected numerous photographs and drawn many plans and sketches — 138 at that point. But in those days photographs cost a lot to print, and quality paper had been in short supply during the war. Percy solved the problem by rendering all photographs as line

Fig. 38 "A Master Plan for New York," published in the *New Republic* (20 November 1944); also published as an appendix in *Communitas*

Fig. 39 Riverview Community Housing Development Proposal, Long Island City, 1944–46: perspective rendering (cat. 18a)

drawings in his bravura sketchbook style. Even the requisite bibliography was transformed into a distinctive Percival Goodman drawing, and they used it as a frontispiece (fig. 37).

The production schedule was slow. When McKeon sent the manuscript to the press in September, the brothers had assumed it could be published by the following spring, and they hurried into print the last in the series of policy proposals that had begun with "Architecture in Wartime." When "A Master Plan for New York" appeared in November (fig. 38), the interested reader was informed that their book was due out in the spring of 1945. In fact it would be the spring of 1947 before *Communitas* saw the light of day. This was all to the good, however, for the brothers now had time and incentive to develop some important new ideas in their book.

Percy was newly married, and so was Paul, whose first marriage had broken up while he was writing the most utopian sections of the book. Together with their new wives, they spent most of the summer on Fire Island, where Percy settled down to work on illustrations and layout ("every damned page")[32] and Paul on the text. Although there was still some tinkering with phrasing — notably in the titles of the three paradigm plans — the most significant changes were now additions. Half a dozen sections of the book were augmented by new material, typically placed at the ends of chapters to bring some present application to the discussion. Their original discussions of the garden city and industrial planning, for instance, now concluded with analyses of how housing and factories always seemed to be planned in total isolation from one another, ignoring commuting time and mindlessly imposing petit bourgeois standards based on "sociological abstractions," rather than what makes a good place to live.

Some suggestions for immediate action were gathered together in four appendices that included their "Master Plan for New York" and a proposal that Percy had worked out some years earlier for developing Long Island City, a blighted industrial area just across the 59th Street Bridge from Manhattan (figs. 39–40). Both of these might be read as indirect assaults on the well-known park commissioner Robert Moses, since every professional would know that his okay was required for all such undertakings. Moses had indeed vetoed Percy's Long Island City proposal; and in default of a master plan for the city, it was Moses's systematic development of commuter routes and faraway recreation facilities that left Manhattan to flight, blight, and bankruptcy in the next generation.

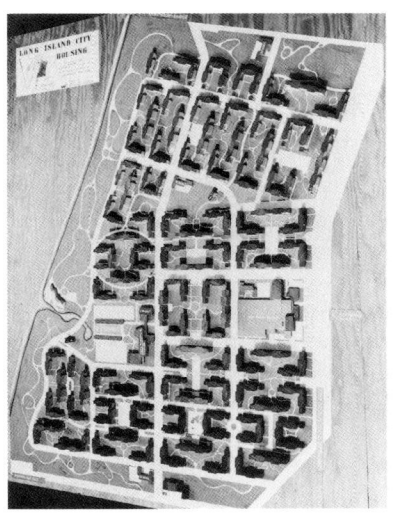

Fig. 40 Riverview Community Housing Development Proposal, Long Island City, 1944–46: model (cat. 18b)

Neo-Functionalism

By far the longest single addition to *Communitas* — and the most important — was a section placed at the end of their second paradigm, the New Commune. Like "A Master Plan for New York," it was partly borrowed from a magazine (*Politics*, December 1944), but the original article in this case was not a corollary study so much as an attempt to formulate the very essence of their book, giving their overall approach its own name and place in the history of modern planning.

From their earliest studies of Wright and Le Corbusier, the Goodmans kept coming back to the nature of functionalism and what its axioms and slogans meant for the planner. By the time of *Communitas*, they agreed that functionalism was much more than an artistic method; philosophically applied, analysis of the relations of formal means and practical ends should lay bare the social and economic assumptions of any plan. Accordingly, in their manual of modern plans, they "start with the technology and ask: What is expressed or presupposed about domestic life? psychology of work and leisure? education? political initiative? aesthetics? economic institutions? practical realization?"[33]

Once this survey was complete, their three paradigms served as case studies of functionalist analysis "in reverse," starting with abstractions such as "efficient consumption" or "planned security with minimum regulation" and then creating plans that would enable those ways of life. Thus functionalism could be used as a technique for criticizing already existing communities or as a theoretical method for exploring the means to particular social ends.

None of this was really new, although no one from the Bauhaus or the International School had ever used functionalism so methodically as a tool of social analysis. It was only after sending their book off to Chicago in the fall of 1944 that the Goodmans worked out one last step in this sequence, which constitutes their unique contribution: "[T]he function itself must be subject to formal criticism: Is it clear, ingenious, rational, proportionate to other functions? Is it worthwhile?" Neo-functionalism was their name for an attitude toward planning that asked these final questions of ethics and propriety in the commonwealth. The planner "must find as much significance in the functions as possible," but he must "also see that the functions are as significant as possible."[34]

In introducing their three paradigms, the Goodmans had distinguished them according to the particular way each one dealt with the moral dimension of planning:

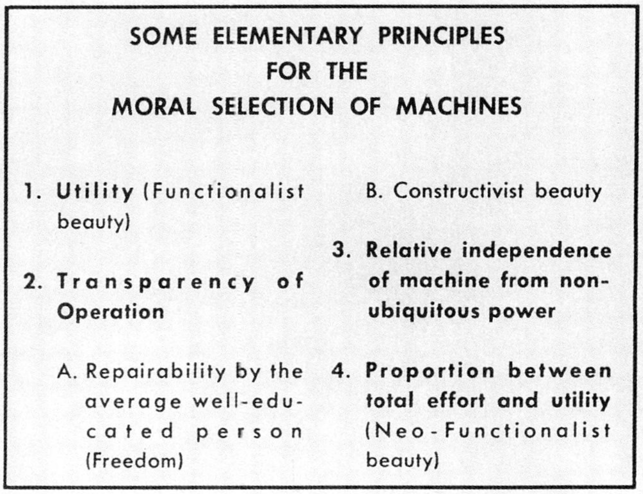

**SOME ELEMENTARY PRINCIPLES
FOR THE
MORAL SELECTION OF MACHINES**

1. Utility (Functionalist beauty)

2. Transparency of Operation

   A. Repairability by the average well-educated person (Freedom)

B. Constructivist beauty

3. Relative independence of machine from non-ubiquitous power

4. Proportion between total effort and utility (Neo-Functionalist beauty)

Fig. 41 Chart of Principles, from *Communitas* (1947)

> Our concerns are how to make the multitude of goods good for something, how to integrate the work and culture, how to keep an integrated community plan from becoming a plan for complete slavery — perhaps, above all, to help keep the now-to-be-developed countries from repeating the same course as the United States and Europe.[35]

Only the second paradigm, "integrating work and culture," had the neo-functionalist attitude built into its plan. "Eliminating the difference" between city and country, work and leisure, public and private life meant providing a structure for ongoing creative adjustment of ends and means. In the New Commune, where the workplace was the center of political initiative and the city square an ongoing town meeting, planning would be part of life, subject to continuous scrutiny on ethical as well as aesthetic and technical grounds.

To have to ask the question "What is it good for?" was already a sign of trouble — that workers no longer knew the whys and wherefores of their labor. Viewed from a slightly different perspective, neo-functionalism was the Goodmans' answer to the psychosocial crisis of modern industrial society, the loss of "the forthright connection between what a man makes and what he uses." Here is how they formulated the problem:

> To take an idyllic case, to a vacationist in the woods the production of a shelter or a meal is enriched by, and is continuous with, the immediate consumption. In the historical self-subsistent family farm just such forthright connections are woven into an entire way of life. The evils of factory towns are remediable, but this loss is in the nature of mass production and is irremediable. Even worse, the machine analysis of production creeps into the attitude of consumption. This is the case of a person who eats calories and vitamins instead of food; whose notions of order and cleanliness do not spring from sensibility and judgment but from the prevalence of air-tight packages . . . ; and whose wants are automatic responses to the advertising that sells the mass products.[36] . . . The multiplication of commodities and the false standard of living, on the one hand, the complication of the economic and technical structure in which one can work at a job, on the other hand, and the lack of direct relationship between the two have by now made a great part of external life morally meaningless.[37]

In more Marxist terms, we are facing here the alienation of labor and its corollaries, the commodification of goods and services, the reification of experience, and so forth. A neo-functionalist attitude would not in itself repair these rents in the social fabric, but to bring the "forthright connection" back into awareness was essential to any possible remedy.

It was not realistic to go back to the woods, nor, at the other extreme, was it practical or desirable that everyone have the expertise and authority of a planner. It was more important to have the neo-functionalist *attitude,* the habit of questioning ends and means rather than merely accepting what was already in place. This in turn would require that premises and implications be clear enough for ordinary citizens to judge them. Once neo-functionalist criteria had been formulated explicitly, much would follow. An example of such criteria was their chart of "Elementary Principles for the Moral Selection of Machines" added to the final draft of *Communitas* (fig. 41).

Although the Goodmans sometimes spoke of neo-functionalism as a principle or set of principles like these, they more often characterized it, as I have been trying to do, as an attitude — "a delicate one, difficult for Americans to grasp clearly." To teach a principle, it might be sufficient to state it and locate its place in more comprehensive conceptions or systems — you could make a chart like this. To encourage an attitude, something like a story or picture was needed, but it was not so easy to imagine a "hypothetical" life. In their first draft they interrupted the exposition to express this difficulty in an imaginary dialogue:

> PERCIVAL: You're a novelist, not just a sociologist! Why do you keep describing this great luxury city of consumers' goods in such arid analyses, almost formulas? This won't come home to anybody; this won't rouse any feeling on the subject.
> PAUL (*terrified*): What am I supposed to do?
> PERCIVAL: Can't you give an imaginative picture of what the people *are*, not just their functional relations? You know — a short story — you know how to write up these things.
> PAUL: I'm at a loss. Where would I get the first words if not from . . . my necessity. But a man can't be *personally* at stake (thank God!) just by wanting to.[38]

Of course, the Department Store City, to which Americans were already inured long before the advent of the downtown shopping mall, was not difficult to portray convincingly, though the facts kept slipping into satire and ridicule. But the other paradigms seemed much less amenable to lifelike rendering. The Goodmans tried to call up the right atmosphere by remembering moments in their own lives when the "forthright connection" of work and pleasure seemed most intact — being a student in Paris or Manhattan — but their vignettes are pale and spiritless in comparison with their social and architectural inventions.

The new material brought into the book with the account of neo-functionalism finally caught the expressive lilt that they had been looking for. Rather than hypothetical fantasies or nostalgic snapshots, we are invited to contemplate actual conditions of our urban scene, for example, the thriving ailanthus tree, the lowly plantain weed, both of them hardy survivors in the world of asphalt and autos. Why not *cultivate* what promises so fair? "At least we can *begin* with all the powers of nature on our side."[39] Certain other conditional possibilities demanded a more vigorous application of the new attitude, though also based on familiar facts of life: the rivers of New York could be rescued from the commuter highways for parks and beaches, swimming and sailing; the great art of the ages could be freed from its lock-and-key museums and restored to churches and city squares, to uplift the spirit of the passerby as in Florence or Venice.

These were ideas that engaged an artist's imagination, and the Goodmans' illustrations of neo-functionalism brightened their pages with vivid reminders of what the good life could be like. Some were obviously utopian — though not far-fetched or impractical, just against the tide — while others were modest proposals, easily managed. To inculcate an attitude it was not necessary to move heaven and earth. As Paul often said in the period of the New Left, it was enough to change "two percent of this and four percent of that."[40] The direction of change, increasing competence and autonomy, was the significant thing, for that was what healed alienation and anomie.

Finding an Audience

When their book finally appeared in the spring of 1947, its reception was mixed. It was not reviewed widely — sixteen notices by 1950 — but the *New York Times* praised it, and so did some major architectural journals. Even *Fortune* magazine paid respectful attention. Back when Columbia University Press consulted its experts, the prediction had been that architects and planners would welcome the book while sociologists would condemn it. By and large that is what happened, yet two notable exceptions presaged a very different fate for *Communitas*. The most contemptuous review appeared in *Commentary,* where the housing expert Charles Abrams seemed irritated by everything about *Communitas,* from the book's "oblong" shape (it would not fit in his bookcase) to its "light-minded" tone and "cartoon" illustrations. Most of all, Abrams was bothered by the "jumbl[ing of] the authors' social views with their views on physical planning."[41] He obviously spoke for the old guard of social science as well as the planning technocrats attacked in the book. Ironically enough, but surely a sign of the times, the longest and most favorable review came from an academic sociologist, David Riesman, who in the manner of a new generation of "committed" scholars — like C. Wright Mills — praised just what Abrams condemned.

Communitas would itself end up as part of this wave of engaged social criticism. A new edition became feasible in 1960 after Random House agreed to publish *Growing Up Absurd,* Paul's call to arms that radicalized college students across the country. Although unknown outside the profession, *Communitas* had been well thumbed by architects and planners, and the original two thousand copies had sold out. Random House bought the rights and scheduled a run of seventeen thousand in a format to match the paperback *Growing Up Absurd.* On its new cover the order of authors was reversed, Paul's suddenly marketable name coming before his brother's, though Percy's was still first on the title page. The editor at Vintage was the social scientist Nathan Glazer, the blurbs came from Riesman and Lewis Mumford, and the recommended category for shelving in bookstores was "sociology" rather than "architecture" or "planning." For the next decade the book's appeal (more than one hundred thousand more copies) would be to the growing ranks of the New Left. Looking back on it in 1973 the anarchist planner and activist Colin Ward, writing

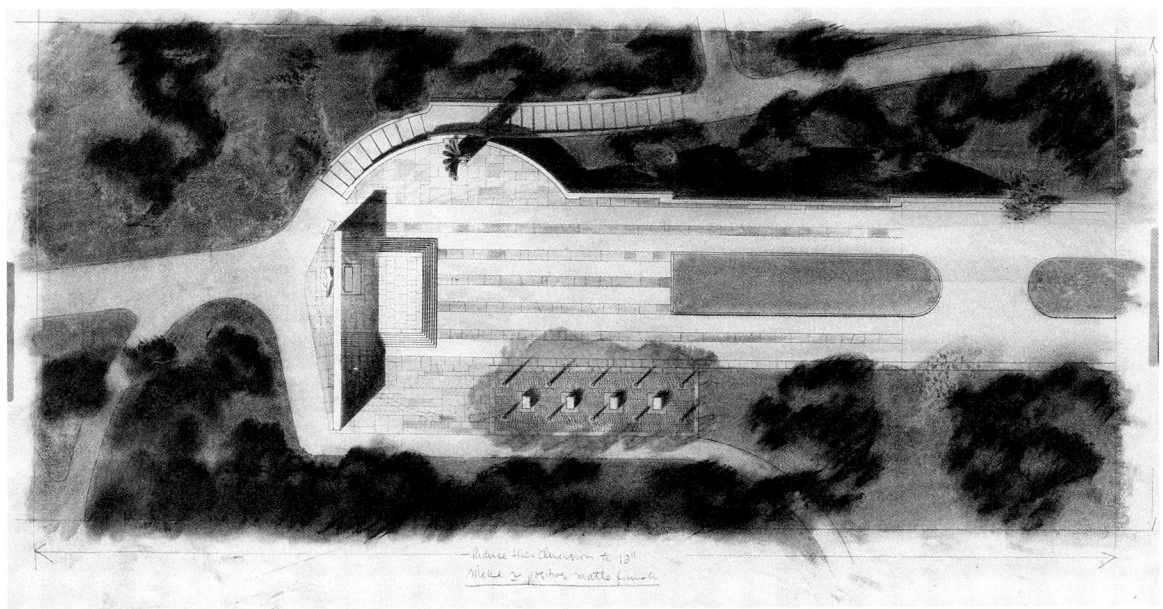

Fig. 42 American Memorial to Six Million Jews of Europe (competition), 1949–50: shadowed plan (cat. 22c)

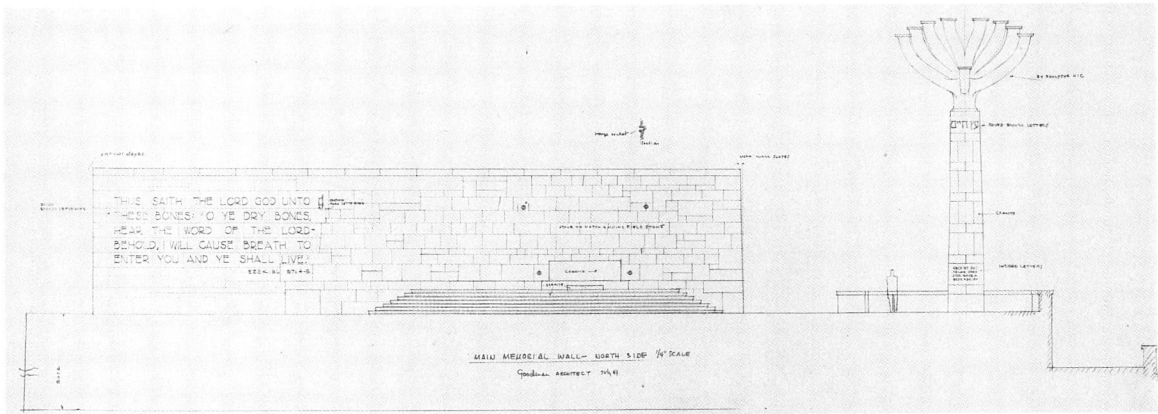

Fig. 43 American Memorial to Six Million Jews of Europe (competition), 1949–50: elevation (cat. 22d)

in the journal of the Royal Institute of British Architects, would sum up its stature and influence by saying it was "a book with more ideas to the page than any other I have read. Ironically prophetic, and with a quirky nobility, it speaks to our condition today more directly, and more immediately, than any later analysis of our dilemmas and aspirations has been able to do."[42]

Reverberations of a Classic

Between 1947 and 1960 both brothers had concentrated on other things. Even before the publication of their book, each had found the new path that would preoccupy him for several decades. Paul added psychotherapy, then social criticism, to his literary work, while Percy began his long career designing synagogues. Even so, they still found occasions to collaborate. When Percy needed a biblical text to serve as a theme for his Riverside Park memorial to the Holocaust victims (figs. 42–45) — eventually vetoed by Robert Moses because it would "distract" motorists on the Westside Highway! — he called on Paul to come up with something from Ezekiel. Soon

Fig. 44 American Memorial to Six Million Jews of Europe (competition), 1949–50: proposed location (cat. 22a)

Fig. 45 American Memorial to Six Million Jews of Europe (competition), 1949–50: Percival Goodman at proposed location (cat. 22b)

Paul turned the doomed project into a short story, "A Memorial Synagogue," introducing Percy as one of the characters. All of this transpired soon after their book was published. A dozen years later Percy told Paul about an H. H. Richardson church sold by its Unitarian congregation and torn down for real estate development. "The Architect from New York" was so pat a story of American disdain for any but commercial values that the *New Yorker* rejected it as too obviously "made up" — but it happened to Percy just as Paul set it down.

The closest and most fruitful collaboration of the brothers after *Communitas* began with the founding of the Jewish Museum of New York. The commission for its design came to Percy at the very beginning of his work in the Jewish community, late in 1944, when he was first thinking through his own attitude toward Jewish traditions and their religious significance. His younger brother had always been much more concerned with matters of faith and scripture. As Percy once told me, "Paul was religious and in his curious way a traditionalist. And of course a preacher. But for his nasty, Goodmanesque intransigence, he would have made a topnotch rabbi."[43]

Neo-functionalist conversations between the brothers now took a specialized turn, focusing on how Judaism might be expressed in redesigning the Felix Warburg Mansion on Fifth Avenue as a cultural museum. As it happened, their proposals called for more extensive alterations to her former home than Mrs. Warburg wanted; so while Percy supervised limited renovations, Paul reworked their initial ideas in still another collaboration, this time with his friend Benjamin Nelson, a sociologist and historian of religion. Percy was thus a silent partner in the published version of their "Project for a Modern Jewish Museum," but during the late forties he and Paul co-authored a series of similar essays on Jewish architecture, giving rise to further discussion in the letters columns of *Commentary* — and not a few commissions for Percy's office.

What was it that drew Percy into this new career as synagogue architect? When he himself tried to explain it, he often began by pointing out that for much of his life he had hobnobbed with rich Jews, who often owned the department stores and grape juice factories and Westchester homes that he was called upon to redesign. Connections made that way put him in favor with boards of trustees and building committees during the great exodus of the American Jews to the suburbs after the war.

After his work on the Jewish Museum, Percy was invited to take part in a conference called by the Union of American Hebrew Congregations to discuss what the building programs after World War II should strive for. His presentation made him "an instant expert on synagogues. The speech apparently conveyed what people wanted to hear. . . . I was pushing for what I considered to be a modern architecture."[44] After that came the essays in *Commentary*, which reached a still wider audience, many of whom would be responsible for choosing the architects of new synagogues.

Once the invitations began to arrive, an important factor in Percy's new vocation was surely the neo-functionalist challenge: to design a temple that could be modern in style, rich in decoration, responsive to its users, and founded in a tradition thousands of years old. Yet even this motive tells us little about Percy's deepest reason for devoting the rest of his life to the houses of worship of his fathers. Percy was often interviewed in his later years; and when asked about his Judaism, sooner or later he would say something like this:

> Hitler . . . led me, like many other Jews, to wonder: "Where do I belong?" and "Who the hell am I?" . . . One insight followed another. It's hard to pinpoint what mattered most. Nothing specific — unless it was the museum — precipitated my awakening. It didn't happen overnight. . . . The upshot was, well, that I am Jewish. It had nothing to do with religion.[45]

To start with then, a Jew is a Jew. The Jewish Museum project broadened this new self-awareness in Percy by teaching him that being a Jew meant being part of a culture and tradition and, most of all, part of a congregation, a Jew among Jews. The brothers spelled it out in their essays for *Commentary*:

> The sense of the congregation as taking part in the service is the fundamental religious function of the synagogue. If there is anything true in religion that is specifically Jewish, it is this integrating of the individual actors and their community: there is no representative and there is no non-human sacrificial act. The phalanx of prayer shawls, and the rising from the ranks of those called on and their returning to the ranks; ultimately this is the whole of it.[46]

Neither the Jewish Museum nor the later Holocaust Memorial could be realized in the way Percy and Paul had envisioned, but Percy's fifty synagogues, built over the next twenty-five years, gave him ample room to say over and over, in the language he knew best, what it meant to him to be a Jew. In essence it was this:

> Suddenly there occurred the fact that six million Jews were slaughtered in three or four years, just because they were Jews. We do not know in what ways other groups would react to such a happening, but among the Jews it seems to have had the following effect: they became aware of themselves as a physical community, a congregation.[47]

These essays and proposals were to be the last work the Goodmans did together. Although they saw each other frequently during the fifties and sixties — their growing families were very close — busy careers left the brothers few opportunities for new collaboration. Not long before

Paul's death in 1972, Percy tried to interest him in a sequel to *Communitas,* "but he said that he had no time and that he no longer believed in schemes for improving the human condition."[48] Percy persisted without him.

Because so many of the issues and dilemmas of planning had changed over the years, the rhetoric and certain premises of their book seemed out of date to Percy. Issuing *The Double E* on the thirtieth anniversary of *Communitas,* he emphasized one enormous new factor that they had not foreseen in 1947: "Limits, not free choice; scarcity, not surplus, are now the facts that will condition our future."[49] Percy proposed a fourth, "ecological" paradigm to take account of these new facts, but in working it out he was still "collaborating" with his brother. *The Double E* is full of quotations from Paul's polemical writings in the sixties, and the analysis of the situation for planners a generation after *Communitas* still relies on the neo-functionalist attitude they had formulated there: the need for a more rational standard of living and a prudent attitude toward technology, a syndicalist reevaluation of work, a bio-regionalist approach to social and economic organization. *Communitas* had not really become obsolete, and even today readers concerned about global trade, global media, or global warming will find insights in the Goodmans still worth taking to heart — even though it is late in the day for us to be heeding their counsel.

Long before their book and long after it, singly as well as jointly, they were teaching the neo-functionalist lesson summed up there. As early as 1932 Percy had written a page that might have been printed verbatim in either *Communitas* or *The Double E*:

> Today we cannot build for posterity, the mists of uncertainty hang over the future. Our loyalties and allegiances are provisional, our systems of producing and living are temporary, subject to changes that are portentous in their implications. . . . That technological science points the way to a promised land of material benefit is obvious. That the lack of moral and spiritual values may lead (and with the same tools) to a cataclysm instead is also obvious. . . . The next years will prove whether we can acclimate ourselves to this new world. . . . So our plan is not a complete one — it is not a plan for living the ideal life materially or spiritually. It is a compromise, a tiding over, a place to wait and a place to work for what the next three generations will bring forth.[50]

Percy's cautionary advice might serve as preface to any plans proposed in the last century or the next one. The same could be said of Paul's call for utopian restraint in the speech "The Future of Man's Environment," given in 1967 at the Smithsonian Institution in Washington:

> [C]an we directly apply our best theories to human and social situations? I think not, for to preplan too thoroughly is to kill life; and the more subtle the theory the more dangerous the attack. This is the invidious sense of "social engineering." Prudence and science are one thing, determining how people are to live and breathe is another. It is probably best just to open a space in which they can live and breathe in their own way. That is, we should aim at decency, not excellence. We cannot draw the lines a priori, but in every case there is something to plan for and much to refrain from planning for. This often means when to technologize, to achieve a decent background, and when not to technologize, to achieve freedom.[51]

Fig. 46 Study for Baltimore Synagogue, drawing, 1948

The same spirit of prudence and moderation permeated all of their thinking, and the idea of an "interim plan" in *Communitas* — a delaying action against planners and developers, especially in the Third World — will never be out of date, although it has certainly been out of fashion, and much of the damage the Goodmans predicted is already done.

As readers may have noted, perhaps with some sense of paradox, there are two sides to the "utopianism" of *Communitas:* one of them the yearning for a golden age that the child in Percy never relinquished, the other Paul's faith, also grounded in childhood experience, that ordinary people could make a satisfactory world for themselves out of whatever materials came to hand, given face-to-face community and freedom from coercion.

For Paul there was a dystopian corollary to his faith: the more that decision making was taken over by planners, the less likely that people would be willing or competent to choose wisely for themselves. It was this concern that led Paul to say in 1972 that he "no longer believed in schemes for improving the human condition." But to Percy this seemed a despairing view, and he could not accept Paul's answer as adequate to his own architect's urge to perfect the world. These conflicts between the utopian impulses of the two brothers are surely what made their work together so fruitful but also so susceptible to misinterpretation by those who do not come to *Communitas* with the neo-functionalist attitude already somewhat ingrained.

One last twist of irony comes of these paradoxes. In 1990 a new edition of *Communitas* was published, with the basic text unchanged but framed now by a laudatory preface (Paul Goldberger) and an afterword (Percy's fourth paradigm from *The Double E*). Both of these choices Percy made during his last illness. By the time the book was printed he had followed his famous younger brother, his nemesis Robert Moses, and many an anonymous sociologist to the grave. Buried, too, was the entire literature of "postwar reconstruction" which had culminated in *Communitas:* the Beveridge Plan in Britain, the Progressive Urban Studies of the National Resources Planning Board in the States, the many books of Lewis Mumford and Colin Ward — all of it paved over by freeways and parking lots and shopping malls. Just how much of the past had been swept under the rug may be suggested by the fact that the new publisher of the book was none other than Columbia University Press. The head of the press wrote Percy during his final illness to acknowledge the mistake made long ago in rejecting what was now recognized as a classic, and to express satisfaction in being allowed to correct that error. But, of course, reprinted classics do not get much attention in a world fixated on an avalanche of new discoveries, new problems, new solutions, and new disasters.

It seems to me that the real import of this last edition of *Communitas* lies in the dark shadow that the passage of time has thrown across its message. For example, the contrast between the utopian attitudes of the two brothers is now highlighted by the inclusion of Percy's updated paradigm, boldly cast in the rhetorical style of *News from Nowhere* — that is, utopian *fiction*. It is strange to move from the New Commune, with its city squares and ailanthus trees, to the backward glance from the year 2020, which serves as premise to *The Double E.* From Edward Bellamy to Ursula Le Guin, the never-never land of the future has always run the risk of doll house quaintness, no matter how cogent its analyses. And yet Percy's fantasy of a better world finds a saving grace in its utter modesty and restraint. The environmental crisis had confirmed lessons learned over the years from his foot-dragging, anarchist brother and freed him from the architect's obsession to build the perfect city. Instead of trying to solve every problem with cutting-edge technology and social engineering, Percy's fourth paradigm wholeheartedly embraces the neo-functionalist attitude, imagining a history of modest retrenchments, repairs, and remediations rather than a diagram for paradise. Would that we might claim such a history when 2020 rolls around!

Paul Goldberger's preface brings out the difference between these two versions of utopia in still another way. On the one hand, he praises the emphasis of *Communitas* on livable neighborhoods and a truly urban aesthetic, reminding us that the attractiveness of city life depends on places to sit, walking distances, and elbow room, in the tradition of Jane Jacobs or the "pattern language" school. On the other hand, Goldberger has his reservations about the three paradigms of *Communitas,* which he seems to regard as "actual plans the Goodmans propose" — as if they had never moved beyond the blueprints of Le Corbusier and Wright. What is even more surprising, and perhaps indicative of our own end-of-the-century plight, is Goldberger's preference for the Goodmans' "defense of the city as a marketplace," which he thinks worth taking seriously "as a source of choice above all, and in this sense . . . far more topical."[52] We've come a long way when a shrewd critic fails to hear the sarcasm reverberating in the Department Store City.

Goldberger is right about one thing: many passages in *Communitas* do speak of the paradigms as *programs* for a more rational order of life. The truth is that both utopian impulses — to build a better world and to trust in people to build their own world, for better or worse — are at work in *Communitas,* and its genius lies in the way Paul and Percy inspired and chastened one another: Percy's Department Store City saved by satire, Paul's New Commune underwritten by willingness to settle for a little breathing space instead, and hope for the future, inherent in Percy's "interim" plan.

In any case, the long-term influence of *Communitas* has not been limited to architects and planners and will continue to spread among the heirs of the New Left: bio-regionalists, environmentalists, Greens — all the citizens who have acquired the neo-functionalist attitude themselves, not necessarily by reading the Goodmans but by living and working in the atmosphere of social controversy and initiative that remains the best legacy of the sixties. *Communitas* helped create this new attitude by ridiculing consumerism and the sacrosanct standard of living; reevaluating the idea of decent poverty and self-subsistence; bringing ethical criteria to the choices of technology; calling for a new balance of urban and rural life; reconceiving regionalism on ecological premises; generally encouraging old-fashioned virtues like prudence, frugality, and modesty; and, most of all, inculcating a healthy suspicion of planners and plans that promise more than meets the eye — even including all these worthy goals and benefits.

Sources

In addition to my own conversations and correspondence over many decades with both Goodman brothers and their families, especially Naomi Goodman and Sally Goodman, I have consulted interviews conducted with Percival Goodman by Suzanne O'Keefe, Bernard Rosenberg and Ernest Goldstein, Robert Meredith, and Dennis L. Dollens as cited in the notes. Unpublished materials are located primarily in the Avery Architectural and Fine Arts Library of Columbia University (for Percival Goodman) and the Houghton Library of Harvard University (for Paul Goodman). Other important sources include the Benjamin Nelson Papers in the Rare Book and Manuscript Library of Columbia University (for the original typescript of *Communitas*) and the Richard P. McKeon Papers in the Joseph Regenstein Library of the University of Chicago, and the archives of the John Simon Guggenheim Memorial Foundation, the Columbia University Press, and the University of Chicago Press.

Notes

1. From an unpublished speech to students at the University of California, Berkeley, 12 February 1965.

2. *Architectural Forum* 62 (January 1935): 112.

3. Percival Goodman, "Notes on Community Planning," *Architectural Progress* 6:2 (February 1932): 4.

4. Percival Goodman and Paul Goodman, *Communitas: Means of Livelihood and Ways of Life* (Chicago: University of Chicago Press, 1947) vi.

5. Notes on Community Planning,"4.

6. Paul Goodman, "A Rationalistic Architecture," *Symposium* (July 1932): 299.

7. Paul Goodman, "A Romantic Architecture," *Symposium* (October 1931): 518.

8. *trend* 2:2 (March–April 1934), 2:3 (May–June 1934), and Le Corbusier, *When the Cathedrals Were White* (New York: Reynal & Hitchcock, 1947 [orig. French ed.1937]) 211.

9. Paul Goodman and Percival Goodman, "Frank Lloyd Wright on Architecture," *Kenyon Review* 4:1 (1942): 23.

10. Ibid., 27.

11. Ibid., 22–23.

12. Percival Goodman, Guggenheim application, 1942 competition (submitted autumn 1941).

13. Ibid.

14. From interviews with Suzanne O'Keefe (2 May–21 October 1979), Columbia University Oral History.

15. As quoted by Vivian Vorsanger, "Designers at the Fair," *Printers' Ink Monthly* 35 (September 1937): 22.

16. "The Mean, The Maximum, and The Minimum," *A Ceremonial: Stories 1936–1940*, vol. 3 of *The Collected Stories*, ed. Taylor Stoehr (Santa Barbara, CA: Black Sparrow Press, 1978) 207.

17. Ibid., 205.

18. *Communitas,* 128–29.

19. Ibid., 61.

20. Ibid., 129.

21. Ibid., 62.

22. Ibid., 72.

23. Ibid., 128.

24. Ibid.

25. Account of the genes s of *Communitas* compiled from unpublished interviews with Percival Goodman by Robert Meredith (31 October 1972) and Suzanne O'Keefe (2 May–31 October 1979). Compare Dennis L. Dollens, "Interview with Percival Goodman," in *Artist of the Actual: Essays on Paul Goodman*, ed. Peter Parisi (Metuchen, NJ: Scarecrow Press, 1986) 145–47.

26. Meredith and O'Keefe interviews.

27. "The Mean, The Maximum, and Minimum," 204.

28. *Communitas,* 88.

29. Meredith and O'Keefe interviews.

30. Dollens, "Interview," 147.

31. Richard P. McKeon Papers, University of Chicago (see note on sources).

32. Dollens, "Interview," 147.

33. *Communitas*, 17.

34. Ibid., 9.

35. Ibid., 128.

36. Ibid., 15.

37. Ibid., 59.

38. Ibid., 74–75.

39. Ibid., 100.

40. Paul Goodman, "Politics Within Limits," in *Crazy Hope and Finite Experience*, ed. Taylor Stoehr (San Francisco: Jossey-Bass, 1994) 73.

41. Charles Abrams, "The City of the Future," *Commentary* 4:5 (November 1947): 500.

42. Colin Ward, "The Utopian Community," *RIBA Journal* 80:2 (February 1973): 96.

43. Letter to the author, 20 August 1982.

44. "The Architect from New York" (interview with Percival Goodman), in *Creators and Disturbers: Reminiscences by Jewish Intellectuals of New York*, ed. Bernard Rosenberg and Ernest Goldstein (New York: Columbia University Press, 1982) 316.

45. Ibid., 315.

46. Percival and Paul Goodman, "Creating a Modern Synagogue Style; Tradition from Function," *Commentary* 3:6 (June 1947): 544; (reprinted in this volume, pp. 62–65).

47. Percival and Paul Goodman, "Modern Artist as Synagogue Builder" *Commentary* 7:1 (January 1949): 52 (reprinted in this volume, pp. 66–71).

48. O'Keefe interviews; compare Dollens, "Interview," 150.

49. Percival Goodman, *The Double E* (Garden City, NY: Anchor Books, 1977) 4.

50. Percival Goodman, unpublished notes for "Notes on Community Planning," Department of Drawings and Archives, Avery Architectural and Fine Arts Library.

51. Paul Goodman, "Two Points of Philosophy and an Example [contribution to a symposium]," in *The Fitness of Man's Environment* (Smithsonian Annual II) (Washington, DC: Smithsonian Institution Press, 1968) 31.

52. Paul Goldberger, "Preface" to *Communitas* (New York: Columbia University Press, 1990) x.

Synagogue Architecture

Fig. 47 Congregation Sha'arey Zedek, Detroit (Southfield), 1956–63: exterior detail (cat. 25i)

Kimberly J. Elman

The Quest for Community: Percival Goodman and the Design of the Modern American Synagogue

In the years just after World War II, Percival Goodman began designing synagogues. Jewish by birth, yet unfamiliar with the traditions of his faith, Goodman was deeply affected by the tragedy of the Holocaust. The killing of six million Jews had awakened in him a deep sense of belonging to a larger Jewish community. Until this time, he had lived a wholly secular existence in New York and Paris, with little concern for organized religion. The end of the war signaled a profound and urgent shift in Goodman's architectural and theoretical output. His heartfelt commitment to sustaining Jewish community life in America now superseded the earlier dedication to social housing and ameliorative city planning proposals that had characterized his work during the 1930s. He also seems to have distanced himself spontaneously from the commercial and residential clients that had previously sustained him economically while he was pursing his more socially committed architecture. Thus between 1947 and 1979, when he discontinued architectural practice, Goodman would come to realize more than fifty synagogues across the United States.

Communitas, written by Percival Goodman and his brother Paul during the waning years of the war, may be seen as a bridge between these two modes of thinking. This book, not published until 1947, certainly seems to represent the culmination of the radical social thinking that Percival had embodied in his prewar visionary projects such as the Working City of 1931 (figs. 18–20) and the Community Service Homes of 1932 (figs. 11–15, pl. IV), both of which aimed at a comprehensive re-evaluation of the way that people lived and worked in the urban environment. Yet at the same time, the book foreshadows the Goodmans' interest in the American Jewish community and the way in which it could survive, adapt, and prosper in the aftermath of the war. One particular passage from *Communitas* seems to evoke the communal mandate of the traditional Jewish temple:

 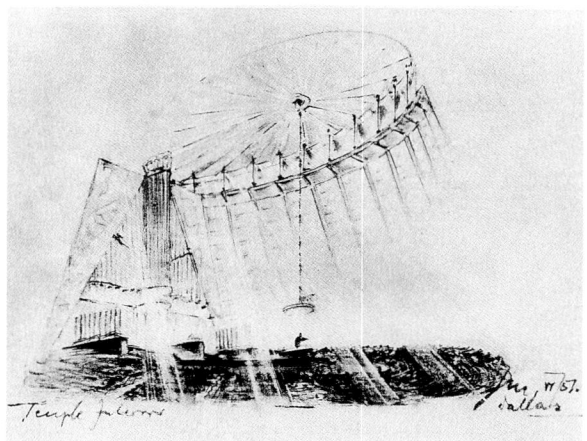

Fig. 48 Children in a classroom in Fairmount Temple, Cleveland (Beechwood Village), 1950–55

Fig. 49 Eric Mendelsohn. Temple Emanu-El, Dallas, 1951: proposal

> For a community is not a construction, a bold Utopian model; its chief part is always people, busy or idle, en masse or a few at a time. And the problem of community planning is not like arranging people for a play or a ballet, for there are no outside spectators, there are only actors; nor are they actors of a scenario but agents of their own needs — though it's a grand thing for us to be not altogether unconscious of forming a beautiful and elaborate city, by how we look and move. That's a proud feeling.[1]

Simultaneous with the Goodmans' collaboration on the book, information about the atrocities in Europe became increasingly available. The emotional impact of these events caused the brothers to re-embrace Judaism; neither had been religious before, although Paul had been a Bar Mitzvah. They read, discussed, and contemplated ways that they could bring the intensity of their other pursuits to the Jewish cause. In this climate, they saw an opportunity to reconcile their positions on the nature of community, as first outlined in *Communitas*, together with the demand for a new type of synagogue that would accommodate the diverse needs of the newly settled suburban congregations. This led to the development of a proactive position on synagogue design that redirected, as it were, the social commitment that underlay their prewar approach to community planning. Percival Goodman's personal dedication to architectural modernism had now to be combined with his newfound awareness of the necessity for maintaining Jewish communities in the decentralized landscape of postwar America.

The country experienced unprecedented economic prosperity as a result of the wartime economy, and the dispersed Jewish community thrived together with the rest of America. Many families moved out of the old urban centers and into new suburban developments that were isolated from their traditional urban neighborhood with its local synagogue. This new landscape was quite different from the small, segregated enclaves where most Jewish immigrants had first settled. Many families in the suburbs lived in neighborhoods where there was a mix of religious affiliations, with the Jewish families being in the minority. In order to retain their congregations many synagogues were compelled to relocate to the suburbs, where land was cheaper and they could provide large complexes that served not only as houses of worship, but also offered classrooms, social halls, and recreational facilities. Goodman characterized this change as follows:

> The most important element differentiating the church of today, whether it be Catholic, Protestant, or Jewish, from the past, is programmatic and its implications are equal perhaps to the dif-

Fig. 50 "The New Synagogue," article by Percival Goodman in the *Brooklyn Jewish Center Review* (October 1953) (cat. 36)

ference between the monastic Romanesque church and the great cathedrals of the late middle ages. This change lies in the emphasis on community activities, for increasing importance is given the school and social arrangement, with a corresponding diminution in the facilities for worship. The church or temple is becoming a community center.[2]

Because the community had lost the closeness provided by the urban environment, the synagogue itself now had to fulfill multiple duties that were not required in the former setting, such as sponsoring social gatherings, encouraging professional networking, and organizing youth activities to insure that the younger generation would not stray from their Jewish roots (fig. 48).

Percival Goodman was among a number of prominent architects who developed an interest in the design of the modern synagogue. Well-known figures such as Eric Mendelsohn, Philip Johnson, and Frank Lloyd Wright also designed synagogues in the decade following the war. Mendelsohn's B'nai Amoona (1949) in Saint Louis has a dramatic parabolic roof in the main sanctuary that terminates in a high wall of windows; in his most ambitious project, for Temple Emanu-El (1951) in Dallas, the main sanctuary would have been inside a grandiose tower (fig. 49), but Mendelsohn died before it could be realized. Johnson's cubic composition in stone, glass, and steel for Kneses Tifereth Israel (1954) in Port Chester, New York, is characteristic of the preferred aesthetic of his commercial and residential work. Wright's famous Beth Sholom (1954) in Elkins Park, Pennsylvania, exemplifies his ability to build for a variety of religious denominations while consistently achieving an acute sense of spirituality through his bold use of color, distinctive forms, and innovative interior planning strategies.

In an essay that they co-authored in 1949 for the magazine *Commentary*, Paul and Percival estimated that there were then eighteen hundred new synagogues in the planning stages.[3] This represented a significant number of commissions after the lean years of the war when most architecture offices closed or worked at just a fraction of their previous capacity. It is clear that the Holocaust became a rallying point for many of the Jewish architects who were involved in this activity; architects like Mendelsohn had escaped from Europe and others such as the Jewish American Louis Kahn, who along with many gentiles, shared in the tremendous sense of grief and incomprehensible loss that afflicted the society as a whole.

The explosion in synagogue building was accompanied by discussions about the appropriate style for new building (fig. 50). Traditionally, synagogue design had been impeded by the lack of a coherent building mandate in the Jewish faith. In an issue of *Commentary* from 1947 where Paul and Percival published their first synagogue essay, Franz Landsberger provides an overview of the historical significance of this debate and explains the theological basis for the confusion.

> The synagogue, as is well known, was not the earliest abode of Jewish worship. It was preceded by the Tent of Meeting in the wilderness and later by the Temple. . . . The synagogue was not a "house of habitation" for God, nor were animal sacrifices offered there. These sacrifices pertained only to the Temple in Jerusalem. The synagogue was a community gathering place in which the word of God, was read and expounded and in which the congregation offered prayers to God. When the Second Temple was destroyed in 70 C.E. and the sacrificial offering finally came to an end, the synagogue became the only center of Jewish worship and as such it has remained to this day.[4]

Without a clear direction, most synagogues before 1945 were built in historical styles that were unrelated to the Jewish faith. Moorish, neoclassical, and colonial were popular choices that often reflected a particular local tradition or served to enhance the image of the synagogue as a religious building equal in stature to the churches and mosques to which it would inevitably come to be compared.

After the war, many architects were active in redefining the role of style in the formation of the synagogue as an institution, strongly arguing for a modernism that would be expressive of the renewed relevance of the liturgy (see figs. 51–52). Eric Mendelsohn wrote in 1947 that

> it has been said that religious structures must be "traditional" in order to impart a sense of the sacred, that the dignity and emotional significance of such buildings can only be expressed through historical associations. To admit this is to deny that religion is an important part of our contemporary society. It is frequently said that contemporary design will not "harmonize." Certainly even the most beautifully conceived contemporary building will suffer if it is arbitrarily forced into a jungle of faked period pieces. This is why it is doubly important to select a site that will do justice to the building and not mar its harmonious integration with its surroundings.[5]

And Percival Goodman added in 1953,

> There can be no question of "modern" versus "period" styles. The building cannot be an imitation of some past way of building for an imitation cannot be as good as the real thing and so is an abom-

Fig. 51 Temple Beth El, New London, Connecticut, 1948–53

Fig. 52 Temple Beth El, New London, Connecticut, 1948–53

ination. Our modern ways of building are what they are, have their own expressive vocabulary and must be used.[6]

Recalling Sullivan's famous motto "Form follows function," and their own interpretation of this tenet in the chapter "Neo-Functionalism" from *Communitas*,[7] the Goodmans looked to "the tradition of the congregation and the service"[8] for inspiration.

In his synagogue buildings, Percival Goodman emphasized the conceptual propositions of Judaism through a specific formal vocabulary. Because of widespread public sentiment that all religious building, including churches and mosques, should be done in the modern style, it was important to Goodman that his work capture the essence of a uniquely Jewish philosophy. At the heart of this endeavor was the proper representation and execution of the tripartite division be-

Fig. 53 Congregation Sha'arey Zedek, Detroit (Southfield), 1956–63 (cat. 25h). The model shows the initial project for the synagogue complex with liturgical, social, and educational spaces.

Fig. 54 Temple Beth El, Springfield, Massachusetts, 1950–53: view from the back of the sanctuary into the lounge and the partition for the social hall (cat. 24e)

tween the liturgical, the educational, and the social parts of the synagogue complex. He explains how all three parts can be given equal consideration in the design of a synagogue:

> Our religion, unlike the Christian, is horizontal: all is holy, the temple, the home, the mountain, and the valley. The Christian concept is vertical: from a point on the ground, man aspires to God. So all is profane except this aspiration. Our faith makes it possible for me to design the social parts, the educational parts and the worship hall as a unity for all our activities shall be a hymn in His praise.[9]

In each of Goodman's synagogues, these three parts were integrated into a single design proposition that aimed to fulfill with equal success, all of the needs of the congregation (fig. 53).

One of the most serious problems faced by any congregation was the discrepancy between the number of worshipers at an average Sabbath service and the large number of members who only attended on the major holidays. Instead of ignoring this growing problem, Goodman and many of his contemporaries devised a compromise system of partitions that would allow the congregation flexibility in the amount of seating available on a particular day. To supplement the permanent main sanctuary, Goodman's preference was to attach the lounge and the social hall, or in some earlier examples the school classrooms, to the sanctuary with a set of movable partitions or heavy curtains serving as dividers (fig. 54). This was a strategy that became instantly popular with many congregations and remains one of the most recognizable features of synagogues from this era.

One aspect of Goodman's design strategy that sets him apart from all of his contemporaries and secures for him an honored place in the history of synagogue building is the relationship between modern art and architecture in his synagogue designs (fig. 55). In his book *Contemporary Synagogue Art* (1966), Avram Kampf writes about the integration of art into synagogue design:

> Goodman's approach to this problem is unique. He thinks that structural symbolism alone is inadequate; and that art and the artist have a significant function in the architectural endeavor. Per-

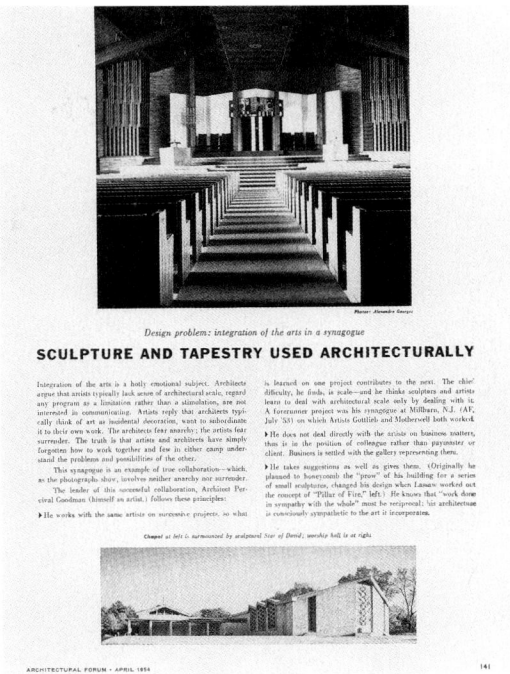

Fig. 55 Article about Temple Beth El, Springfield, Massachusetts, in *Architectural Forum* (April 1954)

haps because his conception of a synagogue is based more on the idea of a gathered congregation rather than on an abstract theological concept, he provides spaces in his architectural plans for artworks; here they can articulate their own themes, without being dominated by the architecture. The work of art is given a place to breathe and unfold; it is a part of the total design, yet it speaks with a voice of its own.[10]

Goodman sought the involvement of contemporary artists to both beautify and activate the ritual spaces through the thoughtful creation of appropriate objects that would enhance the congregation's experience in the synagogue. He commissioned exterior sculptures, lobby murals, ark curtains, and ritual objects — such as the menorah, the eternal lamp, and the kiddush cup — that functioned both as objects of art and of utility. For Goodman it was important that artists be brought into a project early in the design so that their perspective could be taken into account throughout the process. In Millburn, New Jersey, where Goodman built one of his first synagogues, he commissioned a young Robert Motherwell to design a large mural in the entrance lobby of the building (fig. 56, pl. XII). Motherwell became a frequent collaborator on Goodman's synagogue projects, along with sculptors such as Ibram Lassaw, Seymour Lipton, and Herbert Ferber (figs. 57–59).

Percival Goodman's philosophy of synagogue design can be best understood through his large body of built work. Although stylistically many of Goodman's synagogues can be seen as products of their own time, his effort to find an appropriate vocabulary for the design of Jewish ritual space elevates his project above the mere search for a suitable style for the synagogue. His quest was for an architecture that would complement, yet not overshadow, the congregation and their celebration of the liturgy, the two aspects of Jewish community life that always remained at the center of Goodman's understanding of his faith.

Fig. 56 Congregation B'nai Israel, Millburn, New Jersey, 1949–51: lobby, with mural by Robert Motherwell (cat. 23b)

Fig. 57 Congregation B'nai Israel, Millburn, New Jersey, 1949–51: view of exterior with Ibram Lassaw's sculpture *Burning Bush* (cat. 23c)

Fig. 58 Fairmount Temple, Beechwood Village (Cleveland), 1950–55: sculpture by Ibram Lassaw

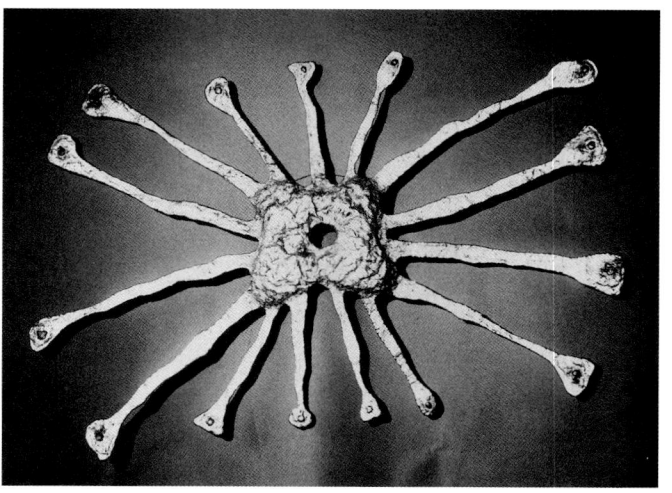

Notes

1. Percival and Paul Goodman, *Communitas: Means of Livelihood and Ways of Life* (New York: Vintage Books, 1960; original ed. 1947) 19–20.

2. Percival Goodman, "The Challenge of Church Design", manuscript, p. 3. Department of Drawings and Archives, Avery Architectural and Fine Arts Library. Published in the *Journal of the Royal Architectural Institute of Canada* 28:1 (January 1951).

3. Paul and Percival Goodman, "Modern Artist as Synagogue Builder," *Commentary* (January 1949): 53 (reprinted in this volume, pp. 66–71).

4. Franz Landsberger, "Expressive of America," *Commentary* (June 1947): 537.

5. Eric Mendelsohn, "In the Spirit of Our Age," *Commentary* (June 1947): 542.

6. Percival Goodman, "The New Synagogue," October 1953, manuscript. Department of Drawings and Archives, Avery Architectural and Fine Arts Library. An edited version of this essay appeared in the *Brooklyn Jewish Center Review* 35:8 (October 1953).

7. *Communitas*, 17–22.

8. "Modern Artist as Synagogue Builder," 53.

9. "The New Synagogue," 4.

10. Avram Kampf, *Contemporary Synagogue Art* (New York: Union of American Hebrew Congregations, 1966) 41.

Fig. 59 Chapel of Temple Beth El, Gary, Indiana, 1952–54: eternal light by Seymour Lipton

Percival and Paul Goodman

Tradition from Function
Reprinted from *Commentary* (June 1947): 542–44

In view of the numerous building projects initiated by Jewish communities following the end of World War II, in 1947 Commentary *published several articles on synagogue architecture. In the March issue an article by Rachel Wischnitzer-Bernstein appeared; in June "Creating a Modern Synagogue Style: A Discussion" was published, with contributions by Franz Landsberger, Ely Jacques Kahn, and Eric Mendelsohn in addition to that by Percival and Paul Goodman. — ed.*

As Rachel Wischnitzer-Bernstein has adequately shown, there is no living tradition of construction and style in the architecture of synagogues. The floundering attempts to invent a tradition by rationalistic analogies and *ad hoc* history result, as in most modern public building (the synagogues are neither better nor worse), in a painful superficiality, ludicrous a year after completion. On the contrary, it is just those synagogues, like that in Newport, Rhode Island, which were the plainest handling of a contemporary way of building, that turn out to age gracefully and to take on a certain venerability. Yet there is a tradition *in* the synagogue: the tradition of the service, of the sacred objects and furniture, and — to a degree — of the iconography — its symbols and decorations — and there is also a tradition of the congregational functions of the building.

In all these there is variation from rite to rite, national group to national group, and generation to generation: what the Sephardim do and what the Ashkenazim do, what the Orthodox do and what the Conservatives do, what the Talmud-learners do and what the American social workers do. But this kind of historical and experimental variation within unexpressed limits is just what is meant by a tradition.

The point of view of these notes is that a tradition of synagogue-building can be drawn from the tradition that exists, i.e., *the service and the congregation*; it cannot be imported where it does not exist, and should not exist, in the construction and style. The authors are functionalists. Now the meaning of functionalism is that the principle of design is the living plan, the arrangement of the actions of the users; the architect must look for his design to the service and the congregation, employing whatever means most simply and directly serve their functions. If he attentively and actively looks to the concrete functions, rather than passively accepting the generalities of a "building committee," he cannot fail to make a traditional synagogue. To say it paradoxically, what is needed is more attention to the letter and less to the spirit.

1. To show what is meant by functionalism in synagogue design, let us take some examples from the service. First, the fundamental act of the service, the reading of the Law. This comprises, orthodoxly, taking the Scrolls from the Ark, carrying them in procession to the reading desk, calling up the men of the congregation for the reading, raising high the Scrolls for all to see, dressing them again, and returning them in procession to the Ark. This complicated choreography contains a wealth of material for functional design.

For instance, in the Spanish synagogue Sheeray Tefila in New York, the Ark and the desk are counterposed across an open plain, the benches of the congregation rising sideways steeply from the plain. This arrangement brings out with much beauty the processional of the Torah between Ark and desk, the reader does not have his back to the audience, the parts of the congregation can see each other and those called on are in evidence as they come forward. (There are also certain disadvantages in the arrangement.) The point is that an inventive solution of the manifold parts of this action cannot help being profoundly expressive architecture. And what if the architect keeps in mind also such a special ceremony as the dance of Simhat Torah?

We have space here for just one more example of the relation of service and plan; let us choose the outdoor booth for Succoth. Obviously this calls for a garden plot, which during warm weather can serve also for collations, and — perhaps most important — as a milling-round space for such of the congregation as go outside during long services. The landscaping of such a garden is a difficult problem of design; the solution of the difficulty will prove to be expressive and traditional.

2. Now concerning decoration: It is a principle of functionalism that the chief care and expense should be given to that which gets the most frequent and attentive use.* What is to be embellished is not the columns that hold up the roof but the things that are intimately handled and scrutinized. (By the same principle, the construction as a *whole*, its proportion and color, must be clear and expressive, for they exert an omnipresent pre-conscious effect.)

In the synagogue this calls for a much closer integration between architecture, sculpture, and painting than we have seen. Decoratively, the role of the architect is to provide a setting for the sculpture and furniture of the Ark, the desk and light, the Scrolls, just as all these in turn are just the adjuncts of the service and the sense of congregation. What we look for is a team of artists in which the functionalist architect plays to the vision of a Lipchitz and a Chagall. In every synagogue the Ark is a focus of attention; why should not the sculpture of it be given to a master? (On this point it would certainly be useful to have a clarification of the "graven image" injunction. The non-naturalistic icons of the great modern artists might be, oddly, just the most traditional decoration conceivable.)

At risk of being polemical, we must mention two current abominations: the memorial stained glass and the eternal *electric* light. The first is a functional impossibility: the service is throughout a reading of prayers and every one has a book, the light simply must be bright and white. Further, with the Jews as with the Protestants, the visible congregation is of the essence: the mysterious illusive brilliance of real stained glass is glorious, but it is not ours. As to the second point, what is the symbolism of an eternal light that requires no care, that does not threaten to flicker?

3. Concerning the congregation, we must consider both the combination of congregational functions and the architecture of the congregation in the service. The congregational functions are traditionally: the prayer service, the study of the adults, the study of the children, festive occasions, the social activities of the sisterhood, the adolescents, etc. These create problems of planning for a number of rooms and for the possible flexible transformation or combination of rooms. There is the suggestion of Ben Bloch, outlined by Mrs. Wischnitzer-Bernstein: "The prayer hall a single unit with the social hall — provided with a collapsible wall and reversible seats — the two rooms joined (for the large crowd) on High Holidays." This is a typical solution that must be studied on its merits in each case. We must not forget the maxim that "an all-purpose object is rarely good for anything."

The sense of the congregation as taking part in the service is the fundamental religious function of the synagogue. If there is anything true in religion that is specifically Jewish, it is this integrating of the individual actors and their community; there is no representative and there is no non-human sacrificial act. The phalanx of prayer shawls, and the rising from the ranks of those called on and their returning to the ranks; ultimately this is the whole of it. Architecturally, *this* must be in evidence: the rabbi, the cantor and his choir, are adjuncts. And what profound, what terrible difficulties are implied in this word *congregation!* For instance, what of the woman's place in the Orthodox rite? Obviously we are here beyond the realm of discussions of buildings, yet who cannot see that apart from these things there is no plan for a building?

4. But the same difficulty — and worse! — meets us if we consider the heart of architecture, the city plan. For the first topic of architecture is not the building but the town square. It is a topic touched on by Mrs. Wischnitzer-Bernstein when she writes: "In the Middle Ages it had been the practice to enter synagogues at the side — inconspicuously — and there was no doorway in the western façade. The synagogue had to refrain from bringing itself strikingly to notice." It is a question of choice of site and the functional relation to other buildings. Now in America we have no town squares at all: no place that people do not pass through but where they stay because it

is the concourse of work, love, and culture.

The problem is not what building dares call notice to itself, but what building has a claim to do so. If, as we believe, every building with a real work, love, and culture function has such a right, we cannot plan without studying the integration of these functional buildings. As architects, can we cowardly avoid raising this question in the reader's mind?

But to end on a more pleasant note. Speaking of tradition, Mrs. Wischnitzer-Bernstein mentions the two Temples, but she fails to speak of the chief architectural passage in the Bible, the great chapters, Exodus 25–27, describing the construction of the Tabernacle. If the reader will consult this remarkable set of specifications he will grasp what we intend in these notes better than we can express it.

The passage begins with the materials that are to be gathered from the congregation: *"Of every man whose heart maketh him willing ye shall take My offering"* — the metals, the tent linen, the oil for the light, the wood for the furniture. It proceeds first to the main architectural feature, the Ark. This is specified as a movable furniture sculpturally embellished with cherubim, whose posture is described in detail. Next are specified the other sacred objects and furniture: the Table and the Candlestick of seven branches. Next, the tent to contain these things, all in bright linen "blue, purple, and scarlet" embroidered. The objects are then disposed in the Tabernacle, the Ark behind the veil, the Table and Candlestick before it, and the Altar. Lastly, the Court of the Tabernacle, for the meeting of the congregation.

"Thou shalt command the children of Israel to bring pure olive oil beaten for the light, to cause a lamp to burn continually. In the tent of meeting, outside the veil before the Covenant, Aaron and his sons shall set it in order, to burn from evening to morning." The religion has changed — in principle for the better; the totemic sacrifice and the priestly caste are both gone. They have been replaced by a tradition of learning and a congregation. But the method of functional analysis of the structure can be confidently recommended to architects; and there is no dearth of "traditional" iconographic ideas.

*See the authors' "Notes on Neo-Functionalism" in *Communitas* (Chicago, University of Chicago Press, 1947), Ch. viii.

Percival and Paul Goodman

Modern Artist as Synagogue Builder: Satisfying the Needs of Today's Congregations
Reprinted from *Commentary* (January 1949): 51–55

Of all branches of culture, the plastic arts have been the last to be cultivated by modern Jews. With the opening of the ghettos and the Enlightenment, Jews moved rapidly to leading places in academic sciences, law, general letters, music — just as for a millennium previously they had well cultivated medicine, philosophy, poetry, and theology. Yet as little as fifty years ago one could find almost no great names of Jewish painters, sculptors, and architects. (The reasons for this tardiness are both complex and, to us at least, obscure.) But now in two or three generations there are innumerable Jewish names in the plastic arts: sculptors, painters, stage-designers, etc. Among Americans alone, from Jacob Epstein to William Zorach, from Max Weber to Abraham Rattner, from Mordecai Gorelik to Lee Simonson; and hosts of the young.

These are, of course, just artists of Jewish lineage, with varying degrees of Jewish home background. We need not expect from them a Jewish art at all, any more than a Jewish science or a Jewish music. How is their development relevant to a rebirth of what is even more specific, a Jewish religious art?

With respect to technique, we do not know what a Jewish technique in painting, sculpture, or architecture would be. With respect to subject matter, we should like to distinguish two classes: first, there are the subjects of Jewish genre realism, no different in kind from any other local depiction of the home life and street scenes of any other minority group. This kind of subject — its greatest extension has been in literature both in Europe and America — springs from sentimental or naturalistic, anti-sentimental impulses; and among the Jews it has perhaps the added pathos that the locale depicted is vanishing, has in many places already vanished. There has been no more continuous decline, and sometimes sudden and catastrophic finish, than of this Jewish scene. And this particular vanishing happens to have a peculiar religious significance, since in the last thousand years so much of Judaism has consisted just of minute observances in family life in tight communities. It is unlikely that this kind of painting, for instance, can — as has sometimes occurred with other national genre styles — develop into a big style; the theme, the locale, are going and gone; and the religiosity embodied in them has little life. We are thinking of the countless effigies of rabbis holding scrolls, synagogue interiors, old men at study; all done in a chiaroscuro that is murky rather than dramatic, too learned to have the *élan* of the primitive, but learned in German and Russian academies rather than in the French schools that had some forward drive. (There are, of course, exceptions, like the genre pieces of Chagall and Ben-Zion.)

The second class of Jewish subject matter among the artists, however, happens to be in a very favorable position, as favorable as the genre subject is unfavored; and the relevance of this kind to religious art is at once apparent. This is the grand-manner symbolical, allegorical, or ritual subject, freighted with a philosophical significance, and often drawing on Biblical material. Let us mention the recent big-branched candlesticks or the sacrificial images of Lipchitz as examples, or Chagall's illustrations of Bible texts. This kind of subject is analogous to that treated by great modern Jewish writers, Buber or Kafka. The reason that this kind is in a peculiarly favorable position seems to us to be the following: among the great Western theologies the Jewish has been the least subject to the corrosive effect of modern science and philosophy. Without making theological judgments, it is sufficient for our purpose to say what few will deny, that Jewish theology has suffered least because it affirms least, and it affirms what, in one sense or another, very few people would contradict: God is one, not a body and the Messiah will come: these three propositions are almost the whole of the Orthodox creed.

And with these, subject to continual reinterpretation, there is a vast corpus of heroic stories and magical legends. These ancient stories, mainly the Bible stories, are archetypal in the psychoanalytical sense: Abraham is the father in every man, Adam is the innocence in every man, Jacob is the wrestler, etc.; when subjected to psychological and anthropological critique, these stories prove to be precisely relevant to us today. They are too legendary ever to be less than true.

The situation of modern artists, no matter what their background, is such that, in search of spiritual and heroic subject-matter, they find themselves on surest ground and with least inner doubt, in treating the Biblical or again the Hellenic symbols. (This has of course been true since the High Renaissance.) The more strong-minded they are, the more likely they are to treat these symbols, as Michelangelo did, or as Mann, Gide, or Cocteau do today. Furthermore, if the artist is concerned to portray social progress, the only great symbols to hand, unsullied by history and institutional or bureaucratic embarrassments, are those of the Prophetic tradition, the Peace of Isaiah or the Bones of Ezekiel. These symbols — the proposition that the Messiah will come — are the essence of social hope.

We have then premised, so far, a great tribe of Jewish artists; a vanishing local naturalistic scene; and on the other hand, a wealth of relevant heroic subject matter, already treated by many Jewish artists, and attractive to all artists in the grand manner.

Suddenly there occurred the fact that six million Jews were slaughtered in three or four years, just because they were Jews. We do not know in what ways other groups would react to such a happening, but among the Jews it seems to have had the following effect: they became aware of themselves as a physical community, a congregation. We mean in the barest physical sense. Not in any especial cultural way, not in a theological way (we do not hear anywhere a particularly authoritative prophetic voice); perhaps somewhat in a political way, in Zionism, for obviously Zionism is profoundly influencing all Jews, the non-Zionists and anti-Zionists as much as the Zionists. But most of all, and most simply of all, the reaction has been the sense of the co-presence of a certain identity and certain rudiments of a tradition, what we are calling the sense of being a physical congregation.

This has been true of Jewish intellectuals equally with other Jews. Whereas previously they had no especial concern with Jewish matters, now they are concerned with Jewish art, theology, the Bible, etc. (One of the authors of this article is in such a case.) To say it pessimistically, the general cultural and social ambiance seems so unreal that the physical congregation of the Jews appears to be a likely reality.

Omitting the debate and the action concerning Zionism, the chief effects of this congregational sentiment have been twofold: an increase in Jewish social work, philanthropy, and community centers — but these have always been strong Jewish drives, for many reasons; and secondly, an entirely new impetus in synagogue building. It is to this impetus that we must now turn.

It is estimated that there are eighteen hundred new synagogues being planned in the United States. Perhaps more important than this figure for our purpose: it is being proved possible to employ for the design of these structures architects and artists of world renown.

Let us mention the Liturgical Movement in several of the Christian churches, as described for instance by A. C. Hebert. Between the Liturgical Movement and this new building of synagogues there is an important similarity and there are important differences. The similarity is that the emotional and practical side of worship, the ritual, iconography, plastic design, and construction are brought to the fore. The differences are, first, that among the Jews there is no strong tradition, one might almost say no living tradition at all, of synagogue design and decoration — therefore serious artists must begin *de novo* to find a plastic interpretation for the tradition that does exist, namely the tradition of the congregation and the service.

We must insist a moment on this absence of plastic tradition. Conceive a meeting of an architect and the building committee of a Jewish congregation. They discuss the style. Georgian? Perhaps Colonial, like that delightful place in Newport? Or maybe to make it look like a Christian Science church? Or, again, Moorish because this is "traditional"? Specifically, what about the fenestration? Colored or clear? Broad? High? Obviously, in planning a church such a muddle would be inconceivable. Certain plastic presumptions compel themselves. The belfry will aspire; stained glass or no stained glass will depend on the theology. If, as in many modern Swiss churches, for example, a contemporary spirit is asked for, this will turn out as a modern statement of traditional arches and proportions, traditional verticals.

Certainly no blame attaches to the Jewish muddle; it simply reflects the late-coming of the Jews into the plastic arts, for a plastic tradition does not come from nowhere or from theologians, it comes from the work of many great artists. What is the way out of this muddle? Categorically: it is to employ the best modern architects working in their best functional and constructivist style. And so also with the painting and sculpture.

But a second, more hopeful, difference from the Liturgical Movement is this: there is no need, as in the Christian movement, to bring back the congregation into the service, reviving very ancient customs in order to do so; for it is the essence of the Jewish service to be the prayer and act of the congregation. The problem of design is simply to affirm this essence in a functional and beautiful way and to delete the aberrations that have crept in.

Perhaps we can make clear this important congregational point by describing the problem of the bimah or reader's desk. In the traditional Jewish service, the central act is the reading of the Law, passages of the Law and the Prophets being read in sequence, the whole Bible complete every year. For this reading members of the congregation are called up to the desk, more than a dozen during the service, counting the reading, undressing of the scrolls, etc.; and this group rotates through the congregation. Now for the Orthodox, this reading was done from a little platform in the middle of the floor, the congregation seated about, the reading directed toward the Ark on the east wall. (The congregational reading is the Offering.) The prayers of the cantor and his choir were also often, perhaps usually, offered from this middle space, from the midst of the congregation.

But in the past century or so there grew up, among the Reform especially, an opposed conception of the main plan: namely, to face all the seats to the front as in a theater or lecture hall, toward the rabbi who leads the service and who lectures. This is clearly an imitation of the Protestants, but it is quite inappropriate to the Jews, because the rabbi is in no sense a priest or minister: he is not sacramental nor is he expected to have any prophetic inspiration; he is just one of the learned men, employed in the communal division of labor to give his time to congregational problems. The only religious actor is the congregation, and this is brought out by the central position of the bimah.

The central bimah gives scope for the colorful procession of the Scrolls from the Ark to the bimah and back, with song and honor, before and after the reading. From the bimah the opened Scroll is raised in the midst of the people, with the words: "This is the Law that Moses put to the people of Israel by God's mouth, by Moses' hand."

From the congregational function of the plan and design, many other things follow. For instance the lighting: the lighting must be clear, white and bright, and general, for the chief object of awareness is the sense of the whole congregation by each member of it. Again, it seems to us mistaken for the voices of the choir to come from some invisible place; they must rather raise from the midst.

On the other hand, so long as the fundamental tradition of the congregational service is maintained, the rest is free for invention — for there is no recent tradition of decoration and furniture, or of music, which has proved itself great, whether Orthodox or Reform. On the contrary, a study of the ancient furnishings of the tabernacle as described in Exodus can only make us see how paltry and colorless the recent centuries have been. Instead of the great sculptured branched candlestick we have had small bare things. An Eternal Light burns before the Ark, and this light has degenerated into an electric light. Also, both the ancient texts and the archeological remains of ancient buildings show the structure embellished with every kind of human and animal figures, re-telling the history, symbolically projecting the meanings; the present restriction to a couple of jumping lions has become customary, but it is not traditional. And the same holds for the instrumentation of the music; the Orthodox disallow instruments, the Reform and Conservative employ the Protestant organ, but if the proscription is to be forgotten then the tradition seems to call for strings, pipes, and brass.

The congregational sense of the Jews, we said above, expresses itself in the synagogue and its service, and in the philanthropy and community center. This twofold conception can be seen in the present building impetus, for the programs given by the building committees call almost invariably for a group of buildings, three in function: a synagogue, a social hall, a school.

Now the architects and artists are in a peculiar position. On the one hand, they try to carry out the purposes and express the feelings of their employers — to make the program function beautifully. On the other hand, the very act of analyzing function and expressing meaning makes the artists soon turn on their employers with persistent embarrassing questions and paradoxes; they point out inconsistencies in the program. To say it strongly, the building committees are not willing to have the functions really function, and the artists reach toward feelings that the committees are afraid to feel. Inevitably these paradoxes crop up in considering the synagogue buildings as a community center, for the Jews share with the rest of the population a lamentable failure and coldness of the sense of community; but the honest analysis of function and the expression of meaningful feeling demand that the community commit itself.

They ask for a complete school building; but, especially among Reform Jews, the building will function only on Sunday mornings. Yet no worthwhile educational program is possible without a staff giving full time and attention to just this work — in short a full-time school. The building must be "better than a public school building in order to attract the young"; yet no activity is proposed to make the building useful or interesting. What is the functional architect to do?

To give a particular instance: more or less elaborate musical provisions are called for in the synagogue, but they shy away from employing a competent musician to train a school choir, yet this would, again, be the essence of a congregational service, as well as a benefit to the general culture. The demand for a large school building shows a dumb awareness of the obvious necessity of the new generation to the survival of any congregation, and even the peculiar importance of study for the People of the Book; but actually to face the concrete functions of a going school — purpose, curriculum, staff — requires more commitment than anybody is prepared for.

They urgently demand a social hall; often the committee is willing to get along with the old house of worship, but it must have a new social hall. This is not unreasonable, because the Jews are a community within the community. All right, what are the functions? Mainly — it turns out — an annual banquet, an occasional lecture, wedding, or *bar mitzvah* celebration. A stage is asked for, but they do not seriously plan for a theater group in or out of the school. So for an occasional evening of use (food better than the usual institutional food, to be sure) there is a large expenditure on stone and steel. Many of the new buildings are suburban, the old congregations having left the center of the city. The sites are spacious, pleasant; but the aspiration seems to be toward a country club as the model of community activity.

It is interesting that a rectory, a house for the rabbi, is not asked for. The rabbi prefers to live elsewhere, otherwise "he cannot have a life of his own." He prefers to devote to this "profession" an eight-hour day. Besides, it is understood on all sides that the building will be permanent, unlike the rabbi; no use consulting him or relying on him too much for liturgical improvement or educational program; either he is looking for a larger place or the congregation is looking for a man who is more of a go-getter. Too often the rabbi is a pessimist: "The congregation is ignorant — they know nothing" — or an opportunist: "Our important people wouldn't like that."

Even so! The fact is that there is a physical Jewish community spending many millions on new buildings, looking for community function and asking artists to express the meaning of the religion.

To sum up: for the first time in modern history there is a tribe of Jewish artists; none of these has ever worked in religious building; at the same time, the greatest of them, like many other great modern artists, are concerned with the Biblical archetypes, the Prophetic tradition, and the simple sublime spirituality of Jewish theology. Then, there is the Jewish community suddenly brought to a new awareness of itself as a congregation and expressing or about to express a large part of this sentiment as a plastic action, building. Lastly, there is no strong recent tradition of design and decoration; there is need to go back to very ancient traditions, to reinterpret them in the freest contemporary way, and this is just what the great artists would do anyway. (In modern times one could not employ free artists under other conditions.) And on the other hand, there is a strong continuing tradition of the congregational service that must be liberated from its excrescences, and a sense of community concern that must fight its way to expression.

What it will all come to is impossible to predict. The whole point of the argument we have advanced is simply that this is something new among the Jews; it is a peculiar set of circumstances. One would be embarrassed to have to show any achieved works; there has not been time. But there are already interesting sketches, plans, blueprints, and, we hope, a lively spirit in the air.

Portfolio of Percival Goodman designs

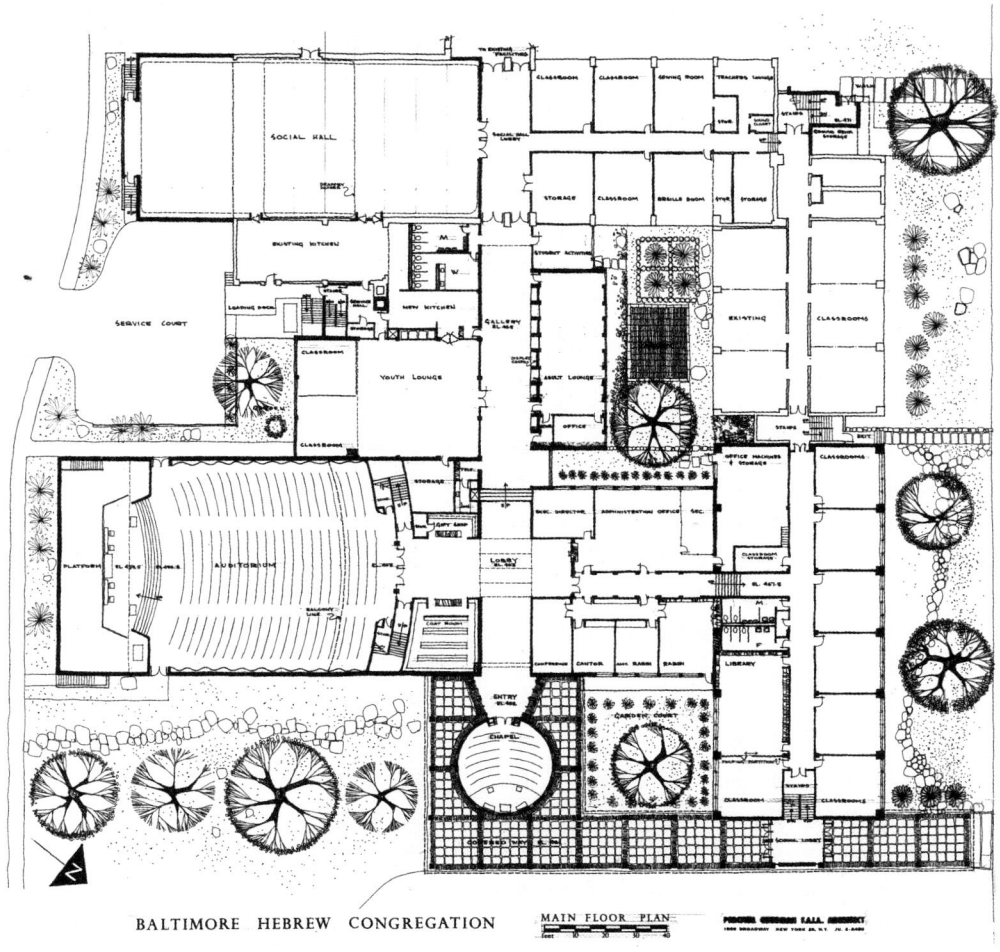

Fig. 60 Baltimore Hebrew Congregation, 1948–53: initial main floor plan

Fig. 61 Baltimore Hebrew Congregation, 1948–53: view toward the back of the sanctuary

Fig. 62 Baltimore Hebrew Congregation, 1948–53: rendering of exterior

Fig. 63 Baltimore Hebrew Congregation, 1948–53: exterior view

Fig. 64 Baltimore Hebrew Congregation, 1948–53: rendering of main sanctuary

Fig. 65 Baltimore Hebrew Congregation, 1948–53: view of ark

75

Fig. 66 Baltimore Hebrew Congregation, 1948–53: sculpture by Arnold Henry Bergier

Fig. 67 Baltimore Hebrew Congregation, 1948–53: eternal light by Seymour Lipton

Fig. 68 Congregation B'nai Israel, Millburn, New Jersey, 1949–51: view of exterior, with sculpture by Herbert Ferber

Fig. 69 Congregation B'nai Israel, Millburn, New Jersey, 1949–51: view of sanctuary with ark curtain by Adolph Gottlieb (cat. 23d)

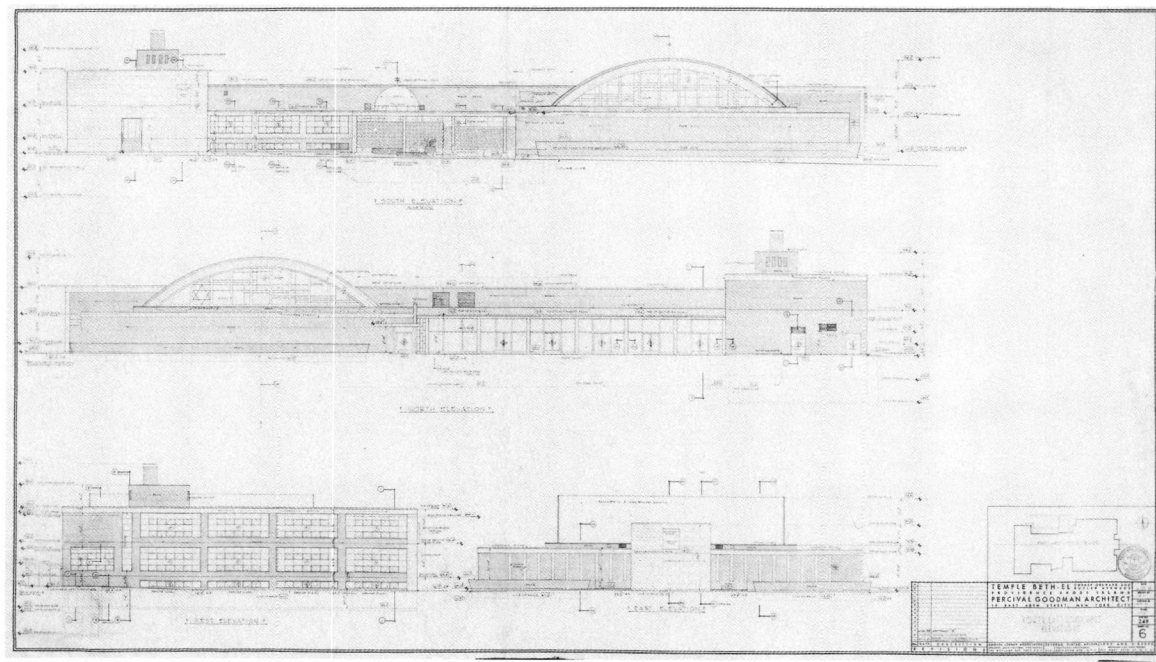

Fig. 70 Temple Beth El, Providence, 1948–55: exterior perspective (cat. 20b)

Fig. 71 Temple Beth El, Providence, 1948–55: north, east, south, west elevations (cat. 20c)

Fig. 72 Temple Beth El, Providence, 1948–55: rendering of entrance (cat. 20a)

Fig. 73 Temple Beth El, Providence, 1948–55: entrance (cat. 20f)

Fig. 74 Temple Beth El, Providence, 1948–55: chapel (cat. 20h)

Fig. 75 Temple Beth El, Providence, 1948–55: view of sanctuary, from aisle toward the ark (cat. 20i)

Fig. 76 Temple Beth El, Providence, 1948–55: view from lobby into sanctuary (cat. 20j)

Fig. 77 Fairmount Temple, Cleveland (Beechwood Village), 1950–55: initial proposal

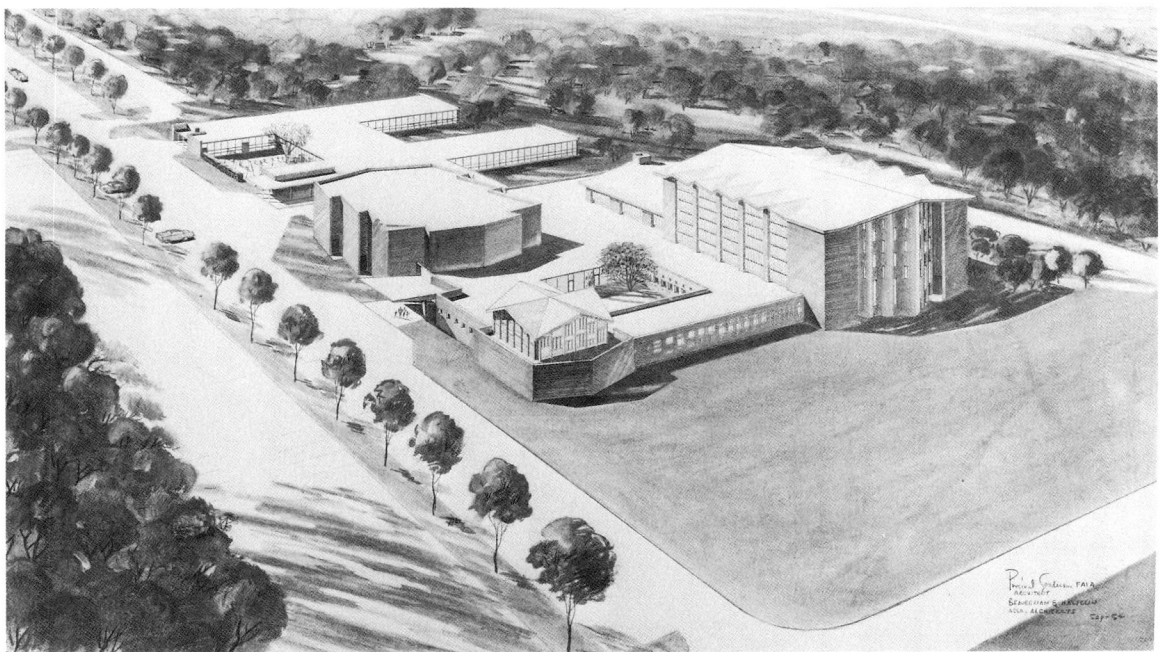

Fig. 78 Fairmount Temple, Cleveland (Beechwood Village), 1950–55: aerial rendering

Fig. 79 Fairmount Temple, Cleveland (Beechwood Village), 1950–55: exterior view

Fig. 80 Fairmount Temple, Cleveland (Beechwood Village), 1950–55: rendering of entrance, 1954

Fig. 81 Fairmount Temple, Cleveland (Beechwood Village), 1950–55: entrance, mosaics on column by Abraham Rattner

Fig. 82 Fairmount Temple, Cleveland (Beechwood Village), 1950–55: chapel tapestries by Abraham Rattner

Fig. 83 Fairmount Temple, Cleveland (Beechwood Village), 1950–55: sculpture by Ibram Lassaw for main sanctuary

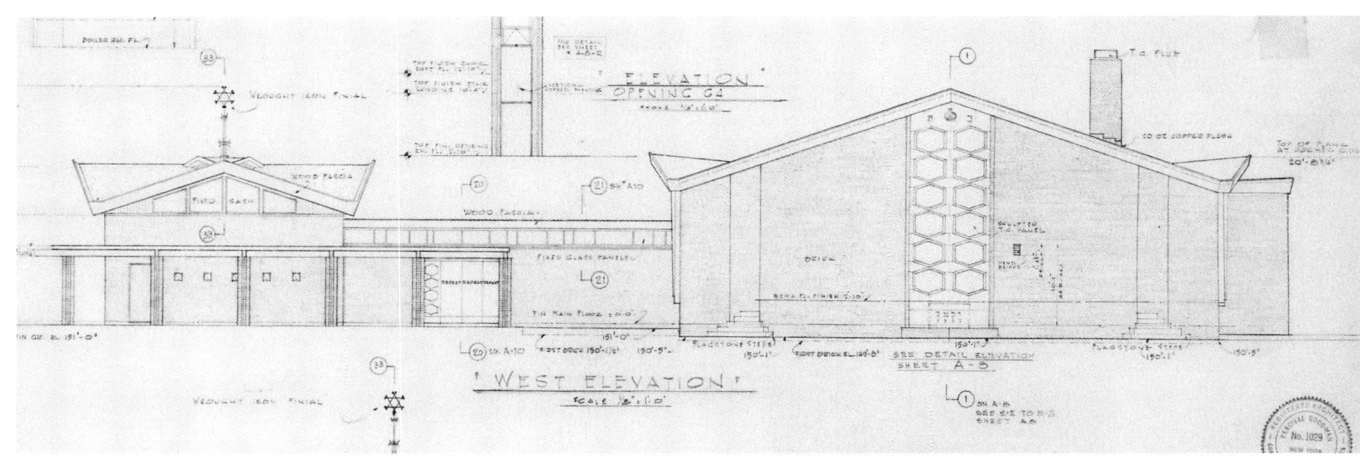

Fig. 84a Temple Beth El, Springfield, Massachusetts, 1950–53: west elevation

Fig. 84b Temple Beth El, Springfield, Massachusetts, 1950–53: west elevation, exterior view

Fig. 85 Temple Beth El, Springfield, Massachusetts, 1950–53: main sanctuary (cat. 24d)

Fig. 86 Temple Beth El, Springfield, Massachusetts, 1950–53: façade with sculpture *Pillar of Fire* by Ibram Lassaw (cat. 24f)

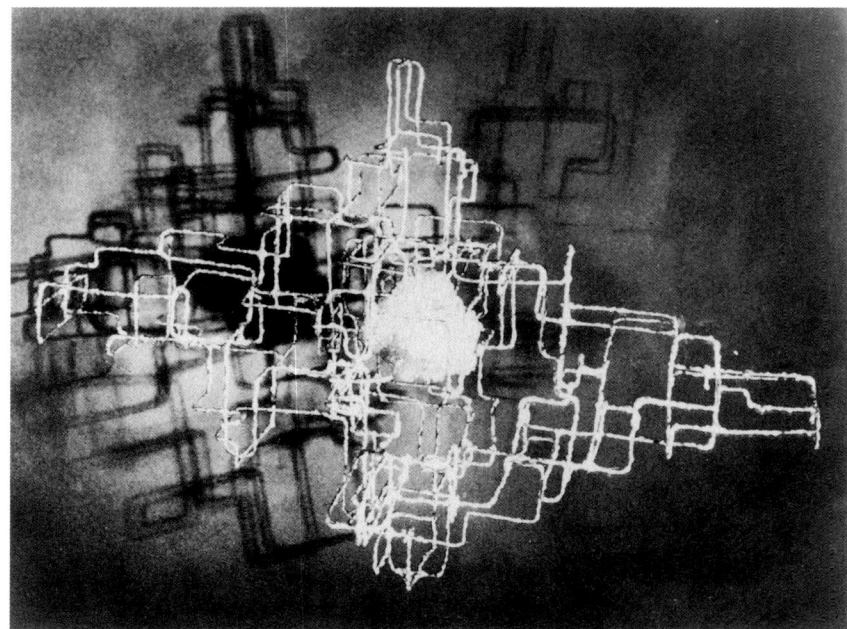

Fig. 87 Temple Beth El, Springfield, Massachusetts, 1950–53: eternal light by Ibram Lassaw (cat. 24g)

Fig. 88 Temple Beth El, Springfield, Massachusetts, 1950–53: ark rug from chapel by Robert Motherwell (cat. 24i)

Fig. 89 Temple Beth El, Springfield, Massachusetts, 1950–53: tapestry by Adolph Gottlieb, representing the twelve months of the year, destroyed by fire in 1964 (cat. 24h)

Fig. 90 Temple Beth El, Springfield, Massachusetts, 1965–66 (rebuilt after fire of 1964): exterior view (cat. 24o)

Fig. 91 Temple Beth El, Springfield, Massachusetts, 1965-66 (rebuilt after fire of 1964): view down center aisle of main sanctuary (cat. 24n)

Fig. 92 Temple Beth El, Springfield, Massachusetts, 1965-66 (rebuilt after fire of 1964): sanctuary and bema (cat. 24m)

Fig. 93 Temple Beth El, Gary, Indiana, 1952–54: entrance tower

Fig. 94 Temple Beth El, Gary, Indiana, 1952–54: rendering of exterior

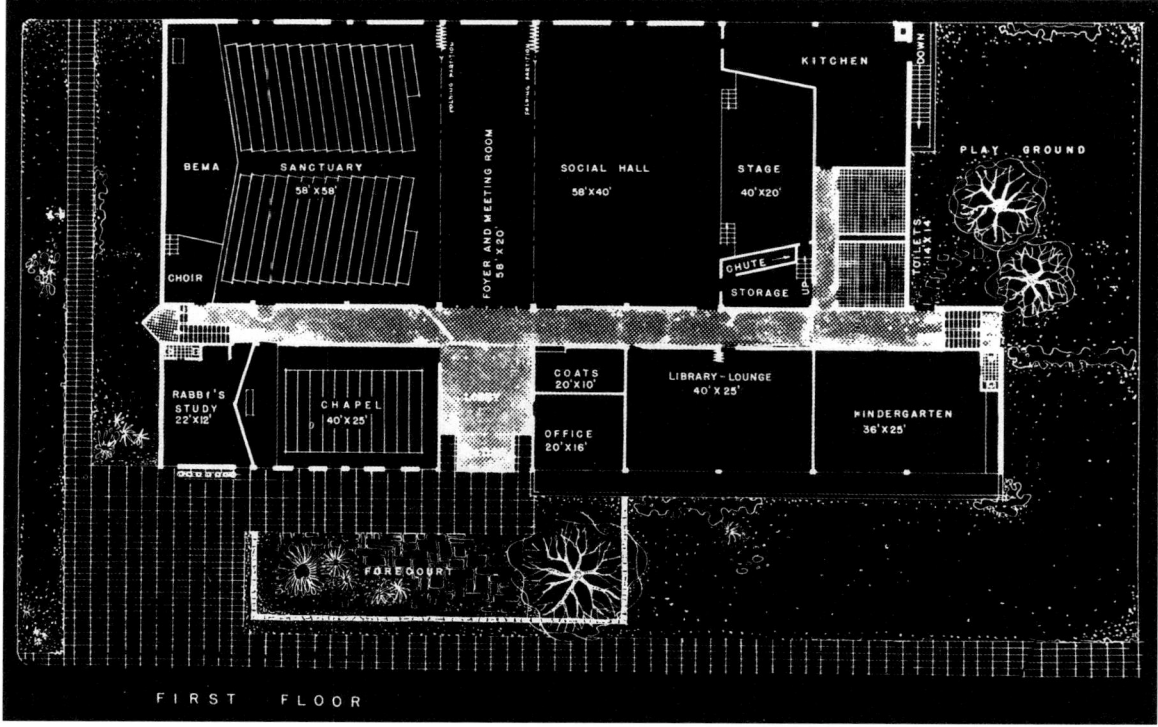

Fig. 95 Temple Beth El, Gary, Indiana, 1952–54: first-floor plan

Fig. 96 Temple Beth El, Gary, Indiana, 1952–54: menorah by Seymour Lipton

Fig. 97a Temple Beth Sholom, Miami Beach, 1953–54: rendering of oceanside elevation

Fig. 97b Temple Beth Sholom, Miami Beach, 1953–54: rendering of main sanctuary elevation

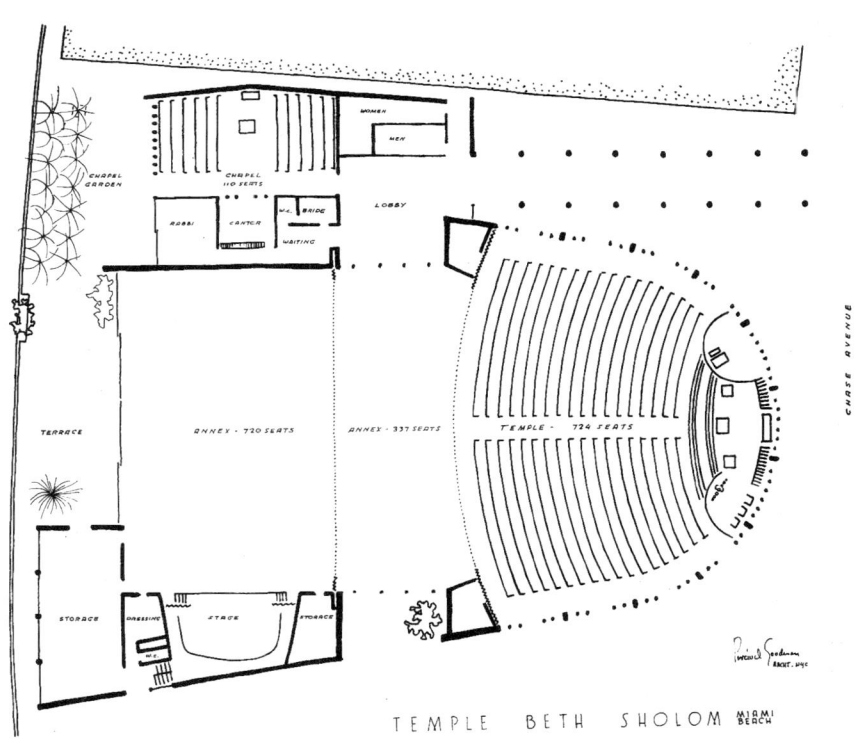

Fig. 97c Temple Beth Sholom, Miami Beach, 1953–54: floor plan

Fig. 98 Temple Beth Sholom, Miami Beach, 1953–54: rendering of main sanctuary interior

Fig. 99 Temple Beth Sholom, Miami Beach, 1953–54: view of bema

Fig. 100 Temple Beth Sholom, Miami Beach, 1953–54: sanctuary dome under construction

Fig. 101 Temple Beth Sholom, Miami Beach, 1953–54: sanctuary dome as completed

Fig. 102 Congregation Sha'arey Zedek, Detroit (Southfield), 1956–63: exterior view of sanctuary (cat. 25g)

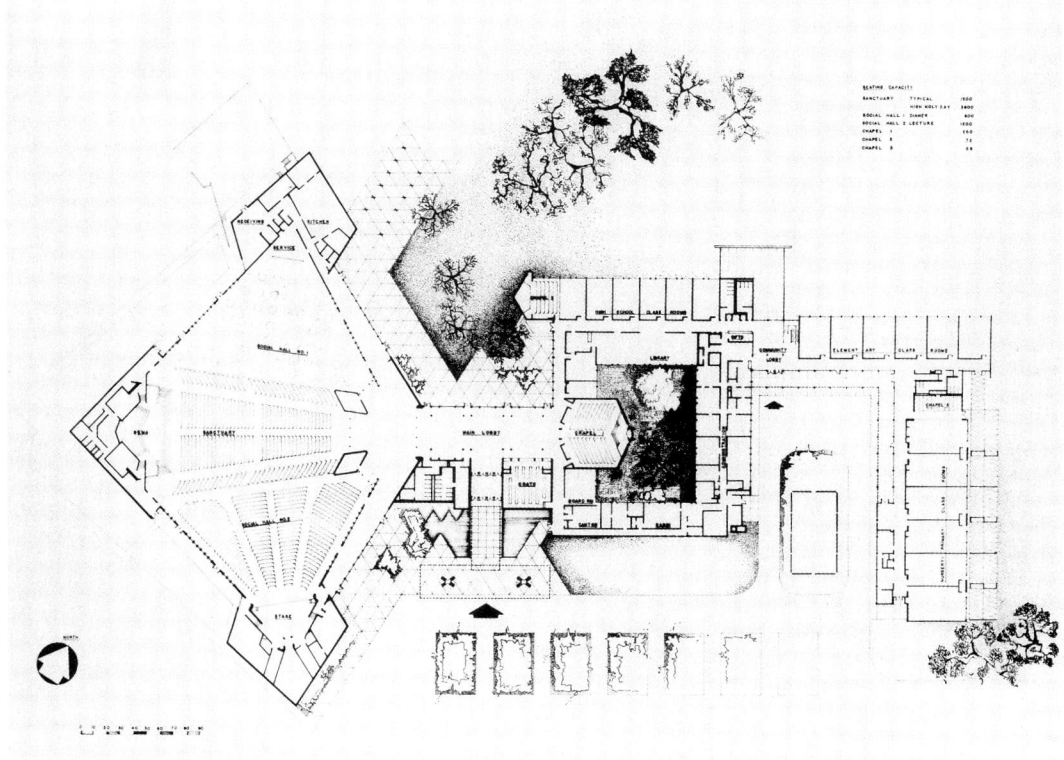

Fig. 103 Congregation Sha'arey Zedek, Detroit (Southfield), 1956–63: main floor plan (cat. 25d)

Fig. 104 Congregation Sha'arey Zedek, Detroit (Southfield), 1956–63: detail of concrete forms, sanctuary façade (cat. 25j)

Fig. 105 Congregation Sha'arey Zedek, Detroit (Southfield), 1956–63: view of chapel façade and interior courtyard

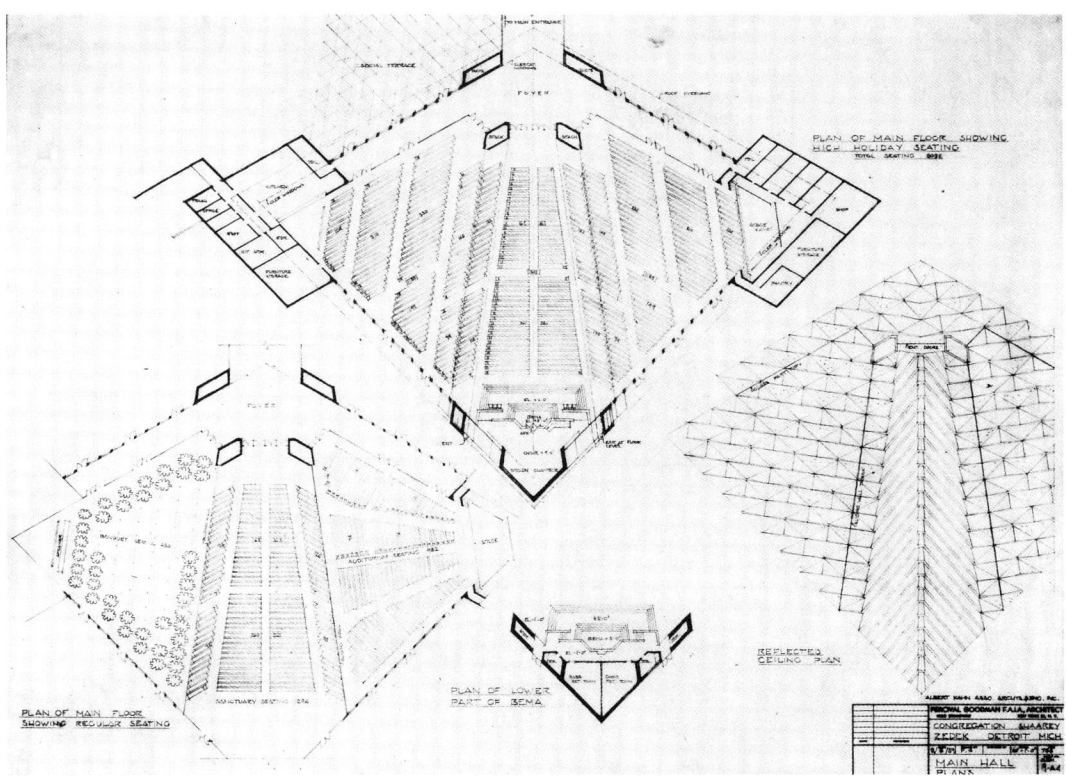

Fig. 106 Congregation Sha'arey Zedek, Detroit (Southfield), 1956–63: plan of main floor of sanctuary showing holiday and regular seating (cat. 25e)

Fig. 107 Sha'arey Zedek, Detroit (Southfield), 1956–63: view of the main sanctuary from the ark (cat. 25l)

Fig. 108
Congregation Sha'arey Zedek, Detroit (Southfield), 1956–63: view of ark in the main sanctuary (cat. 25k)

Fig. 109
Congregation Sha'arey Zedek, Detroit (Southfield), 1956–63: view of ark area under construction (cat. 25n)

Fig. 110 Congregation Sha'arey Zedek, Detroit (Southfield), 1956–63: view into the sanctuary from the social hall

Fig. 111 Congregation Sha'arey Zedek, Detroit (Southfield), 1956–63: view of lobby

Fig. 112 Temple Beth El, Rochester, New York, 1960–63: view of main façade (cat. 26h)

Fig. 113 Temple Beth El, Rochester, New York, 1960–63: looking upward at the main façade

Fig. 114 Temple Beth El, Rochester, New York, 1960–63: exterior view

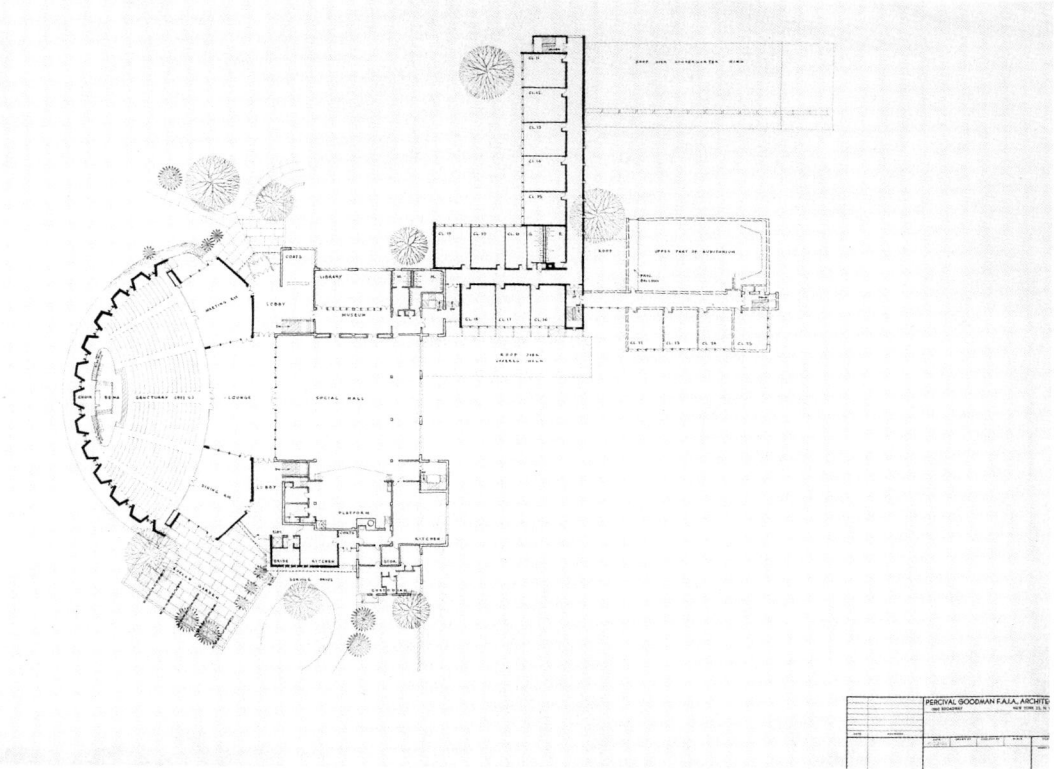

Fig. 115 Temple Beth El, Rochester, New York, 1960–63: initial floor plan showing a different sanctuary façade (cat. 26d)

Fig. 116 Temple Beth El, Rochester, New York, 1960–63: rendering of initial proposal for the sanctuary façade (cat. 26a)

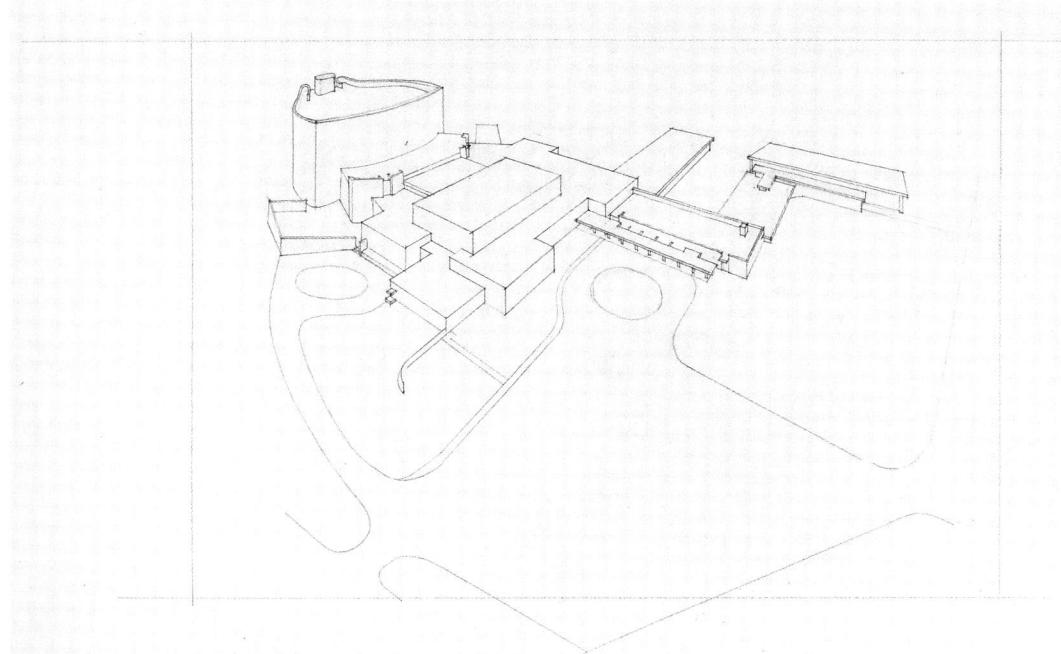

Fig. 117 Temple Beth El, Rochester, New York, 1960–63: axonometric drawing of general layout of synagogue complex (cat. 26e)

103

Fig. 118 Temple Beth El, Rochester, New York, 1960–63: rendering of the main sanctuary façade (cat. 26c)

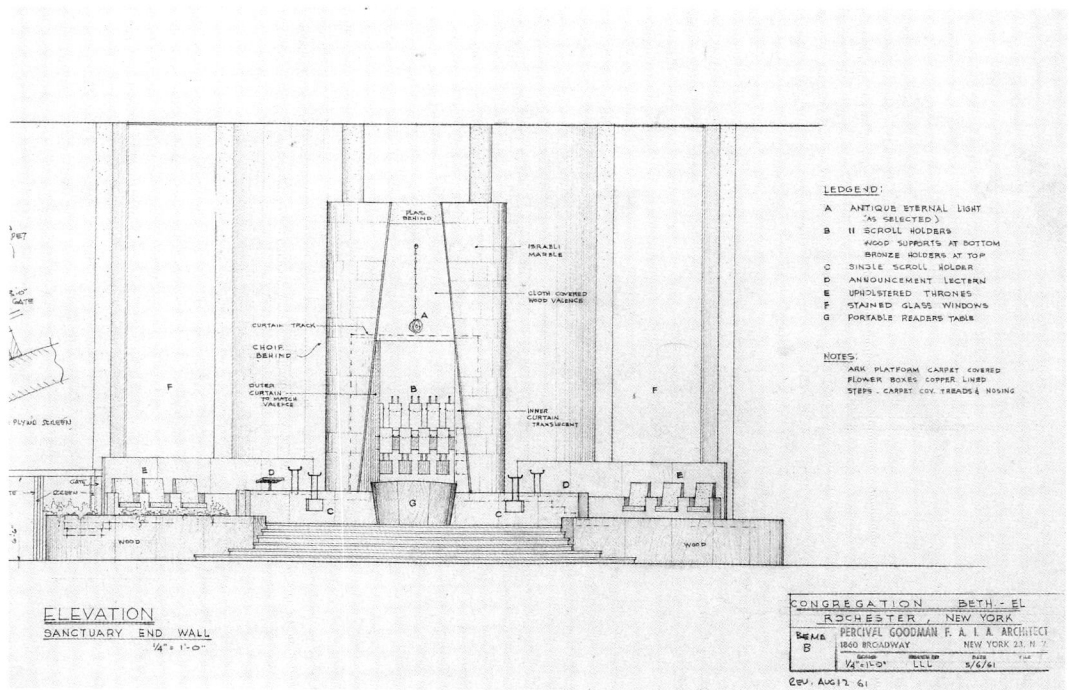

Fig. 119 Temple Beth El, Rochester, New York, 1960–63: elevation of end wall of sanctuary (cat. 26f)

Fig. 120 Temple Beth El, Rochester, New York, 1960–63: view of sanctuary, toward bema (cat. 26j)

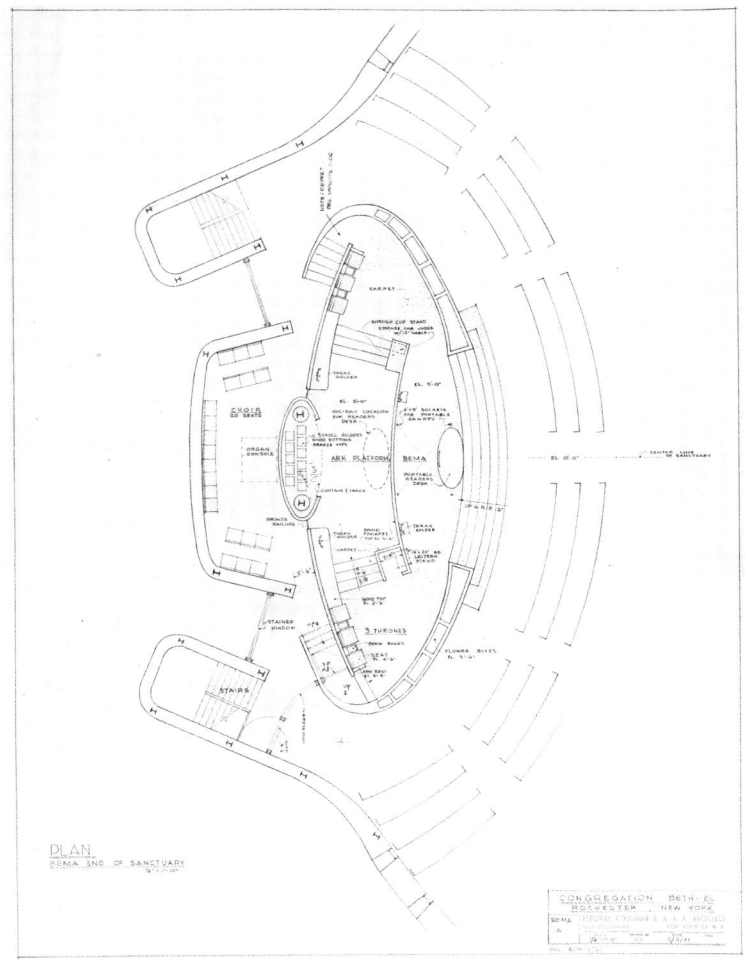

Fig. 121 Temple Beth El, Rochester, New York, 1960–63: plan of bema end of sanctuary (cat. 26g)

Fig. 122 Temple Beth El, Rochester, New York, 1960–63: bema and ark in main sanctuary (cat. 26k)

Rabbi Martin Freedman

A Client's Perspective

Percival Goodman — architect, planner, artist, writer, social critic, environmentalist, teacher, and designer — was in many respects a polymath both in his interests and accomplishments. His architectural career embraced an extensive range of buildings and plans. In the latter half of his career, however, he became preeminently distinguished as a builder of synagogues and temples and, between 1945 and 1986, designed and built more than fifty Jewish religious and community structures. His important creative work in this area significantly transformed the American synagogue.

Goodman's synagogues were modern, artistic entities that consistently reflected his creative, aesthetic vision and inspired both reverence and beauty. He designed religious buildings for Orthodox, Conservative, and Reform Jewish congregations, repeatedly demonstrating his keen ability to convince diverse synagogue building committees to reach for beauty and incorporate in the temple "not simply what the client has seen, or what he thinks he wants, but what is really needed."

The importance of art in the synagogue was a natural outgrowth of Goodman's concept of viewing the temple as a totality. His architectural design encompassed not only the physical structure but the complete interior of the religious building as well. For this reason, his desire to use great art and artists in sculpture, stained glass, tapestries, murals, and fabrics was a natural extension of his imaginative design for the uncompromisingly modernist temple. His aesthetic vision compelled him to seek works of art from some of the outstanding artists of our time, such as Motherwell, Frankenthaler, Ferber, Gottlieb, Lassaw, Rattner, Pinart, Lipton, and others. The nonfigurative art of abstract expressionism, by not contravening the traditional objections to

Fig. 123 Barnert Temple, Paterson, New Jersey, 1963: exterior view

human representations, was ideally suited to Jewish houses of worship. He convinced many of his clients of the need for modern art in their synagogues and succeeded in commissioning many contemporary artists to create pieces for the beautification of temples. When he could, he would commission local artists who had connections with the congregation or community.

The materials that Goodman used in his synagogue designs reflected a strong sense of place, and he always endeavored to incorporate local elements in developing his design. He was never satisfied in simply replicating his designs, but always sought to bring some local aspects into play in order to achieve a unique practical and spiritual vision. An example of this was his dramatic and striking design of the Barnert Temple in Paterson, New Jersey (1962), which reflected the nineteenth-century use of red brick in the factories of the silk textile industry (many of whose owners had been members of the Barnert Temple). He utilized the brickwork in a soaring roof line rising sixty-five feet over the Ark with a slanting roof containing ten dormers to admit fractured beams of light. In 1963 the Barnert Temple won an award as the best community structure built in New Jersey that year; it was further singled out by the French magazine *L'Arche* as one of the outstanding synagogue community buildings in the United States in 1963 (fig.123–124).

One of his early synagogues, in Millburn, New Jersey (1951), set a pattern for modern religious structures that was emulated by many other architects. His successful design for the expanding sanctuary was to be replicated countless times throughout the nation. His pervasive influence on temple buildings in the Reform Jewish movement came as a result of his role as a consultant and as a reviewer of construction plans of other architects throughout the nation. As a consultant for the Synagogue Commission of the Union of American Hebrew Congregations for more than a quarter of a century, his impact was clearly felt in the many critical evaluations he wrote. Meticulous in meeting the practical details of synagogue construction without stifling the creative spirit, he consistently reached for exciting, dynamic, and modern options in overall design.

It is interesting to note that as a child Percival Goodman had very little Jewish education. He often remarked that he "was a religious agnostic whose Jewish vision was powerfully awakened by the events of the Holocaust." He also rediscovered his Jewish heritage in the writings of Mar-

Fig. 124 Barnert Temple, Paterson, New Jersey, 1963: interior view of sanctuary

tin Buber and the person of Abraham Joshua Heschel. After World War II, his developing sensitivity for creating beauty in Jewish ritual and synagogue life also reflected the influence of his brother Paul. His wife, Naomi, worked with him for many years in the interior designs and furnishings of his buildings. Both Percival and Naomi Goodman experienced over the years a profound and intensive deepening of their Jewish sensibilities.

In the obituary in the *New York Times* of 12 October 1989, Paul Goldberger described Percival Goodman's synagogues as "assertive modernist structures that reflect Mr. Goodman's belief that the vocabulary of modern architecture can be transformed into something rich enough to express powerful religious feelings. We shall miss the power of his presence." Shortly after his death, the Fairmount Temple of Cleveland, Ohio, published the following notice in the *Times*:

> His social ideas are enshrined in his architecture. For more than three decades we have worshipped, studied and assembled to pursue mitzvot (religious commandments) in a synagogue building whose light and spaces enhanced our search and our participation. He has an enduring memorial here.

In a poem written by his brother Paul, entitled "For My Brother (Manner of Pindar)," are the lines:

> An artist is lucky who is busy
> With what is necessary! He
> Invents what people do not know they want
> But they see it come to be with surprise,
> Pleased in the end.

It is patently clear that Percival Goodman was such an artist.

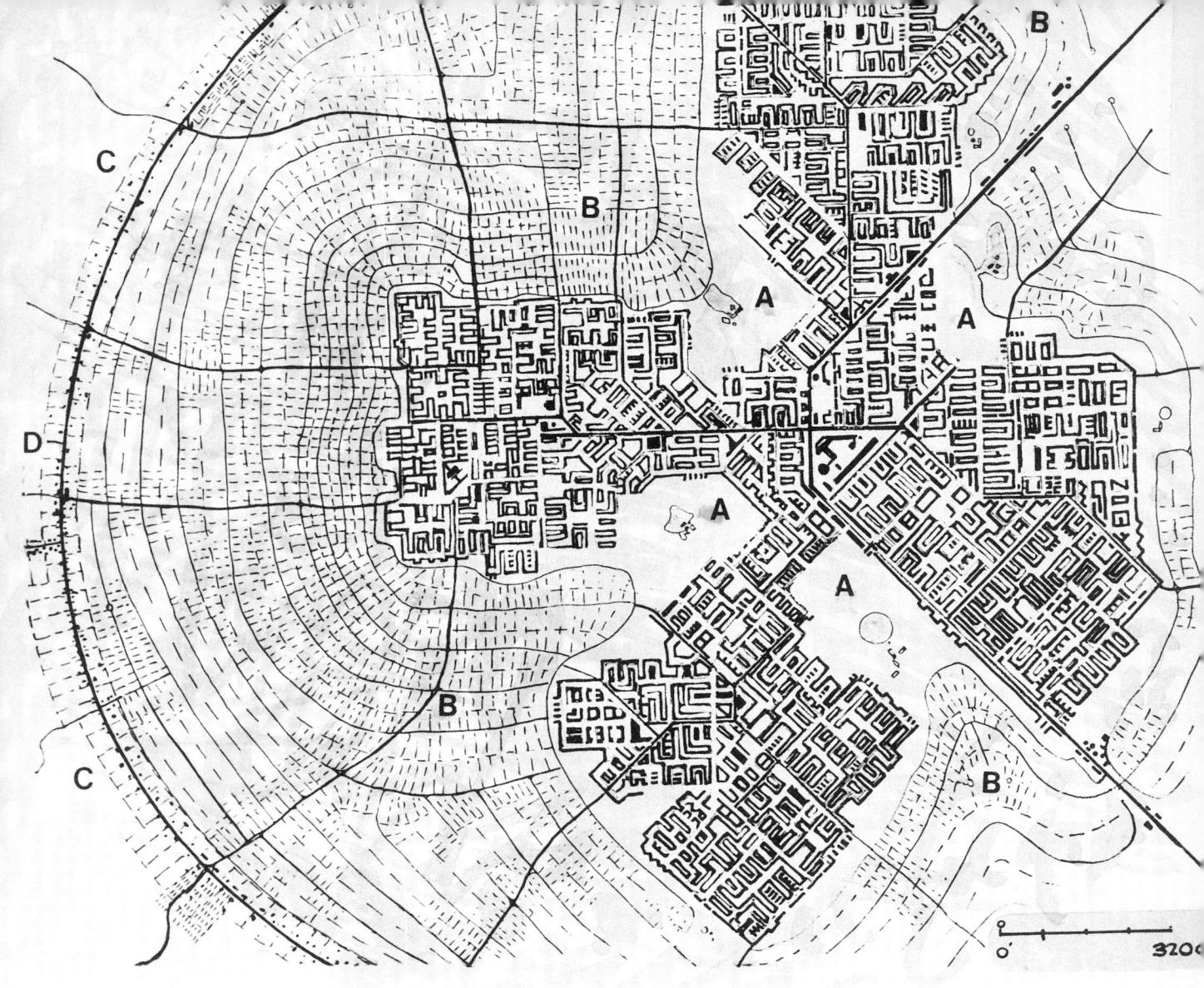

Fig. 125 Drawing for the ideal city from *The Double E* (1977). "The principles are: (1) to have most functions within walking or bicycling distance, and (2) to have nothing zoned in isolation except nuisance industries. (A) Recreation areas, (B) kitchen gardens, (C) the ring road, (D) farms."

Robert Fishman

Utopian Freedom: Percival Goodman's Social Thought

Percival Goodman planned many ideal communities, but perhaps his most utopian concept was his ideal of planning itself. For Goodman, planning was not a limitation but an enlargement of freedom. As he and his brother Paul Goodman argue in *Communitas*, "for the first time in history we have, spectacularly in the United States, a surplus technology that allows for the most widely various community-arrangements and ways of life."[1] But the bewildering varieties of technologies and choices have tended to paralyze action. Only comprehensive planning can make these options real by intelligently relating means to ends: showing how changes in the built environment can serve to realize society's values. Long-range, comprehensive planning is thus society's most fundamental assertion of freedom.

Yet the Goodmans also well understood the dangers to democracy inherent in comprehensive planning. If planning is indeed the assertion of certain fundamental values, how can these choices be justified and enforced in a pluralistic society? As the Goodmans point out, "Different people in a place want different things, and the same people want different things."[2] Like other utopians, the Goodmans never entirely escape this problem. Indeed, their own preference for the decentralization of power and population made comprehensive planning all the more paradoxical within their own framework.

The Goodmans respond to this problem by attempting to introduce choice and freedom into utopian thought itself. They treat their own and others' plans not as blueprints to be implemented but as intellectual "paradigms" that teach the varied relationship of design to values. These paradigms are essential to the education of citizens, who learn to make their own choices by critiquing and combining the paradigms. Thus, where other utopian thinkers either ignore or

Fig. 126 Goodman's drawing of La Ville Contemporaine of Le Corbusier, for *The Double E* (1977)

dismiss all other plans but their own, the Goodmans discuss a full range of twentieth-century utopias from Le Corbusier to the Israeli kibbutz in their "Manual of Modern Plans." For many readers of *Communitas*, these insightful, sympathetic yet critical discussions of such disparate plans as Ebenezer Howard's Garden City, Le Corbusier's Radiant City (fig. 126), and Frank Lloyd Wright's Broadacre City represent the most useful part of the book. The Goodmans not only offer their own three paradigms as three possibilities among many; they introduce fundamentally different values (hence fundamentally different designs) into their own proposals.

In *Communitas* the Goodmans saw the fundamental choice facing American society as between consumerism and community. Although their own preference was of course the latter, they nevertheless tried to give consumerism its due by presenting a kind of "utopian consumerism" in the paradigm they called "A City of Efficient Consumption." Their two preferred utopian paradigms were titled "A New Community: The Elimination of the Difference Between Production and Consumption" and "Planned Security with Minimum Regulation."

Thirty years after *Communitas* and five years after his brother's death, Percival Goodman returned to the utopian field in his book *The Double E*, which was based on the crucial relation of "*Economy* (the management of expenses) and *Ecology* (the mutual relationship between organism and environment)."[3] Here he offers a definitive synthesis of the two communitarian paradigms of *Communitas*, but these positive hopes are balanced by his growing concerns over the dual crises of economy and ecology. He sees the advanced economies of the West entering a new era of limits and scarcities, and he sees both city and suburb as caught in a downward spiral which only radical action can remedy. His vision of the cities of his time catches the essence of their urban crisis:

> The future? For the people, poverty and failure in slums where discontent and frustration feed on each other. For the city budget, a population needing housing, schools, hospitals, and social services with no means to pay for them. What were once the advantages — centralization of resources, variety of choice, and a large producing and consuming population — turn into a sink of human and vehicular congestion and pollution, physically unmanageable and financially bankrupt.[4]

Yet the suburbs of metropolitan areas were in Goodman's estimation scarcely better. They were "ecological disasters" whose faults lay in "sprawl and spread, in the highways and the traffic required by sprawl and spread, in the industries and their wastes, in the people's garbage, end product of a society where artificially generated cravings are taken for healthy appetites."[5]

Not surprisingly given these concerns, Goodman dropped completely the consumerist utopia in *Communitas* from *The Double E* and concentrated instead on a radical communitarian alternative for both existing cities and suburbs. But for my purposes I want to start with the early consumerist paradigm, because it is the necessary foil for Goodman's positive beliefs. Moreover, this paradigm — however ironically intended — took on a life of its own and had a vitality and inventiveness often lacking in the Goodmans' designs for their preferred community. Indeed, this paradigm would prove to be the most prophetic part of *Communitas*. These two communitarian idealists anticipated certain key elements in our postwar consumer society long before our most hardheaded developers or retailers adopted them. By a strange alchemy, *Communitas* came to resemble one of those works of godly piety where the devil got the best lines (fig. 127).

Although *Communitas* was published in the early postwar period, the Goodmans' understanding of consumerism retained the markings of their experience of the Depression, which seemed to prove that the techniques of mass production were so powerful that they were constantly in danger of flooding the market with excess goods, leading to persistent business crises and unemployment. Hence, an ideal consumer society must be organized to maintain a high level of demand. The Goodmans rose to this challenge by imagining a society whose built environment was relentlessly organized around the principle of the constant stimulation of desire for ever more varied material goods.

The Goodmans aptly subtitle their consumerist paradigm "the metropolis as a department store" because here consumption has completely engrossed the public spaces of the city. They imagine a metropolitan area of some five million people because only so large a number could

Fig. 127 "Street scene in the cylinder: always perfect shopping weather," from *Communitas* (1947)

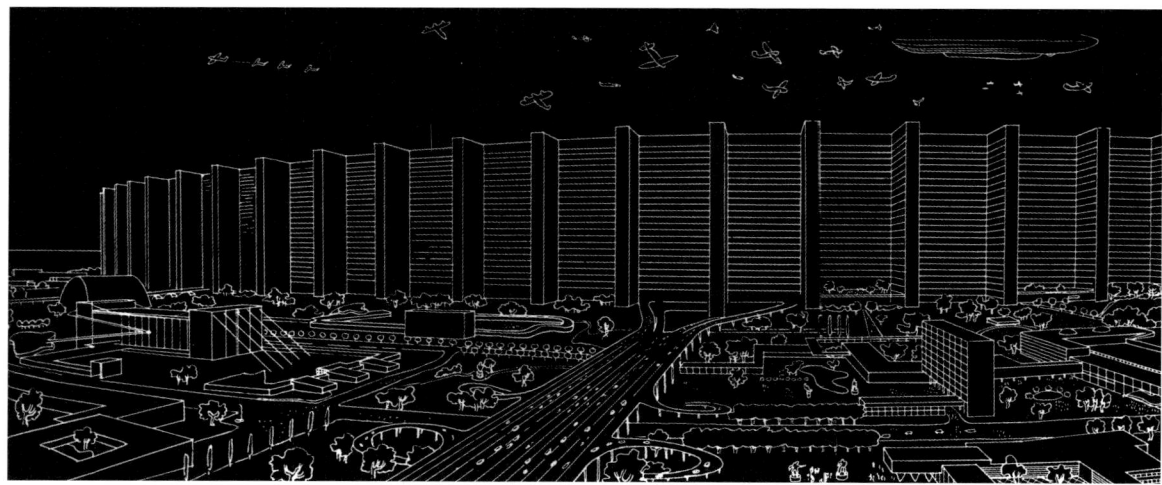

Fig. 128 "View of the air conditioned cylinder from the university zone," reverse drawing by Goodman for *Communitas* (1947); also reproduced in *The Double E* as "City of efficient consumption"

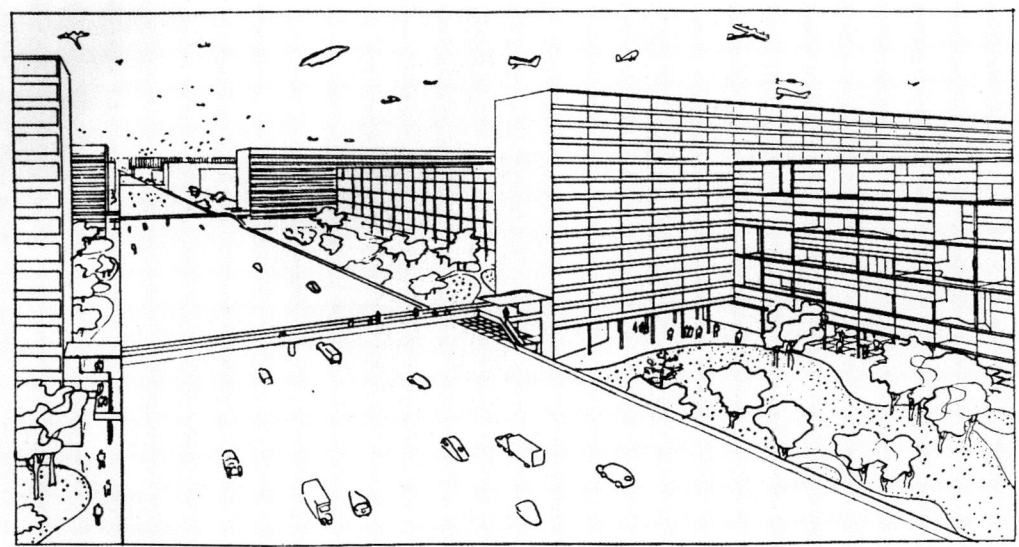

Fig. 129 "Along a radial highway in the residential zone," from *Communitas* (1947)

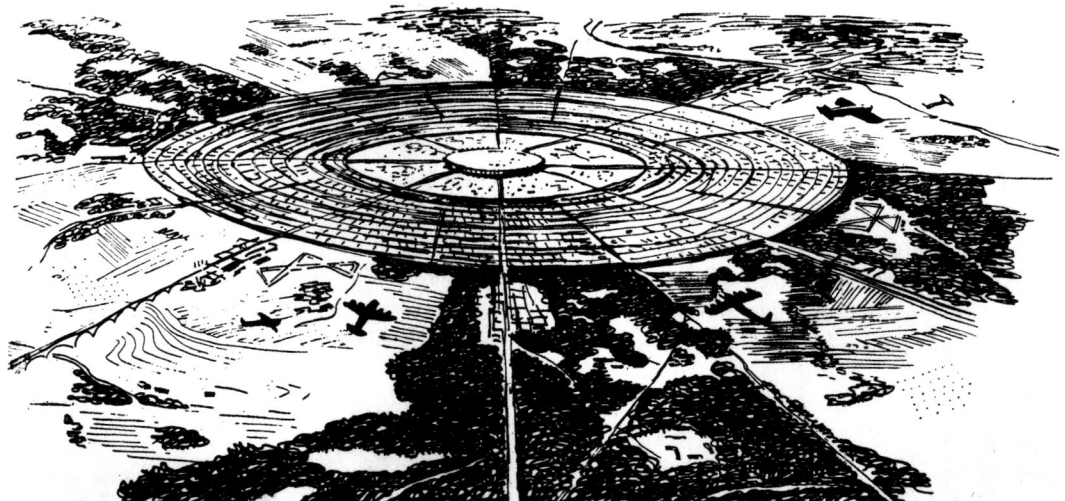

Fig. 130 Bird's-eye view of the ideal radiocentric city, from *Communitas* (1947)

generate the varied and changing demands to keep the production system constantly occupied. The downtown core of the metropolis is a single twenty-story megastructure, one mile in diameter, completely enclosed and climate controlled (figs. 18–20). Within the megastructure the streets are pedestrian promenades or "corridors" for the display of goods sold in the shops within. "Everywhere, in every corridor, as at a permanent fair, are on display the products that make it worthwhile to get up in the morning to go to work, and to work efficiently in order to have at the same time the most money and the most leisure."[6]

The upper floors of the megastructure contain some light manufacturing but are mostly devoted to offices. The roof is an airport, and underground are the mass-transit links, roads, and mechanical plant that service the core functions. Beyond the core is a university district (figs. 128–129) — presumably to teach the skills to produce the goods — and then residential districts. There a mixture of social classes would be permitted and even encouraged insofar as the presence of the less affluent promoted consumption among the better off to show their superiority. At the edge of the metropolis is open space, here conceived as a form of leisure consumption for jaded urbanites (fig. 130). Politics in the metropolis expresses itself not through elections but through consumer choice; and, in case this city somehow fails to consume all the products it has produced, a yearly carnival or saturnalia clears the shelves for the next season.

The Goodmans' depiction of a totalizing environment where advertising and design merge to promote consumption comes uncomfortably close to the main lines of American postwar development. The core megastructure is, among other things, an extraordinary prophecy of the enclosed shopping mall, whose realization was still almost a decade in the future when *Communitas* was published. To be sure, the Goodmans believed that efficient consumption required a single central core and failed to see how a decentralized system of automobile roads could achieve even greater efficiency for consumption by fragmenting their megastructure into dozens of subcenters conveniently located among the suburbs of the region. Indeed, one might regard the "Edge Cities" as defined by Joel Garreau — developments of more than five million square feet including retail, office, residential, and entertainment spaces — as the definitive (if decentralized) realizations of the Goodmans' sardonic vision. Almost in spite of themselves, the Goodmans captured the sheer power of consumerism as a system shaping both the built environment and personal relations. Their paradigm raises the uncomfortable issue of what alternatives could possibly compete with this utopia of wish fulfillment.

This is the problem that Paul and Percival Goodman confront in their two other paradigms in *Communitas*, and that Pericival Goodman would take up thirty years later in *The Double E*. The weakness of consumerism, as they originally saw it, is that it divides production and consumption. The world of work is separated from the home both spatially and spiritually. The worker commutes to a sphere of discipline, regulation, and stress and hopes to be rewarded by an abundant and satisfying home and leisure environment. The real result of this dichotomy, as Paul

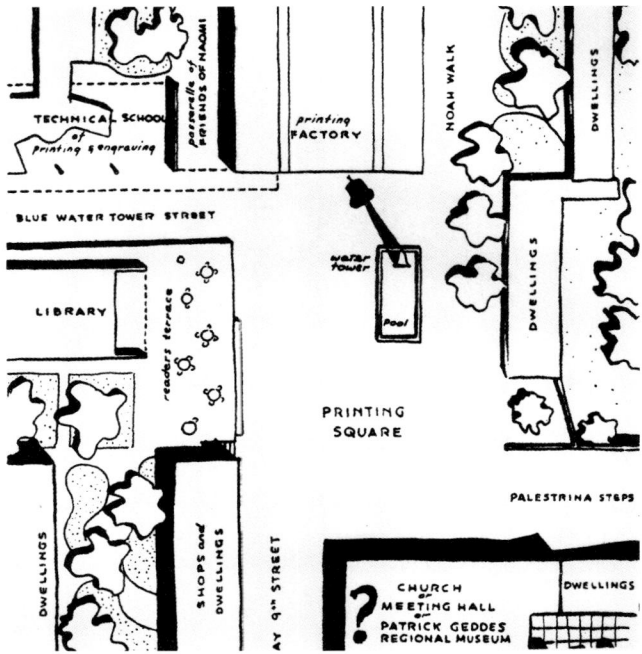

Fig. 131 "A square in the town: integration of work, love, and knowledge," from *Communitas* (1947)

Goodman argued in his influential book *Growing Up Absurd* (1959) is that "our abundant society is at present simply deficient in many of the most elementary objective opportunities and worth-while goals that could make growing up possible. . . . It thwarts aptitude and creates stupidity. . . . It discourages the religious convictions of Justification and Vocation, and it dims the sense that there is a Creation. It has no honor. It has no community."[7]

To these arguments Percival Goodman added another in 1977: if the consumerist utopia was culturally bankrupt, it was also doomed by what he called the double E of economic limitations and ecological unbalance. Goodman wrote in the midst of the deep recession of the mid-1970s that followed the energy crisis brought on by the Arab oil embargo. As he saw it, this double crisis of economy and ecology meant the need for a total rethinking of the American corporate economy and the American way of life. He proclaimed that "global resources will soon be inadequate to support us in the style to which we have become accustomed" and we must therefore "expect and plan for large-scale changes in the way we build our houses and our towns." No longer can these changes be made in a context of almost limitless choices. "Who could have guessed how quickly our appetites would grow, how quickly our surplus would diminish, and how badly we would choose?"[8]

For Goodman in 1977, the rebirth of the communitarian spirit was more than one choice among many (the one he and his brother preferred), as it had been in *Communitas* (fig. 131); in *The Double E* communitarianism is above all a necessary response to the crisis where "limits, not free choice, scarcity not surplus, are now the facts that will condition our future." The consumerist utopia (as well as virtually the whole "Manual of Modern Plans") therefore disappears from *The Double E*. Instead he presents a synthesis of "A New Community: The Elimination of the Difference Between Production and Consumption" and "Planned Security with Minimum Regulation" as a single paradigm representing the "right" choice.

What then is this synthesis? If, as Percival Goodman argued, planning is choosing the right relations between ends and means, what are the ends, i.e., the values, and what are the means, i.e., the physical form and social organization? We might begin by observing that Goodman's ideal city is a synthesis of two traditions. The first (in opposition to the industrial revolution) is judged the good society by its capacity to provide meaningful work. The great figure of this tradition was William Morris, but behind him stood the American transcendentalists like Henry Thoreau, who warned in *Walden* that "we have become the tools of our tools," and Ralph Waldo Emerson, whose poem "Two Laws Discrete" is quoted in *The Double E*:

> There are two laws discrete
> Not reconciled
> Law for man and law for things;
> The last builds towns and fleet,
> But it runs wild
> And doth man unking.[9]

The second tradition saw the Garden City or New Town — the city consciously planned and limited in size to be both a genuine community and in balance with nature — as the best setting for civilized life. Its great figures were Ebenezer Howard and Goodman's contemporary Lewis Mumford. Central to both traditions was John Ruskin, whose defense of craftsmanship against industrialism and the industrial city echoed through the nineteenth and early twentieth centuries. Goodman appropriately quotes in *The Double E* Ruskin's famous adjuration in *Sesame and Lillies* that cities be "kept in proportion to their streams and walled around, so that there be no festering and wretched suburb anywhere, but clean and busy streets within and open country without, with a belt of beautiful garden and orchard around the walls, so that from any part of the city perfectly fresh air and grass and sight of far horizon might be reachable in a few minutes walk."[10] Goodman omitted the walls, but he kept the spirit.

Fig. 132 Drawing of an 1870 invention called the Pedespeed which Goodman posits as a means of personal transportation in the city, from *The Double E* (1977)

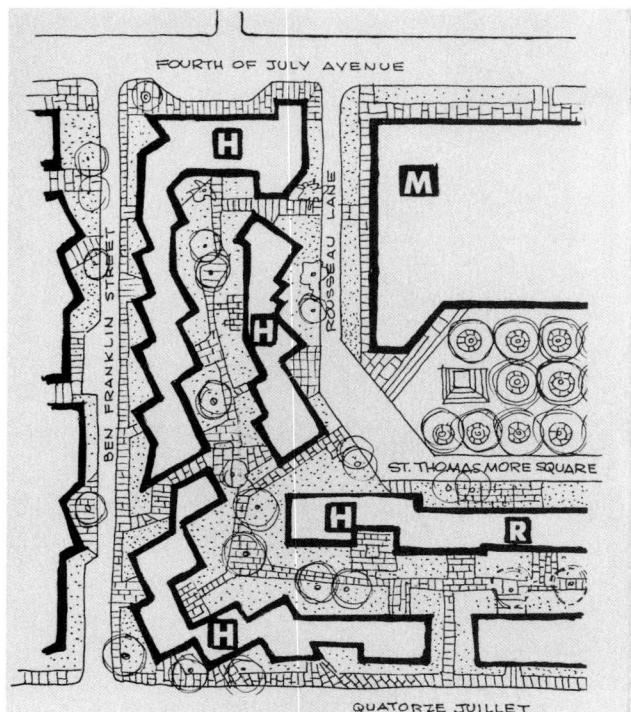

Fig. 133 "Street pattern: (M) Museum of Discarded Technology, (H) households, (R) restaurant," drawing for *The Double E* (1977)

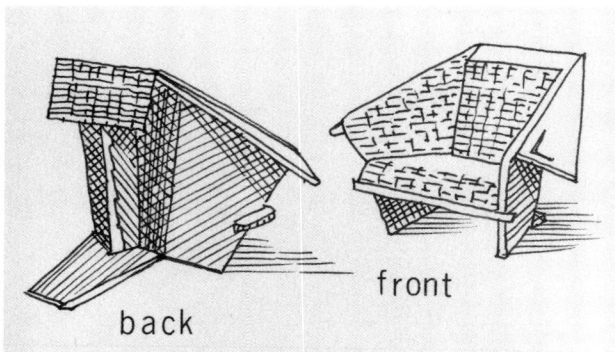

Fig. 134 Frank Lloyd Wright chair as an example of the "intermediate style" which emphasizes quality over quantity, drawing for *The Double E* (1977)

Fig. 135 "A quiet street," from *Communitas* (1947)

The ideal city of *The Double E* (Goodman does not give it a name) is a "bounded community," that is, a settlement whose success is defined not by how quickly it grows but by how effectively it stays within its optimum limits. He envisioned a city of about two hundred thousand people with a density of fifty per acre, sufficiently concentrated so that all its parts are within walking or bicycling distance (fig. 132), and everyone has easy access to the greenbelt that surrounds it. The basic planning and indeed spiritual principle of the city is "mixed use." The close interconnection of work, residence, and public space define the city's basic values (fig. 133). Goodman specifies neighborhoods of three- or four-storied row houses on narrow streets; each building would generally contain both home and workshops, and the streets would lead naturally into plazas that are the public spaces of the cities. As he puts it, "the 'grain' of the street (as urban designers used to call it) is close to Paris before rather than after Haussmann."[11]

Before further specifying Goodman's ideal of craftsmanship and its relation to his economic and ecological concerns, I must first describe the seeming anomaly in his ideal city, the massive industrial "Basic Economy Production Centers" that occupy parts of the greenbelt outside the town. Like other thinkers in the Ruskin/Morris tradition, Goodman had to confront the machine and the relation of craftsmanship to mass production. His response is particularly complex, and derives from work that he and Paul Goodman had done in the late 1930s. The Goodmans had calculated that only a tenth or perhaps a fifteenth of the productive capacity of the nation was needed to provide all its citizens with ample "basic" goods if those goods were produced with maximum efficiency. In *The Double E* Percival Goodman now imagines a mass-production sector of the economy using the most advanced techniques to produce the basic food, clothing, and shelter that constitute a minimal standard of living. Because products are simple and standardized, the costs and environmental impact are limited. Young men and women would be "drafted" to work at these production centers for a limited time, perhaps as little as two years. After this service, all citizens would have the right to draw on the basic sector to the extent of their needs for the rest of their lives.

To be sure, Goodman expected that only a small percentage of the population would be content with these basic goods and would seek further employment in the parts of the economy that produce "convenience, comfort, and luxury goods." Nevertheless, the basic sector would provide a cushion of security for everyone and an earned substitute for unemployment or welfare. With a basic livelihood guaranteed, people would be free to choose jobs that they found truly satisfying. The rest of the economy would be as free as possible, but Goodman clearly hoped that its characteristic unit would be the small workshop whose emphasis would be quality rather than quantity. These would be integrated into the home.

Goodman found in the Ruskin/Morris tradition of craftsmanship the ultimate solution to the crisis of "the double E." An economy that emphasized quality over quantity (fig. 134) would be utterly lavish only in those elements of skill and craftsmanship that make few demands on the

Fig. 136 "The Kitchen Gardens," drawing for *The Double E* (1977)

environment. It would thus conserve natural resources, consume less energy, and provide an unlimited number of satisfying jobs for citizens. These goals would also apply to agriculture in the greenbelt around the city. Agro-businesses that used vast quantities of fertilizer and other chemicals would be replaced by small-scale farms run on organic principles. These would be geared not to a national market but to providing the neighboring city with the freshest possible foods.

Both on the farm and in the city, the integration of home and work would of course eliminate commuting and the waste of time and energy inherent in the "spread city." In his depiction of typical home/workshops, Goodman acknowledged the revolutions of the 1960s in family and in gender roles, and tried to imagine these new kinds of families as the basis of a small-scale crafts economy. He describes a home/workshop in his ideal city that

> is shared by some thirty adults and children in two households. One produces a variety of small parts for an electronics firm while the other designs and makes rather modish women's clothes. The street floor of the house is divided between the workshop and the farm-style kitchen-living rooms, a busy and sometimes noisy place. . . . [Another] house is shared by a sculptor and a painter, a graphics artist and printer, each with their apprentices and households.[12]

Balancing these private worlds of family and work are the public spaces of the squares or "piazzas," which the Goodmans in *Communitas* had described as "the *definition* of the city" (fig. 135). Without the time pressures imposed by long commutes or frantic accumulation, citizens would have ample leisure for the "repetitive small pleasures" of conversation, people watching, food and drink. These squares would be enclosed, traffic-free areas bordered by the full range of activities in the town, from factories and technical schools to libraries, shops, and home/workshops. Compared to the single-minded spaces of the "City of Efficient Consumption" where every inch is designed to maximize purchases, these squares would be what the philosopher Michael Walzer has called "open-minded spaces," places where citizens would be encouraged to explore all the opportunities of the town. Besides the library and the school, there is a building labeled "Church or Meeting Hall or Patrick Geddes Regional Museum" (a reference to Geddes's "Outlook Tower" museum in turn-of-the-century Edinburgh which exhibited a survey of the region and its wider context in world history and culture).[13] Characteristically, the Goodmans thus decline to specify the higher values — spiritual, political, or cultural — that would animate the public life of their ideal city. Nevertheless, one neighborhood from *The Double E* is bordered by Saint Thomas More Square, Rousseau Lane, and Ben Franklin Street.[14]

One crucial value that Goodman does specify is the close relation between town and country. Beyond the built-up areas of the town one finds a large tract of "kitchen gardens" where urbanites could grow their own high-quality fruits and vegetables (fig. 136). Moreover, the family farms of the greenbelt would be closely integrated into the life of the town. For example, much of the education of young people would take place on the farms, where a true understanding of economy and, especially, ecology would be inculcated. Beyond that, the farms would be oriented toward serving their localities rather than the national market.

Indeed, Goodman advocates an inward-looking regional focus for both town and country. While he recognized that no region could be self-sufficient, he hoped that high-quality, distinctive production for local demand would eventually supplant mass-produced goods for a national market. Within each region, therefore, "an awareness of climate and season is fostered, a pride in a place and its distinctive foods and industries, its way of doing things, and its special style in clothes and slang."[15] In short, Goodman envisioned a direction for the American economy that was almost diametrically opposite to the path of standardization and "globalization" that it actually took.

At this point it might be useful (though not decisive) to evaluate Goodman's plans by comparing them more broadly to the actual evolution of American society since 1977. I do not mean to judge him by his qualities as a forecaster. Goodman himself had little respect for those supposedly hard-nosed prognosticators who "attempt to extrapolate the future by projecting present trends"; his method was to "establish goals, then work backward from them to the present." Nevertheless, it is important to understand some of the ways in which his thought embodied or diverged from the trends of his time.

As we can now see, the leadership of corporate America shared Goodman's belief that the dual economic and energy crises of the 1970s constituted a general crisis for American capitalism. The response of corporate leaders, however, was to move in a very different direction from Goodman's. The falling rate of profit in the era of stagflation combined with increasing competition, first from Europe and then from Japan, convinced them to restructure their operations in the direction of lower costs and greater flexibility. This unleashed an era of downsizing that devastated the manufacturing economy of the Northeast and Midwest (some cities like Philadelphia lost almost three-quarters of their manufacturing jobs) as production was moved to low-wage facilities first in the Sunbelt and eventually abroad. When in the early 1980s the high-interest policies of the Federal Reserve squeezed the inflation out of the economy — at the cost of another recession — corporate America was ready to profit from a period of stable prices and relatively low energy costs that has persisted almost to the present. At the same time, the high-technology sector of the American economy emerged as the international center of growth and innovation, with windfall profits for entrepreneurs and investors.

The result was a "second wind" for the American economy in the 1980s and 1990s that superseded Goodman's anticipated limits and scarcity. For the top twenty percent of American households (who now possess half of American income), the result was an explosion of consumerism far in excess of the "absurd" materialism that the Goodmans had protested against in the 1940s and 1950s. While the "middle of the middle class" struggled to hold its own and the poor lost ground, the upper middle class led the nation in an explosion of consumerism that made the Goodmans' 1947 "City as Department Store" seem almost austere. Where Goodman in 1977 had hoped to see a rebirth of the communitarian spirit in response to a shared crisis, we saw instead the triumph of the "me generation" whose symbols were the sports utility vehicle and the tract "mansion."

Nevertheless, a full accounting of the cultural and economic changes since 1977 would show a more nuanced picture. If the consumer society that has emerged in the last quarter-century is in some ways even worse than the one the Goodmans originally criticized, that consumerism has paradoxically been flexible enough to accommodate some of their aims. If, as they claim in *Communitas*, the real politics of a consumer society are found in consumer choices, at least some of these choices have reflected the values that *The Double E* celebrated.

Judged by Goodman's most important criterion, the quality of work, American society has surely experienced a significant improvement, if for reasons very different from the ones that Goodman advocated. To be sure, the further spread of "spread city" and the increasing prevalence of two-earner households has lengthened commuting times for both spouses, worsening the split between home and work that *The Double E* tried to remedy. But in terms of work itself, the restructuring of American manufacturing has moved many of the most routinized production and even service jobs outside the country. (And the worst remaining jobs are now taken by recent immigrants who must take what no one else wants; these are the workers who have in fact been drafted into the equivalent of Goodman's "Basic Production Centers.") Moreover, economic restructuring and the growth of the high-tech economy has de-emphasized the large corporate employers that were the Goodmans' favorite targets in favor of smaller firms that give their employees more autonomy. Today a typical American auto worker might be a woman sitting in front of a computer screen at a high-tech start-up company designing a new part that is likely to be manufactured in Mexico or Asia.

We are not yet in the crafts utopia that Goodman envisioned nor even in its high-tech equivalent, but American workers with more than a high school education have certainly seen their opportunities for satisfying work increase. Ecology too has seen a significant if uneven improvement since 1977, in part due to government regulations but also due to consumer choices. In *The Double E* Goodman placed particular emphasis on issues of farming and diet, not only in his plans for farming in the greenbelt but also in two chapters titled "People and Food" and "Cooking and Eating." Since he wrote, "organic" or "health" foods have indeed become part of the diet of much of the middle class, with some corresponding increase in ecological understanding.

Beyond work and ecology, there is the crucial question of the evolution of the built environment since 1977. From the perspective of Goodman's hopes and values, the picture is largely negative. If the central cities have escaped the bankruptcy that seemed to threaten them at that time, it is only because their downtown areas again became attractive for the "efficient consumption" that the Goodmans forecast in 1947: gentrification, megastores, festival marketplaces, high-rise offices, convention centers, entertainment districts. Beyond these zones of affluence, the continued ghetto poverty seems to justify Goodman's harsh assertion in *The Double E* that the great black migration from the countryside to the city from the 1940s to the 1970s was a profound mistake. "To have destroyed the possibility of people earning a living on farms and in small towns, forcing mass migrations to the cities, was an act of unparalleled stupidity."[16]

But, if big cities remain inimical to Goodman's vision, are we any closer to his alternative, the human-scaled, ecologically sensitive, socially responsible communities? Certainly there are few signs of them in metropolitan areas that now sprawl much farther than the ones that Goodman attacked in 1977 as "ecological disasters." Yet we should recognize at least the beginnings of a countermovement in Goodman's direction. In virtually every metropolitan area one can find a "smart growth" movement to preserve open space, support mass transit, and practice sustainable patterns of growth. In the design professions this movement is concentrated in "The New Urbanism," and Percival Goodman would surely have had a complicated relationship to it. Insofar as the New Urbanism has revived the ideal of the "bounded community" as the remedy for suburban sprawl, it has put Goodman's concerns at the center of the urban design debate. Moreover, the narrow streets, mixed uses, front porches, and public squares of such New Urbanist projects as Seaside Florida and Kentlands, Maryland (both planned by Andrés Duany and Elizabeth Plater-Zyberk) project a "grain of the street" similar to his own. But insofar as these projects have been disconnected from his vision of social change, he would probably see them as merely a variation on "The City as Department Store": The Town as Boutique.

This is only one aspect of the New Urbanism, however. Far closer to Goodman's values and designs is the work of the California-based architect Peter Calthorpe, one of the founders in 1993 of the Congress for the New Urbanism. Indeed, Calthorpe's early work in the 1970s and 1980s seems to come directly out of Goodman's concerns. In *Sustainable Communities* Calthorpe and his co-author Sim Van der Ryn present a plan (never built) for a "Marin Solar Village" fifteen miles north of the Golden Gate Bridge. As envisioned, the solar village included passive solar design of all buildings, a high-tech employment center within walking distance of housing, and extensive fruit and vegetable farms supplied with recycled water and wastes from the village.[17] Calthorpe later developed and refined his ideas into what he called transit-oriented development, where bounded communities would be strung out along light-rail lines, connected to each other and to the regional core, while preserving land beyond the transit lines for agriculture and open space.

In the early 1990s, Calthorpe began working with citizens' groups in the Portland, Oregon, region on a series of regional plans based on their long-standing commitment to fighting automobile-based sprawl.[18] As eventually embodied in the Portland 2040 Plan, the region embraced its own version of "the double e": a sustainable ecology supporting a high-tech economy. The Portland region, if it continues to follow its present trajectory, could well become the most important test case in showing how far this country might go in Goodman's general direction. He would certainly recognize and applaud a region that emphasizes a sustainable balance of town and country, with an "urban growth boundary" to assure the survival of agriculture; a shift to bounded, transit-oriented communities where residents would be within walking distance of both open space and a transit line; an economy oriented toward high-tech craftsmanship in small-scale enterprises; and a distinctive regional identity based on the Pacific Northwest's style of life and environmental ethos. And he would also certainly have some critical comments as well, no doubt including the Portland plan's acceptance of the economic status quo. We miss his combination of a constant questioning of the details of a plan while always seeking a more encompassing vision of utopian possibilities.

Percival Goodman's social thought at its strongest might therefore be called "untimely" in the sense that Friedrich Nietzsche used and praised that term in his essays. "Untimeliness" meant the freedom from conventional wisdom and expectations, the freedom to affirm values and alternatives regardless of their likely reception in the short term. Percival and Paul Goodman issued their first call for community in 1947, precisely when the United States was about to embark on the postwar era of unprecedented individual materialism. Percival Goodman issued his own call for community, for economic limits, and for ecological balance just when American society was about to embark on an even more feverish era of growth and consumption. His thought is not, however, diminished by this untimeliness. He was following the utopian imperative to extend the limits of our possibilities during periods when they seem to shrink to a single inevitable "reality." In *The Double E* Goodman aptly quotes Gunnar Myrdal's exhortation that planning requires "an element of belief in reason as an independent force in history and in the freedom of choice by which man can change reality according to his design, and so turn the course of future development."[19] This commitment to both freedom and planning is the defining essence of Percival Goodman's social thought.

Notes

1. Paul and Percival Goodman, *Communitas: Means of Livelihood and Ways of Life* (New York: Vintage Books, 1960; original ed. 1947) 11.

2. Ibid., 221.

3. Percival Goodman, *The Double E* (Garden City, NY: Anchor Books, 1977) 115.

4. Ibid., 21.

5. Ibid., 22.

6. *Communitas*, 138.

7. Quoted in *The Double E*, 58.

8. *The Double E*, 4.

9. Quoted ibid., 76

10. Quoted ibid., 153.

11. *The Double E*, 165.

12. Ibid., 166–67.

13. This plan is in *Communitas* (163), but the whole spirit of the discussion of public squares is so similar to that in *The Double E* that I have merged the two.

14. *The Double E*, 164.

15. Ibid., 178.

16. Ibid., 297.

17. Sim Van der Ryn and Peter Calthorpe, *Sustainable Communities: A New Design for Cities, Suburbs, and Towns* (San Francisco: Sierra Club Books, 1986), part one.

18. Transit-oriented development and its application to the Portland region are detailed in Peter Calthorpe, *The Next American Metropolis* (New York: Princeton Architectural Press, 1993) and Peter Calthorpe and William Fulton, *The Regional City* (Washington, DC: Island Press, 2001).

19. Quoted in *The Double E*, 93.

Fig. 137 Caricature of Percy surrounded by students of the class of 1950 in the studio, by N. Gökbeler, 1950

Raymond Lifchez and Chiu-Hwa Wang, editors

The Teacher:
Recollections by Former Students and Colleagues

Introduction

Percival Goodman taught the Master's studio class in the School of Architecture at Columbia University from 1946 until his retirement in 1972. By the time he joined the faculty, the historic battle between proponents of the beaux-arts tradition and of the modern movement in American architectural education had subsided.[1] Goodman was one of several young modern designers to join the faculty at that time. He believed, as did other architects of his social and political persuasions, that the responsibility of the architect was "not merely to create physical forms, but also to serve as an advocate for improved social conditions."[2] They were the avant-garde. As a teacher, Goodman made remarkable contributions to this position; his views influenced his teaching program and were soon accepted into the mainstream of architectural discourse. In the 1940s and 1950s, Goodman's ideas pointed forward to the 1960s, when similar views held by sociologists and social psychologists made the social sciences required or recommended courses for architecture students.

As the years passed, Goodman's ideas about teaching evolved, partly in response to the experiences of the students who came to New York to study.[3] Among these, he identified principally with those who came to Columbia from "small colleges" (i.e., provincials) and were probably in a big city for the first time.[4] He believed that to rectify the failing of conventional architectural education it was essential that they discover the importance of the arts in the making of buildings. He saw New York as the city without parallel in which this acculturation might occur.

Goodman took special interest in foreign students. He was concerned that they not be overwhelmed by their American experience in ways that would diminish their respect for their own cultures, especially as at that time most of them were planning to return home upon completing their degrees. It was his goal to educate them in ways that would prepare them for their future roles. With this in mind, he typically would have them at some point make designs for their native lands, beginning with a consideration of the client and the social milieu that the building was to serve and paying attention to the traditional forms and practices that were meaningful. Conversely, he sought to have these students consider how, through their architecture, to create models for a better life, even if it meant that their views challenged conventional practices.

Suzanne O'Keefe's interviews made with Goodman during the years after his retirement form a remarkable document of recollections and anecdotes, illuminating the tenets of his philosophy of education.[5] When queried about his position on the importance to an architect of a professional consciousness informed by the social sciences and the arts, he replied,

> Architecture deals in the first place with the necessity for sheltering the physical body against animals, cold or heat or enemies, whatever. But once you've gotten past that primitive need, then you begin to enter into a whole field which deals with the psychology of people, the sociology of people, the history of people, and so on. It does seem to me, in our modern time, that . . . an extension of the way of seeing and of understanding has been developing, that . . . never existed before. . . . In the twentieth century, we have a new extension, a new perspective, a new horizon. We've gotten on the top of a certain kind of hill, and we can see another space beyond. In order to understand what this was, you had to not look merely at one manifestation, because that isn't what our century is about. The century is spread out into many manifestations. . . . [A]nd I feel that what modern music has to say to not merely a person, but a person as architect. What modern painting has to say, and so on down the line. . . . Not that you're trying to make a Renaissance man or anything like that; I don't think many people are capable of being Renaissance . . . of knowing a lot about everything. However, one can be a Thomas Jefferson or a fellow of that sort. To . . . get the rhythm that is there, and then to play with it and use it for your own particular job: that's what seemed to me important.

Through Goodman, his students came to experience New York as the essential laboratory adjunct to the design studio. He encouraged us to pay attention to its daily life and to its cultural opportunities — to get involved. He constructed his assignments in ways that made this happen: they frequently took us away from the campus and into the city's buildings and streets. On occasion, he would also send us to a colleague for an outside opinion of our work. In the studio he discussed our work in the light of his own experiences, adding a professional sophistication to the issues that we were wrestling with ourselves.

Goodman was personally generous. He made himself available beyond Avery Hall. Our recollections abound with invitations to his family's apartment, to his office, to lunch, to meet professionals who would be of interest — or of help — in a particular situation, or to holiday occasions with his family and friends. In these settings we met New York and foreign luminaries of contemporary culture. The Goodmans' stable of friends and acquaintances was astonishing. There was his advice and support when scholarships or employment were at stake. These recollections are enlivened by a certain confidence that what Percy taught and the example that he set laid a foundation upon which the writers have built personally significant careers.

The contributors to this chapter were his students, fledgling architects in his employment, or both. Their testimonials cover the twenty-five years of Goodman's tenure at Columbia, beginning with those who knew him earliest. As our recollections reveal, we were drawn to Goodman for different reasons and received differently from him. But in what follows, each acknowledges that he was a brilliant and effective teacher, that his humanity was no less evident in his daily life than in the way he taught. He was a positive influence on the kinds of professionals we have become.

Notes

1. Richard Oliver, ed. *The Making of an Architect 1881–1981: Columbia University in the City of New York* (New York: Rizzoli, 1981).

2. Paul Goldberger, Percival Goodman obituary, *New York Times* (12 October 1989).

3. The reminiscences of Percival Goodman: oral history, 1979. Interviewed by Suzanne O'Keefe. Columbia University, Oral History Research Office.

4. Ibid.

5. Ibid.

Fig. 138 Chiu-Hwa Wang with her grand-nephew on a visit to Ray Lifchez, Oakland, 1979

An Original Mind and a Generous Heart

Chiu-Hwa Wang

I knew Percy first as a professor, then as an employer, and finally as a comrade at work and a lifelong friend. Of this multifaceted relationship, it was Percival the Teacher who made a real difference in my life. At a time when I was dubious about having chosen the right profession and critical of the worth of architecture, Percival (like none of the teachers I had known before) raised a curtain, so to speak, and revealed architecture as an integral part of the complex built environment, charged with human emotions and social meaning — beyond form and function, beauty and utility.

In the studio he was a fierce critic. With piercing eyes beneath bushy eyebrows and an exuberant range of mustache (we nicknamed him "the brush"), he used to intimidate the students, especially those from foreign lands, though in time he did mellow, when the mustache was supplemented by a graying full beard.

Percy was talented in many ways: he drew beautifully and made numerous pieces of sculpture and jewelry out of discarded objects (pl. XVI). But the extraordinary fact is that he had an original, provocative mind and a generous heart. I am surely not the only student inspired by him to think and feel with fresh zeal and vigor, as though embarking on a new life. Let me mention just a few events that are particularly meaningful to me.

Shortly after graduating from Columbia in 1949 and starting full-time work in the Goodman office, I became ill with tuberculosis and had to spend two and a half years at a sanatorium. It was for me an emotional as well as a physical crisis, and Percy came to the rescue by allowing me to continue working for him. I designed, while lying flat on my back, the expansion of the Beechwood Synagogue with an auditorium and some thirty classrooms, the first major commission in my life. At the same time he made me read — "an architect must first mature as a human person" — the Bible, Sigmund Freud, Bertrand Russell, Marcel Proust, and much more.

Then in 1960, when I was about to take the architectural licensing examination, I realized that my knowledge of the history of Western architecture was terribly inadequate. Having learned history mostly as a series of names and dates which one memorized only to happily discard, I was astounded to hear Percy's version of architectural history, interwoven as part of the social/economic/political fabric — a fascinating new world. Endowed with a naturally probing mind, and notwithstanding having had very little formal education, he developed penetrating observations, merging history and theory. Twenty years later, when I taught in the universities in Taiwan, "History and Theory of Architecture" and "The Man-Made Environment" became my favorite subjects alongside of design.

Finally, it was Percy who introduced me to the utopian literature of the West — not just the literature, but an attitude, a consuming desire for a better life, a better world. Gerald T. Littlefield, a dear classmate and student of Percy's, captured this attitude in a poem, which has become one of my favorites:

> He who strives for an infinite star
> And misses by far
> His aim
> Is greater than he
> Who climbs a tree
> And proudly carves his name.

Percival Goodman as Teacher

Romaldo Giurgola

My encounters with Percival Goodman occurred in two periods of time, both of which were pivotal in my life. The first started the day after I landed in New York from Italy in 1949 to begin the Master's program in architecture at Columbia University, the second some years later when I lived in New York from 1964 to the late 1980s.

It was on a sunny day in autumn when I first stepped across the threshold of Avery Hall, a building full of Roman dignity, more Roman than the school I had left in Rome. I was received there by the dean, a man who in all respects matched the formality of the building and who eventually led me to the studio upstairs. Percy, as I learned later everyone was calling him, was there with a student, both intent on some papers. After a short while I was introduced to Percy, my critic for the course. Wearing his usual inimitable tweed, he greeted me with a warm and quizzical smile under a heavy mustache, his words spoken in a modulated baritone, which quickly dispelled my previous apprehensions. We began a conversation loosely structured on questions and answers — Percy was a good, subtle questioner which, in fact, extended for the entire length of the course. For me it was an introduction to a new country or, to be more precise, to a city and to a culture that appeared to me much more complex than the one I had left, regardless of how many layers of history Europe may have.

Percy's suggestion for a good reading of New York was to take as many crosstown buses as I could and to take note of things happening in the street as well as at the bottoms of buildings. Of course I did so, my eyes fixed on the intersections of building walls and sidewalks, noting the myriad of events occurring there. After I had become saturated with that exercise, he told me to look at the tops of buildings and to let my imagination run.

I did not know for a while that Percy had designed several religious buildings. He never mentioned his buildings in the studio, unlike the critics in Italy who were inclined to do so frequently.

The major project throughout the term was the design of an office tower for which I was totally unprepared, but which, nevertheless, I approached with great enthusiasm. Percy occasionally referred to the ideas of his brother, Paul, which of course sent me to read their book, *Communitas*. In the fifties, when we were still involved in that release of energy that turned out a society of intense materialistic pursuits, *Communitas* was a courageous and prophetic book. Percy, I realized, used the project of the office tower as an instrument to comment on the students' attitude toward the human condition in the workplace.

As I look again from here in Australia at those sketches included in *Communitas,* I am taken by the effort that Percy made to humanize the rigid aspect of modernistic building representing an equally rigid social program into a more flexible program of social reintegration. The deep conviction that design and physical planning were, as they are indeed today, a major moral, political, and cultural problem was ever present in the teaching and in the design criticism of Percival Goodman. But the influence of Percy on my thoughts became significant when in the early sixties I came back to Avery Hall as chairman of the architectural division of the school. Those years turned out quite differently from what I could have imagined earlier, but they remain the most significant of my life. During the student unrest at Columbia, Percy was one of the few, I remember, to have a full grasp of the events and of their eventual outcome in the midst of a great confusion of minds. He lived those events with the consciousness of the impact that his thoughts made on them, following them with great attention. Known to be passionately involved in the cause, he showed remarkable self-control and reason on that occasion.

After those times of some significant cultural changes, as the more radical thoughts seemed gradually to fade, I met Percy occasionally before my departure for Australia for the design of the new Parliament. His comments were often affected by the realization of the coming fragmentation, dissemination, and frivolous play of "everything goes" in architecture.

Percy was an admirable individualist, in constant search for an ethic at once individualist and communal. His well-known ideological stand gave him a structure and a direction. He taught me about modesty in architecture which, like the technological modesty in building that he recommended so often, is not a self-effacing condition but consists in claiming no more than a particular condition requires. I understood his interest as an architect in religious buildings, as the synagogues that he designed required precisely that attitude.

One evening I visited him at his home near the American Museum of Natural History. He showed me with amusement some sculptural objects he made with crushed aluminum foil shaped in what appeared to be at times figures (fig. 139), at times architectural configurations. Years later I happened to see similar exercises by other architects, but this time built at full scale.

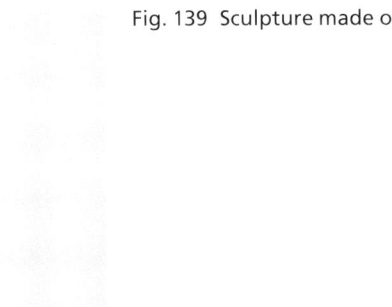

Fig. 139 Sculpture made of aluminum foil (cat. 55)

Fig. 140 Temple of Aaron, Saint Paul, Minnesota, 1954–56: view from the main sanctuary into social hall

Planter of Doubts, Seeker of Truth

Val Michelson

When in June 1941 Hitler's armies invaded the USSR, I was called away from the drafting board to defend what then was my country. Four years later, the end of the war was described by a contemporary Russian bard: "Many more soldiers lie below the ground than live above its surface." I happened to be one of those who remained on the earth's surface. As a displaced person, I was stranded on the shores of the United States in 1949 and two years later dared to present myself at the Master's class in Avery Hall.

My apprehension is difficult to recall now, but I remember its turning into panic when confronted with my first sketch problem: a small general store and an interfaith chapel. No training at the communist version of the École des Beaux-Arts had prepared me for this! How could an American professor understand my predicament? To my astonishment Percy Goodman not only understood my difficulties but had a better grasp of the realities in the world I had come from than I did.

I believe that many others under Percy's tutelage were similarly impressed. In him we met an unusual teacher who refused to hand down any wisdom derived from some proven, abstract, and universally applicable system of professional education. Percy preserved his sympathetic understanding of personal and cultural differences among individuals and guided each of them toward finding his or her own way. For him, the work with each student was an exciting experiment, directed not so much to training a competent professional as to shaping an ethical ideal in the service of humanity.

Maybe because the discovery of our common admiration of Auguste Choisy — Percy often spoke of his intention to translate the *Histoire* — toward the end of my first year at Avery, he decided to take me under his wing: I would be employed in his firm. In the early fifties, a small flat in a partially abandoned tenement house in mid-Manhattan that we called our office perfectly fitted Percy's life style. Space for the draftsmen had been made by pulling down some partitions, the pipe columns staying in place. Two doors formed an entry where, squeezed into one door opening, the secretary (Paul Goodman's wife) sat at a desk. Behind her was Percy's table and a window opening onto a fire escape ladder in a court which was packed with fire escapes from neighboring tenements. In the hot and humid New York summers, all windows were open, and on some of the fire escape landings one could observe waistcoated tailors stitching new jackets or pairs of trousers.

Such was the setting in which I for the first time comprehended the allures and perils of private enterprise. But more to the point, it was here that I began to understand what inspired Percy's design of houses of worship. It was a deep respect for and a desire to serve the communal spirit, rooted in an ancient faith yet needing to be expressed in modern forms. The office was busy. Synagogues — for Springfield, Massachusetts; Tulsa, Oklahoma; Miami, Florida; Gary, Indiana — followed each other, each shaped by a different structural system and the use of different materials. There were many opportunities to test and criticize, to learn from, and to admire Percy's design principles.

Despite the joys of working with Percy, after two years I felt a need to find another venue: with Percy's consent, I committed myself to working for Marcel Breuer. When I came to take leave, however, I was shaken suddenly by an explosion: "It is unheard of! One does not leave like that, in the midst of an unfinished job! Ah, but what can one expect from a Russian!" I was thunderstruck and took flight, feeling totally miserable. Early the next morning my home phone rang. It was Percy, offering an apology for his unwarranted outburst. Dear Percy!

Our friendship remaining intact, we often met when I, an eager disciple, still lived in New York. Later my wife and I stayed with Percy on our infrequent visits to the Big Apple. In 1970, he asked me to represent him as the architect of record for the expansion of the Temple Aaron complex in Saint Paul (fig. 140). And since 1978, *The Double E* was required reading in the course that I taught at the University of Minnesota.

Percy's own words form a fitting conclusion. In a letter written in 1984, he said, "Be of good cheer — architecture is not only a witches' Sabbath (i.e., merchandising); it is the joy of putting down a clean sheet, sharpening a pencil, and thinking, 'This time Ictinus will whisper in my ear; Alberti, Palladio, Scamozzi (or the designers of Chartres?) will move my hand.'"

How much I would like to hear Percy's undying optimism whispered to my ear!

A Tribute to the Man, the Artist, and the Teacher

Costa N. Decavalla

The first time I came across Percy Goodman's ideas and ideals was at the roundtable discussion — called "a great debate" — in the *Magazine of Building*, in its issue of November 1950. It was not a real debate, but it was presented as such. A number of distinguished American architects and architectural critics, including Belluschi, Cherymayeff, Bel Geddes, Goff, Gropius, Hamlin, Hitchcock, Neutra, Pereira, Rudolph, Schindler, and others, among them Percy Goodman, had been asked questions about the U. N. Building in New York. Percy Goodman's comments made their mark: first by questioning the functionality of the actual project, then by making revolutionary suggestions, but most importantly, by showing his ideas in the form of pen-and-ink drawings. And what masterly drawings!

A year later, as his pupil at the Graduate School of Architecture at Columbia University, I discovered that he never used a modern pen for his marvelous drawings. Instead he used a pen holder and steel nib — a good traditional pen from the time when sketching and drawing had their own particular importance as a way to convey ideas. Still later, when I was working in his office in New York, every morning as I uncovered my drawing board, I found Percy's china-ink drawings for the building under study, bursting with ideas and architectural solutions to our design problems. For the two years that I worked for Percy Goodman before returning to Europe and Greece, his drawings every morning, day in day out, made my day, as they say.

At a time when most architects tried to establish their reputation by creating a sort of trademark through an individual mode of architectural expression, Percy Goodman experimented with new forms and shapes in each new project that came into his office. His projects were recognizable not through easily read characteristics but because of their personality and the high quality of the design values that they represented. This taught me the real value of freedom — intellectual freedom and creative freedom.

During my student days at Columbia Percy Goodman, as head of the design studio, was naturally the most important professor for us young architects who came from all around the world. But we never felt that he was our professor. We had the feeling that he was both one of us, sharing our problems and our endeavors, as well as a sort of magician who with his magic words, his fresh and provocative ideas, was opening new horizons for us, the existence of which we never suspected, and new worlds that he constantly prodded us to explore. The design projects that he assigned reflected his cultural and social concerns and aimed at awakening our sensibilities in these directions. He constantly strove to enrich his teaching by inviting very special people as design critics and lecturers. We always felt that his deep concern for others, and in particular for his students, was the driving force behind his teaching. His house in New York was open to us, and every year we spent Christmas Eve in his company, having been invited to share the festivities with his family. For us foreigners, this was a great treat.

Percy Goodman, always an enchanting talker, could be at the same time a revolutionary and a staunch defender of traditional values. My last recollection of him is as a biblical patriarch, in the middle eighties, when as our host, he presided over Passover celebrations in his home in Manhattan. But above all I remember him as a visionary and a fighter. He firmly believed that man is fundamentally good and that there could be a bright future for mankind if certain conditions were met, and those concerning architecture and planning he set out to develop.

Being a man of many talents, his means of expression were not limited to the practice of architecture, planning, art, and teaching, as is attested by his books, beautifully illustrated by himself. It is always a joy to come across his ideas in his writings. There one discovers his profound humanity and compassion in a world where true values tend to give their place to the ephemeral and the trivial. His firm belief in social justice and civilized urban living permeates *Communitas*, while his anxiety and deep concern over the inexorable destruction of our natural and social environment find their expression in *The Double E.*

It is proof of his moral and intellectual integrity that what he preached he practiced. He lived in the middle of the city he cherished and never allowed himself the use of a private motor car. In *The Double E,* first printed in 1977, he expounds on the merits of modest and graceful living and the respect of the environment in contrast to conspicuous consumption, waste, and greed. In a certain way it is what my ancient Greek ancestors used to teach.

Communitas, written in collaboration with his brother, the poet Paul Goodman, was published more than fifty years ago. But when reading it again today, I have the impression that it concerns, more than ever, our present world. I am amazed at the extent to which it has influenced my way of thinking since the early fifties when I first read it and studied its various assessments of our built environment, the problems that it generates, and the provocative ideas about the possibilities open to us. For me personally there is one more dimension that his books represent: they are a living presence. Through them I always have the feeling of Percy's being still around, prodding us to explore new ideas and new possibilities. And that for me is his greatest legacy.

Teacher, Colleague, Friend

Raymond Lifchez

When I arrived at Avery Hall in September of 1955 to enroll in Percy Goodman's Master's class, I discovered that my five years at the University of Florida had not prepared me to be his student. At no time in my undergraduate education had I encountered a teacher quite like him: one who spoke with ease, confidence, and familiarity about those whom I considered to be architectural celebrities and about buildings that I had known only as textbook illustrations. At no time had I encountered a teacher so erudite, who vigorously espoused what he believed in. I was enthralled and intimidated. Those first weeks were painful. My undergraduate years had taught me how, but not what, to draw. My first efforts at design left Goodman relatively speechless. Peering down, after a long pause, his initial comment was generally but one word: "unfortunate." And with that singular remark, instruction would begin.

Goodman's social views contained ideas that began to shape my designs. As I perceived his enthusiasm for my work taking root, Professor Goodman became Percy. I was a willing student and I wanted nothing more than to produce designs that would encourage his appreciation. I found that I could and in doing so, for the first time in my education, I felt some confidence as a designer.

Percy insisted that to be an architect meant to have ideas. He began by asking each of us to conceive of an architectural problem that interested us personally, and to sum it up in a statement about why our interest was worthwhile. He also pressed the point that to be an architect one must believe in what one was attempting to do. Through this way of thinking, design became for me something of a moral imperative — a point of view that was affirmed by the new humanism of the 1960s.

In studio chats, Percy frequently presented some aspect of his practice as a designer, as a critic of urban renewal, or of his pursuit of suitable embellishments for the synagogues he designed. Doing so, he acquainted us with his concerns and conveyed, indirectly, the importance of professional practice for the teacher. Because of the way he encouraged our views, I grew to respect what I sensed was his affection for his students and his wish to deepen our understanding of his values and of our common goals. As a teacher myself I often reflect upon how well Percy did this.

Percy exposed us to a wider circle of design critics by sending us to show our work to other architects when he thought we would benefit. It was typical of him to find ways to broaden his students' understanding of the profession and to introduce us into the culture and worldly affairs that New York City offered. With similar intent, Percy used his midtown office and his home to broaden us intellectually. I was frequently invited to his office to help with competition drawings or to his apartment, where he and his wife, Naomi, included his students when there were architects, artists, and writers whom they thought we would enjoy meeting. How often, even today, in conversation, I refer to those competition-charrettes and social occasions.

Percy's remarkable knowledge of architectural history colored his critiques and inspired me to take courses offered in the Department of Art History. I also had tutorials with James Vanderpool, the Avery librarian. On Percy's recommendation, Dean Leopold Arnaud sent me to the École Americaine at Fontainebleau for the summer session of 1956. And from 1957 to 1959 I continued my studies in architectural history as a William Kinne Fellow at the American School of Classical Studies, Athens, and in Istanbul, serving as a draftsman for a Harvard University research team measuring Byzantine monuments. Engrossed, I considered becoming a historian rather than an architect, which I mentioned in a letter to Percy. His reply was, "Come home. You have a job with Eero Saarinen, if you want it." And I did. Three years later, I returned to Avery Hall to teach and became Percy's colleague.

In the academic year 1968–69, following the Columbia "strike" Percy and I found ourselves together representing the architecture students before the university administration in the difficult process of changing the way that architecture was taught at the school. Although this troublesome experience brought me ever closer to Percy as a friend and colleague, it also made me realize that after fifteen years of an affectionate relationship with the school, it was time for me to leave. In 1970 I came to Berkeley, but my friendship with Percy continued until his death. When I visited New York, he and I sometimes took walks about the city, to see the neighborhoods and buildings through his eyes. He liked being a teacher, and I never tired of being his student.

Reminiscences of Percival Goodman

Rudolf Guyer

I met Percival Goodman for the first time in 1957 when he gave a lecture at the school of architecture of the Ohio State University where I was an instructor. I don't remember what he was talking about, but I very well remember that I was deeply impressed by the clarity of his thinking, the precision of his language, and, above all, the intensity of the expression on his face. There was no small talk around the subject or verbal ornamentation of cloudy thoughts but a very earnest and direct approach to the core of what he wanted to say. As a teacher with a foreign tongue who had some difficulty in expressing himself clearly in English and was able to communicate with his students only in simple terms, I was fascinated by Percival's gift of translating complex thoughts into clear and easily understandable language. After his lecture I wanted to tell him how much I liked his speech but didn't dare to do so, seeing him surrounded by people much more important than a young instructor.

When in 1958 I quit my teaching job and went to New York City to find work in an architectural office to gain practical experience, there was a recession and I met long queues of job-seeking architects at the doors of all large firms. After having looked in vain for almost three weeks, I remembered Percy's lecture, went to his office at 1860 Broadway, and was lucky enough to be hired on the spot. I rushed back to pick up my wife and newborn son, who were waiting in Columbus, and started my job of nine months in Percy's office. In spite of its short duration, it turned out to be one of the happiest and most intense experiences in my life and the beginning of a long friendship, albeit mostly in absentia.

As I recall, the office consisted of one big room with twelve or fourteen drafting tables in two rows. Percy's table was at the back wall beside that of Chiu-Hwa Wang, his associate and right hand. Since my work place was immediately in front of them, I was able to see from very close range that the work on Percy's drafting table was of the same intensity and precision as his lecture at Ohio State. While seemingly a total introvert when he concentrated on a problem, he had at all times complete control of the room in front of him and was ready to intervene immediately and help with sharp-sighted comments when questions arose on one of the projects. His criticism was always constructive, and he left great freedom to his employees as long as he felt they were able to contribute creative work. When he was absent from the office teaching, lecturing, or visiting building sites, his alter ego Chiu-Hwa saw to it that the work process continued in Percy's intentions; their creative teamwork was absolutely symbiotic and wonderful.

Since Percy's wife, Naomi, worked in the office also, the whole setup gave the impression of a large family. At Christmas all employees were invited to the famous Christmas party at the

Fig. 141 Temple Emanuel, Denver, 1953–60: interior view

Goodmans'; and when our baby got sick, Naomi was quick to find a doctor and give advice to my young family, somewhat lost in the big city.

My work in the office at the beginning consisted mostly of design studies, perspective drawings, and colored renderings of projects that at that period were all synagogues. As time went by I became involved with the working drawings of a synagogue in Denver (fig. 141) which called for, among other things, elaborate trigonometric calculations of the complex steel structure. There were no calculating machines and all had to be done by hand, and in feet and inches — an almost impossible task for a European who had studied more ancient Greek and Latin literature than mathematics and who was used to calculating only in the metric system. Nevertheless, the synagogue was built, after my return to Switzerland. When Percy and his family came to visit us there, he told me that when the steel skeleton was erected in Denver, the bent girders would not meet at the top and he had to have my calculations checked by a professional mathematician. As it turned out, they proved to be correct, and the problem on the building site has remained a mystery.

When the Goodmans visited us in Switzerland in 1960, we took a trip to Le Corbusier's Ronchamp Chapel and La Tourette Monastery. I remember the deep impression that the brute force of the two buildings made on Percy. Then we didn't see each other for almost twenty years. But every year we got an invitation to the Goodmans' Christmas party, and that gave us the feeling of still belonging to the family. In 1977 we were able to accept the invitation, and in 1984 we met again and Percy showed us the drawings that he was working on then. I took a series of copies home with me, hoping to get them published in Europe; although I didn't succeed, I continue to keep them as a testimony of his ingenuity.

Percival Goodman

Peter Eisenman

It is commonly perceived that the two major influences on my career were Colin Rowe and Manfredo Tafuri. This is because little is known of my work prior to 1960, when I arrived in Cambridge. What is not known is that I would not have come to Cambridge, nor would my history have unfolded as it did, if it were not for one person — Percival Goodman. In the summer of 1957, I was just out of the United States Army, having been in Korea since graduating from Cornell in 1955. Like many of my Cornell classmates, I had been told that I would be given a position at some prestigious New York office, in my case with Marcel Breuer because of the Cornell connection to Robert Gatje. When my interview with Gatje produced nothing, I was out on the streets of New York, unemployed. I don't know how I got to 1860 Broadway, but I remember my first meeting with Percy, who brusquely told me that he would pay me seventy-five dollars a week and that I would learn to fold drawings and run errands. I think that Percy saw me as a spoiled suburban rich kid; Korea had taught me otherwise. After a year in the office I did learn how to fold construction drawings properly (a procedure that I teach my employees to this day). I left, first for a brief disappointing stay with Edgar Tafel and then an equally disappointing time in Cambridge, Massachusetts, with Walter Gropius's Architects Collaborative. It was then that I returned to Percy for advice. This was the turning point of my education. He said, "Peter, you are wasting your time working your way up the ladder of corporate architectural America. Why don't you come back to Columbia and study with me?" By then we had developed a mutual respect, and Percy's advice meant a lot to me.

Columbia was a wasteland save for Percy, Gerry Kallmann, Marston Fitch, and a few others. Percy had managed at that time to recruit as students two young Englishmen, John Fowler and Michael McKinnell, who were later to become my roommates. Percy's studio that year, 1959–1960, was a hothouse. The energy generated mutually by Percy, McKinnell, and myself was what learning and teaching was all about. Fifty blocks north, removed from his office, Percy was a different cat, more what I would like to believe was his true self: relaxed, philosophical, wistful. His private internal struggle with himself and with his image of his brother Paul was all but subsumed through his life in the studio. There we talked, we thought, we challenged, and we worked like crazy. It was as if we were on some private island; certainly, I cannot say I was in New York.

My year with Percy at Columbia was a revelation for me. It plowed the ground and planted the seeds that are still with me today; the radical, insurgent, intellectual outsider that was Percy somehow remains alive inside me. Am I a legacy? In a way, perhaps yes. But in no way can his successes and failures be imaged in others. Percy was that unique brand of diamond-in-the-rough Jewish intellectual, a unique product of a time and place — New York in the 1920s and 1930s. To see in his work and his students a seamless continuity is to miss the uniqueness of his moment and his being. History may not be kind to Percival Goodman Architect, but it can neither reveal nor take away what he gave to me and his other students. Proust said that memory should not be confused with nostalgia for what was in the past. Memory, he said, should live in the present. That is where Percy will always reside for me.

A Halcyon Year

N. Michael McKinnell

I was twenty-three years old when I came to America in 1958. Of the two scholarships that I had been offered, one at M.I.T. and one at Columbia University, I chose to come to Columbia because residence in New York City would afford me the possibility of listening to jazz music, and because a university seemed more prestigious than an institute of technology. My introduction to America was a summer-long stay with a charming and gracious family who lived on a beautiful estate in Locust Valley on Long Island, all arranged under the auspices of the Fulbright Commission.

I had been trained in architecture at the University of Manchester. My serious education began, however, when after the idyllic summer I arrived in the studio of the Master's class in Avery Hall and there met a diminutive man with a fierce mustache and even fiercer, penetrating brown eyes: Percy Goodman.

Percy, as he was immediately known to everyone in the class except me who with class-conscious English reserve referred to him always as Professor Goodman, set our first assignment. It was short and intended, I believe, to reveal our personae as young architects. At the next session of the class, I had set up my drawing board — huge, antique, and raft-sized — to which I had fixed my paper with thumb tacks which had brass heads the size of quarters, and I was drawing with a T square made of mahogany and equipped with an ebony edge, all brought from England. It was these drafting tools that caught Percy's eye when he came to my desk. Indeed, he made no comment at all on my preliminary sketches but instead asked me to look around at my fellows with their huge rolls of thin tracing paper, which they were all consuming at what to me seemed a profligate rate; their drafting tape, each piece of which they threw away after a single use; and their Perspex T squares. There followed a one-sided tutorial on, among other things, the dangerous propensity of unbridled capitalism to produce a society of consumers urged to engage in a life of unfettered expenditure of material resources; Thorstein Veblen, William James, and Pragmatism; and finally some cutting remarks on European blindness to technological advances and the perils of nostalgia.

Thus began my education and thus it continued. Percy set about precipitating an engagement of all the members of the class with each other and coincidentally upsetting all of our received opinions, prejudices, and — to the extent that they existed — our beliefs. In the beginning he met with no resistance from two of the group. After the first exercise in which I had employed all of the graphic presentation skills that I had been trained to master in England, Peter Eisenman sidled up to me and whispered in my ear with consummate authority, "We do the next project as a team." This began a year-long partnership during which we were inseparable. This was encouraged by Percy, and it was from this that I learned that architecture defies didactic instruction and that students learn much more from each other, particularly if that dialogue is provoked and nurtured by the instructor.

The deconstruction and rebuilding of my embryonic intellect and belief system went on outside of the studio. Percy plunged me and my colleagues into the Jewish intellectual and artistic milieu of New York. At his apartment overlooking the American Museum of Natural History, we were gently drawn into dialogue with the likes of Paul Goodman, Mark Rothko, and Herbert Ferber. It was a world of ideas totally alien to me and it re-formed the life of my mind ineluctably.

For me it was a halcyon year during which what we made as designers was always less important than why we were making it. After graduation, and through Percy's generous intervention, I was given the post of assistant to the first-year master, Gerhard Kallmann. He and I decided to form a partnership with each other. Lacking commissions, we entered the competition for the new Boston City Hall; and, to the astonishment of everyone and most of all ourselves, we won. Percy threw a great party for us and after much champagne drew me into a corner. "You are on top of the world at the moment and I am delighted for you," he said, "but don't for a moment think you will become successful architects in America; neither of you has the slightest capacity for self-advertisement."

I knew exactly what Percy was telling me: that, in his view, success depended on advertisement and advertisement depended on the lie. He was paying me the highest of compliments. But Percy did not know something about me. He and my friend Peter Eisenman had taught me by example that to make architecture at all requires extraordinary energy, commitment, and tenacity. I like to think that it was by emulating those attributes that Percy possessed in abundance that I have achieved any success. He had taught me that my English lassitude and sense of entitlement would no longer do. If any of the buildings that I have designed serves any social purpose, it is because Percy opened my mind to that essential function of architecture.

A Pivotal Mentor

Joshua Jih Pan

Columbia's Graduate School of Architecture and Mr. Goodman's urban design studio there allowed me to have my first encounter with the social aspects of architecture. I had grown up in Taiwan, then under marshal law and constantly facing the threat of war with communist China, where architecture was very much subservient to engineering training. Two years at a professional degree program at Rice University in Houston had given me a wider perspective of humanity and a liberal arts outlook on architecture, but the design studio was still very much oriented toward a single subject/single building approach. In Goodman's studio of 1966–67, our scope was the redevelopment of the South Bronx (figs. 142–144). All of a sudden our concern was with half a borough of New York City, an area plagued by poverty, full of dilapidated buildings, and densely occupied by inhabitants of many ethnicities.

Percy was approaching his retirement then, but I remember clearly that he nevertheless accompanied our group of around twelve students on our first reconnaissance of that part of the city. He pointed out problem areas and nodes of potential, instilling in us a heartfelt compassion for the disadvantaged community. In class, one hand constantly holding a lit cigarette, Mr. Goodman would spend most of the afternoon talking about social, economic, and political problems

Fig. 142 Harlem River Project, 1966: Bronx Market site (cat. 30b)

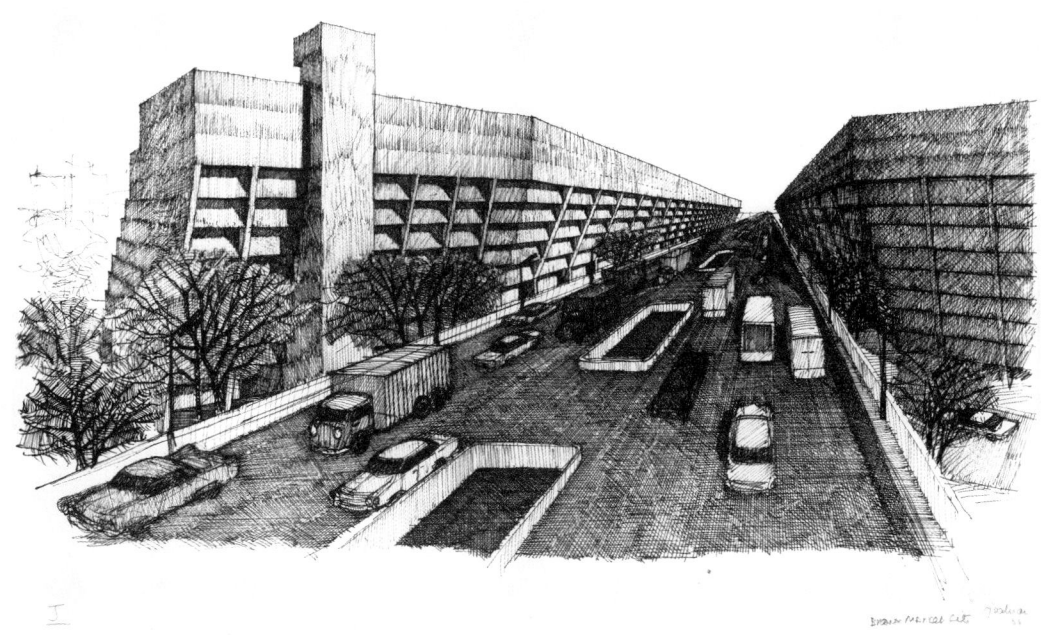

Fig. 143 Harlem River Project, 1966: Bronx Market site (cat. 30c)

and about how an architect, with privileged training and sensitivity, can be of use. His design crits were generally short and precise, but it was his compassionate "preaching" that greatly influenced my attitude toward architecture. This period with Percy and my subsequent internship years at Davis, Brody and Associates, the firm that helped to revolutionize New York City's public housing design in the sixties, was when I also learned how an architect walks out of the ivory tower to become more people-oriented. My lifelong attitude as an architect was thus molded and cast into what it is today. Among the more than three hundred projects completed in the intervening twenty years, I have occasionally had the opportunity to design buildings without restricted budgets. But it was the projects that have had the tightest constraints and budget limi-

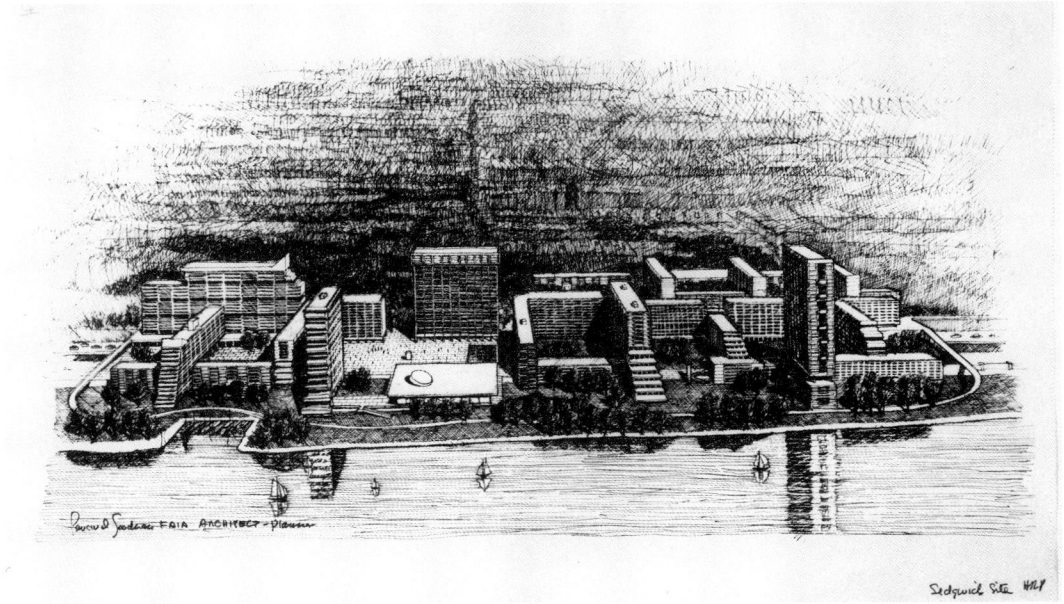

Fig. 144 Harlem River Project, 1966: Sedgwick site (cat. 30a)

145

tations that were most satisfying to me: finding that my expertise made the difference in their fruition. For this, I am greatly indebted to those chain-smoking afternoons.

Our class was very international, with students from England, Ireland, Australia, Canada, Japan, and Taiwan; and I was amazed to observe how genuinely caring and thoughtful Mr. Goodman was to each one of his students with their varied backgrounds and needs. During the year in our design studio I was among the successful students but did a poor job at the year-end thesis design presentation. A professor from another studio jumped all over my proposed design, and I gave up all hope of being selected for the keenly pursued William Kinne traveling fellowship. I was thus elated at commencement to hear my name announced at the end of the list of fellowship recipients. I later learned that it was Mr. Goodman who fought for me, thinking that as a student from Asia I could benefit from travel and study within the United States, which would have an impact on the development of my professional career.

If it is true that every architect has one or two pivotal mentors who help to shape his philosophy in architecture, Mr. Percival Goodman is certainly one of those to me.

Goodman and Utopia

Suzanne O'Keefe

There he was, curly hair, bushy mustache, horn-rimmed glasses, and probably pipe. I was at his doorstep to hear the reminiscences of an influential architect's life. Would Percy Goodman remember me? The date was 2 May 1979. Ten years had passed since I attended his class at Columbia University. I was working as an urban designer at the New York City Department of City Planning when I set off on a fascinating personal mission: interviewing older architects. The idea came to me in 1977, while attending a lecture about Alvar Aalto: if I could talk with Aalto or, more precisely, *listen* to him talk, it might be a step toward understanding and appreciating his brilliant work.

My undergraduate studies in art history, no doubt, had some influence on my thinking. When I discovered that there were preciously few oral histories of architects, I took a course given by Columbia's Oral History Research Office. In 1978 I was awarded a grant from the National Endowment for the Arts to conduct oral histories of older architects. Thus I arrived on a spring day in 1979, armed with my portable tape recorder and no little bit of awe, to interview Percy at his apartment. He had recently moved his office to his home and was busily finishing up projects. In retrospect this was the perfect time for my interview: he was seventy-five years old, sorting through his work, winding down his practice, and thinking about the future.

What I had thought would be three to six interviews of an hour's duration each became a huge underestimate. After beginning with his apprenticeship to his architect uncle, we produced seventeen transcribed interviews, concluding with an in-depth discussion of the synagogues that he built in the early 1950s. During these six months I came to see Percy as a very special architect or, more accurately, as more than an architect. His interests and friendships ran deeply and broadly across the intellectual and cultural wonderland of New York. I found myself immersed in a world of writers, artists, intellectuals, thinkers. In order to prepare questions for the next interview, I eagerly read articles that he gave me and others that I found in the library.

We usually met in the morning. Afterward, I would sometimes have lunch with him and Naomi, his wife. I looked forward to sitting in the Goodman's living room, marveling at his creations made from found objects while we carried on our conversation, sans tape recorder. His ideas on architecture, planning, and social policy were heavyweight; he was thoughtful but intellectually barbed, not seeming to care whom he might offend. The man spoke his mind.

I remember his saying that World War II made him embrace his Judaism, which led inexorably to the deep convictions underlying his design of synagogues. He embraced modernism but never neglected the contributions of individual artists. It seemed significant that he became an architect through an apprenticeship, before winning the Paris Prize in 1925 and studying at the École des Beaux-Arts.

These seventeen interviews were not the first time that he talked and I listened. Percy, essentially always a teacher, had been one of my own teachers at Columbia, during tumultuous times. I entered the Columbia University School of Architecture in the fall of 1968. The class was very small, I believe around twenty, and had few women. The previous spring had seen the architecture school at the forefront of the radicalism that gripped universities as civil rights, Vietnam, and, at Columbia, a proposed gym in Morningside Park came together in a hailstorm of protest.

Although as an undergraduate at New York University I had not been particularly politicized, in the fall of 1969 I took a class on utopian thought offered in the planning department . This was Percival Goodman's class. I was not aware then that he was the co-author with his brother Paul of *Communitas*, a book still in print since 1947, nor did I know that utopias were his lifelong interest. I found myself with planning students and at least one Columbia undergraduate. We read and discussed utopian thought, utopias through history, how they were envisioned, and whether they worked. His course sparked a new interest in me.

Percy had so much to teach and talk about but we never went past the seventeenth interview, though I continued to see him and Naomi for the next few years. I felt privileged to have gained entry into "The Goodman party," an annual event on December 24th, which I attended until 1984. Hundreds of people were there. Later in the evening, the party's distinctive feature, a vegetable bean soup, was brought out to the buffet. Begun as an office party that then moved

Fig. 145 Drawing from the series News from Nowhere (inspired by William Morris's book), in "An Illustrated Guide to Utopias: An Architect's Diary," 1980

to their home, it went on for more than fifty years, Percy claimed. It ended with his death in 1989.

In 1992, I went to see an exhibition of his visionary drawings at the Guild Hall in East Hampton on Long Island. It was on this trip that Naomi took me to their home, a prefab, in Springs. It seemed the perfect Percy vacation home: modern, simple, practical, but beautiful. It was in the exhibition, however, that the ethereal world of author and artist was most vividly revealed. The drawings were done during his last decade (1979–89). In "An Illustrated Guide to Utopias: An Architect's Diary" (1980), he showed his enduring fascination with utopias and in the classical beaux-arts architecture of his youth (fig. 145). Plans, an elevation, and a section of "The Guardian House in The Republic" showed how he thought Plato's Republic looked. The Postmodern Series (1982–83; see pls. XVIII–XX) made pointed fun of the self-conscious classical allusions then in vogue: in "Temple of Gastronomy," for example, imagined to be in Central Park, a stock pot, frying pan, griddle, and wok in the corners belched out different food smells; and in *Houses 1–10* (1983) each house, in the shape of a numeral, was shown as plan and rendering.

Percy began his most ambitious work in 1982 and continued until the end of his life: Illustrated Series of Greek Poems, a collection of more than one hundred works based on Greek mythology. I could see in these marvelous creations that, at the end of his working days, he inhabited a wondrously beguiling intellectual dreamscape in words and drawings. In "The Parthenon Project," he has Pericles discussing the rebuilding of the Acropolis with his companion, Aspasia: "So here it is, your scheme, already no longer a dream, not a shadow or passing breeze but the beginning of reality." "I cannot wait, unroll the plan," was Aspasia's reply. I feel that this is how Percival Goodman approached all facets of his life and career: straightforwardly, with excitement, expectation, and magical wit. In looking at the exhibition, I imagined what I had missed in not continuing to interview him as he developed these drawings.

A Symbol of Urban Design

Patrick Ping-tze Too

As a first-year graduate student in the urban design program at Columbia, when I met Percy in 1971 I didn't know that he was a famous professor. The architecture school catalogue listed him as professor emeritus, and I thought that perhaps he was just a longtime teacher in the university. Nor was I aware that during the 1968 student rebellion at Columbia he had been one of the ad hoc faculty members in support of the students' demands and opposed to the use of police force in dealing with the student riots. I had come to New York all the way from Taiwan to get an education in architecture and urban planning, the student movement was not my concern, and of course I had not yet read his book *Communitas*. This elderly professor who talked in a gentle tone of voice seemed kind and wise. I could not remember most of what he said on that first day of school, but did get an impression of him as a learned old man very much into concepts and ideas about life rather than the design aspects of cities. After listening to our self-introductions, he commented that he always liked the mixture of students who came from different parts of the world and that our international backgrounds were among the reasons that made New York City such a wonderful place for learning. I had a feeling that he must love New York a lot.

Percy, or Professor Goodman as I often interchangeably called him, turned out to be a really great teacher for me and helped make my two years at Columbia the greatest learning experience in my life (though he stopped teaching in 1972, before my second year). I attended his design studio and his seminar on urban design and took an elective course on utopian communities, all of which expanded my knowledge of human societies and ways of life — invaluable lessons in the shaping of urban spaces. This learning process was strangely puzzling at the beginning, yet very enlightening and energizing for me in the end; for I did not realize how much the art or science of "design" was the central theme of Percy's teaching until I gradually found out how wrong I was.

Both in the studio and the classroom, we had many discussions and arguments, some serious, others in good humor. When Percy pointed out that both the creativity and stupidity of human societies were revealed in the way that people lived and shaped their living spaces, I became interested in finding out how great thinkers in the past envisioned and built cities, and how and why societies accepted or abandoned those visions. As I became more knowledgeable, I developed more doubts as well. In discussing this with Percy, instead of trying to indoctrinate me with his beliefs, he suggested that I experiment with my own ideas.

Thus in the summer of 1972, I went with a classmate from France to 101st Street in East Harlem. My idea was to design a children's playground and a teenagers' ball field for two vacant lots. As a semester project for the design studio, only the design on paper had to be handed in to receive a grade, but I wanted much more. After discussing the project with the neighborhood residents, we actually built it as a collective effort with the kids on the block; and my French classmate filmed the total building process. Actually, before starting the work we did go to see Percy at his home for guidance on our "real" project. This interview was also filmed. At first Percy was a little dubious, but in the end he affirmed our effort saying, "First of all, every man has a responsibility to help his fellow citizens when he can, and secondly, while it may be a very small enterprise, make it perfect and beautiful, as a symbol — a symbol of urban design."

After the interview, Percy showed us some of his drawings and paintings (fig. 146). I was very impressed with his paintings, so full of artistic energy and youthful spirit, like the work of a romantic young man. He commended me on my design "talent," which made me blush. At the time I aspired to become a painter as well as a socially useful urban designer, and looking at Percy's art work made me realize that such goals could be achieved, or were certainly worth striving for. I consider myself lucky to have studied under Percy, if only for one year — his last one teaching at Columbia. He had ideas and credos which he showed me without asking me to follow them, encouraging me to search and find my own. After graduating from Columbia, I became a city planner and urban designer with the Planning Department of New York City. Although I have been dealing with the physical environment of the city day in and day out, I have

Fig. 146 *The Prison: In Memory of Piranesi*, 1974, acrylic on Masonite (cat. 44)

never forgotten that better ways still need to be found both in the design of our living spaces and in our life styles.

The playground and ball field that I helped to build in East Harlem have been deserted by the people on the block since the late 1980s, the two lots again becoming covered with weeds. The children from the summer of 1972 must all be grown up and most of them probably have left the neighborhood. I thought of Percy and our discussion on the "symbol" of urban space making and felt a little sad. For sure, it was not architecture nor urban design, but for me it was an indelible, genuine learning experience, something I will always treasure.

Fig. 147 Studio jury in 1949: Percy, Dean Kenneth Smith, Talbot Hamlin (Avery Librarian), and an unidentified student

Fig. 148 Percy and Naomi in Long Island, circa 1959

Naomi Goodman

A Memoir

The first part of this memoir is based on stories and information from Percy, his sister and brother, old friends, and Taylor Stoehr, from his research for a biography of Paul Goodman. Some facts and episodes have been checked or amplified through Suzanne O'Keefe's interviews with Percy in 1979 (in the Columbia Oral History Project). Percy and I met in May of 1944, so the second part is based on my own recollections. As his career during the latter period is better known, and as aspects of his professional work and teaching will be discussed in other parts of this book, I have limited the scope of my memoir.

Part 1

The second of four children, Percival Goodman was born on 13 January 1904 and was named for his grandfather. His father, Barnet, was a partner in a prosperous auctioneering concern. Barnet had wanted to marry his stepsister, Augusta, for some time, but she believed that marriage was not possible because of their kinship. Barnet arranged for them to consult a rabbi who explained that, as they were not blood relatives, they could marry, and so they did.

Percy remembered winter trips to Bermuda as a small boy, when the family lived in a brownstone house on East 16th Street. By the time he was seven (when his brother Paul was born) the household was breaking up. His parents were divorced in a bitter contest. According to Percy, his father had told his mother that, if she divorced him, she would never see him again. This proved true, as Barnet left the country and went to South America.

Augusta was left with four children — Alice, ten; Percy, eight; Arnold, six; and the infant Paul — and no financial support. She had done bookkeeping and dealt with customers for the auction house but had no other business experience. Arranging for her half-sister, Frances, to take care of the children, she went to work as a saleswoman in various women's specialty stores,

Fig. 149 Percival, Alice, and Arnold Goodman, 1911 (cat. 58)

Fig. 150 Sidonia and Benjamin Levitan (Aunt Sadie and Uncle Ben) with Augusta Goodman, circa 1911 (cat. 57)

among other jobs. She kept the family together by living frugally, settling in the less expensive Washington Heights area, and by moving the household whenever she could find a cheaper apartment (fig. 149). Every summer she sent the children and Frances to board in the country, gave up their living quarters, put the furniture in storage, and moved in with a friend. In the fall she would rent another apartment, so the children came back to a different home every autumn, often having to transfer to a new school.

Small for his age, and thin, Percy was not robust as a child. He was considered to have a heart murmur, which certainly was not apparent in later years. Also, he had some tendency to tuberculosis. Since fresh air was believed to help such children, he was sent to spend a winter in Massachusetts, living in the country with a minister and his family. Given Augusta's finances, this treatment must have been strongly advised. Percy drew from the time he could remember. Although he preferred using his left hand, his mother and aunt tried to make him right-handed, following current beliefs. As a result, he used his right hand for skills that he had been taught early, but his left hand for actions that were instinctive for him, such as drawing, and for skills that he had learned later.

Percy was not a happy child. He resented his parent's divorce and his mother's absence. His brother Arnold, a cheerful boy, died of meningitis resulting from a misdiagnosed ear infection. The family's living arrangements did not help. His education and friendships were limited by the frequent changes of school, and these various schools were, by all reports, not very good. In 1914, he was shuttled back and forth four times between two crowded schools. Classmates made fun of his name, which was considered "sissy," and a popular comic strip about an early robot called "Percy, the Mechanical Man" was used to taunt him.

Home was not much better than school. He got on very badly with Aunt Frances. Later, Paul disagreed with him about Frances, remembering her as being pleasant. But Percy was triumphant when suppressed feelings of anger about Frances came out during Paul's analysis. Percy told me that he went to her funeral in order to be sure that she was really dead.

During Percy's childhood, Augusta expressed no interest in religion, so he had no Jewish religious training. A woman of enthusiasms, she became interested in her Judaism in time for Paul to attend religious school and to become a Bar Mitzvah. In her later years, she became a follower of the popular evangelist Aimee Semple MacPherson and moved to Los Angeles.

The family lived near their Aunt Sidonia (Sadie), Augusta's sister, and her husband, Benjamin Levitan, the sisters' cousin (fig. 150). Ben was an architect who had studied architecture in Paris. The families were close and Ben was interested in Percy; Sadie and Ben were certainly helpful to Augusta and her family. In 1917, when Percy was thirteen and had started seventh grade, he asked his uncle for a job. Ben consulted Augusta, who agreed, and so Percy left home to live on his own, becoming an errand boy in Ben's office, which was on 32nd Street between Fifth and Sixth Avenues.

After starting to work, Percy had limited contact with his immediate family, by his own choice. Although his mother would have heard from Ben Levitan about him, and Percy did sometimes come home for a weekend meal, as time went on he visited less and less. Paul recalled occasional visits, when Percy would bring presents that young Paul considered too childish for him. The difference in their ages, and Percy's living separately from the family, kept them apart. Alice, however, two years older than Percy, was deeply involved in family life. She helped to take care of Paul and, dropping out of Hunter College High School at sixteen, started working at M.G.M., where she continued all of her adult life, gradually having more responsible positions.

Percy recalled that the Italian draftsmen in his uncle's office were very kind to him, sometimes chipping in to buy him a hero sandwich when he went to pick up their similar lunches. This was especially welcome as his salary was only six dollars a week; even translated into current dollars, the wages would approximate slightly more than one hundred and fifty dollars a week, which is less than today's minimum wage for the hours worked. After paying his rent, he often did not have enough money for food. At the local Automat he frequently alternated between eating a ketchup sandwich (a five-cent buttered roll with free ketchup) and a mustard sandwich (same system). He believed that he was paid little in an effort to make him return and live at home. Whether he received less than other errand boys, I do not know, but he was certain that Uncle Ben was exploiting him.

Among his assignments was measuring the basement of the old Astor Library on Lafayette Street (now the Public Theater), where he encountered rats of enormous size. One winter, he was sent to deliver revised plans for the so-called upside-down building on Welfare Island (now Roosevelt Island), which was under construction. Ben had designed the building so that truck drivers, who crossed the river on the bridge from Manhattan, could drive directly onto the roof and then take their trucks down by elevator to ground level for deliveries. The steel framing, which had been erected for the four or five floors of the building, was covered with ice. A strong wind was blowing. Percy called up to the construction superintendent, who was at the top level on the opposite side, to say that he had the plans. The man indicated that he should bring them up. The boy started climbing and, when he reached the top level, held out the roll of drawings. The man signaled that he should bring the drawings to him, at the other side. Percy started out across the icy steel girders but could not continue and froze, holding on to a girder for dear life. It took several men to pry him off. He never liked heights in later life.

Another task took place on sunny days, when Percy would take plans up to the roof to make the blueprints from them. He would put the tracing paper drawings in a special frame, with light-sensitive paper underneath them. He had to time the exposure to the sun, then remove the blueprints from the frame, roll them up, and take them down to the office where he washed them in a special, large sink.

When Percy was about fourteen, his uncle felt that he should have more education and sent him to study drafting at the Cooper Union, giving him time off during the working day for his classes. Cooper Union had been set up to train mechanics and draftsmen and did not yet have other architectural courses. Percy spent three months as a student there; and, completing the year's work, he saw no reason to continue. Then his uncle arranged for him to attend the Beaux-Arts Institute of Design in New York, which had been established by architects who had studied at the École des Beaux-Arts in Paris. The institute followed the French atelier system, with students working under a single critic and architects holding informal classes in their offices, often in the evenings. The architects would volunteer to act as critics to young draftsmen, assigning projects that the Beaux-Arts Institute had prepared. Ben recommended that Percy join the Atelier Licht, which consisted of George Licht, an architect who was chief draftsman for the firm of Delano and Aldrich, and Percy. Other ateliers might have as many as ten or twenty students.

Fig. 151 Design for Natatorium, Hotel-Apartment, and Garage, New York, 1930 (cat. 4)

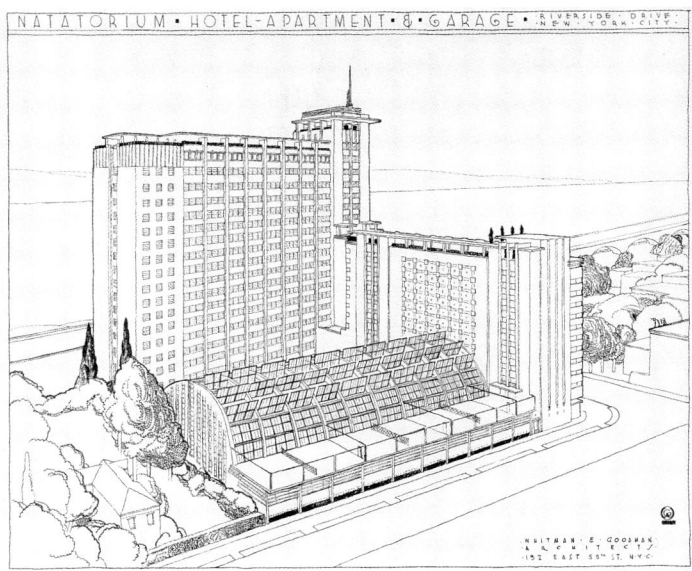

There were also Saturday eight-hour "sketches" at the institute itself. Through George Licht, Percy sometimes worked evenings at Delano and Aldrich, when they needed extra draftsmen.

In addition, Percy read a lot about architecture. The bold sketches of Eric Mendelsohn and pictures of his Einstein Tower were a revelation to him; these sketches were unlike anything he had seen before and opened up exciting architectural possibilities. He read widely in other fields, in an effort to improve his education. In addition to his uncle and Licht, he had other mentors. A second-hand bookseller on Eighth Street recommended books to him and took them back for credit after he had read them. Percy took lessons in drawing, perspective, and architectural drawing from a retired professor named Varon, who was French, and spent one winter living as a boarder with the Varons on Staten Island. They spoke only French at home, which improved Percy's proficiency in that language.

By that time, Percy would have been working as a draftsman, at a somewhat higher salary. Ben's office designed various buildings in the city, including natatoria, a name for swimming pools with other amenities, probably what we would now call a health club. Through the natatoria commissions, Percy met J. Franklin Whitman, a few years his senior, an artist working for his father, a builder of natatoria (fig. 151). Whitman moved from Philadelphia to New York and became a close friend of Percy's, sharing an apartment with him on Minetta Lane.

After working in his uncle's office for a number of years, Percy left as he resented still being underpaid. First he worked for some apartment house architects, who paid much more, and then for John Peterkin. Unfortunately, I have no dates for these changes. At Peterkin's office, he soon became the main designer, creating renderings for skyscrapers, among other assignments. As he explained, these designs were for the exterior of the building only, with classical details. There was no attempt to relate the exterior to an interior plan. Because of Percy's youth (he would have been under twenty), Peterkin generally saw the clients without him. But, in one instance, the designer was needed at a conference, so Percy was called in. The meeting went well, but the clients were amazed that the designer was so young and suggested to Peterkin that he was "robbing the cradle." Jack Peterkin told Percy that he must do something to look older and recommended both growing a mustache and starting to smoke. Percy followed both suggestions and continued the style and habit for many years.

Peterkin was very important in Percy's development. In addition to the design opportunities, he suggested that Percy should spend time abroad and recommended the American School of Fine Arts at Fontainebleau, a summer program that included an architectural division. When he was around eighteen, Percy was given the summer off from work. Knowing that saving was difficult for his young designer, Peterkin held back part of his pay; and upon embarking for France, Percy was given a wallet containing extra money. He spent several summers at Fontainebleau, where — not working by day and studying by night — he enjoyed the first free time he had in many years. He spent time in the painting and sculpture studios as well as studying architecture. While he had been sketching people and landscapes whenever he could, at Fontainbleau he had his first and only instruction in painting and sculpture.

Percy's next quest was for the Paris Prize which enabled a young American to study architecture at the École Nationale des Beaux-Arts in Paris and to travel with a stipend of (I believe) five thousand dollars a year, a large sum in those days of favorable exchange rates. Percy was a runner-up in 1924 and determined to win the next year. His critic would have been George Licht, but Licht was away when Percy was working on the 1925 competition. Percy, however, had become friendly with the architect Jacques Carlu at Fountainbleau. Carlu was teaching at M.I.T. during this period and agreed to be Percy's critic. So Percy went to Cambridge at Carlu's invitation and spent about six weeks in his studio, developing competition drawings for a United States Summer Capitol, the project for that year.

One of five finalists in the 1925 competition, Percy took first prize. At that time, competitions did not have such definite specifications on size, color, et cetera as now exist. Percy, having decided that his project must stand out so strikingly that the judges would hardly be able to see any other design, used strong colors and framed his drawings in heavy gold frames. After winning, he posed for a newspaper picture as a young artist in a smock (fig. 26), at a drafting board covered with sketches, having made up a story about entering in order to be independent from his rich father. The one existing rendering and an elevation are in the Metropolitan Museum of Art (figs. 152–154). (He discussed the competition in detail in Suzanne O'Keefe's interviews.) Only after winning the competition did Percy find out that, to enroll in the Beaux-Arts, a student had to be at least a high school graduate. The judges, who were very sympathetic, agreed to give him an oral examination, which Percy, after a few months of tutoring in mathematics, passed.

Percy had learned beaux-arts skills in the New York ateliers and had followed that approach to win the Paris Prize. Meanwhile, he had been greatly influenced by the modern movement in architecture, both through books and during his sojourn in France, and was deeply impressed by the drawings that Le Corbusier had made for the League of Nations competition and by the work of Auguste Perret among others. The Bauhaus had to be discovered through books, since at that time it was not acknowledged in France.

For four years, Percy was enrolled at the École des Beaux-Arts, where his critic was the architect

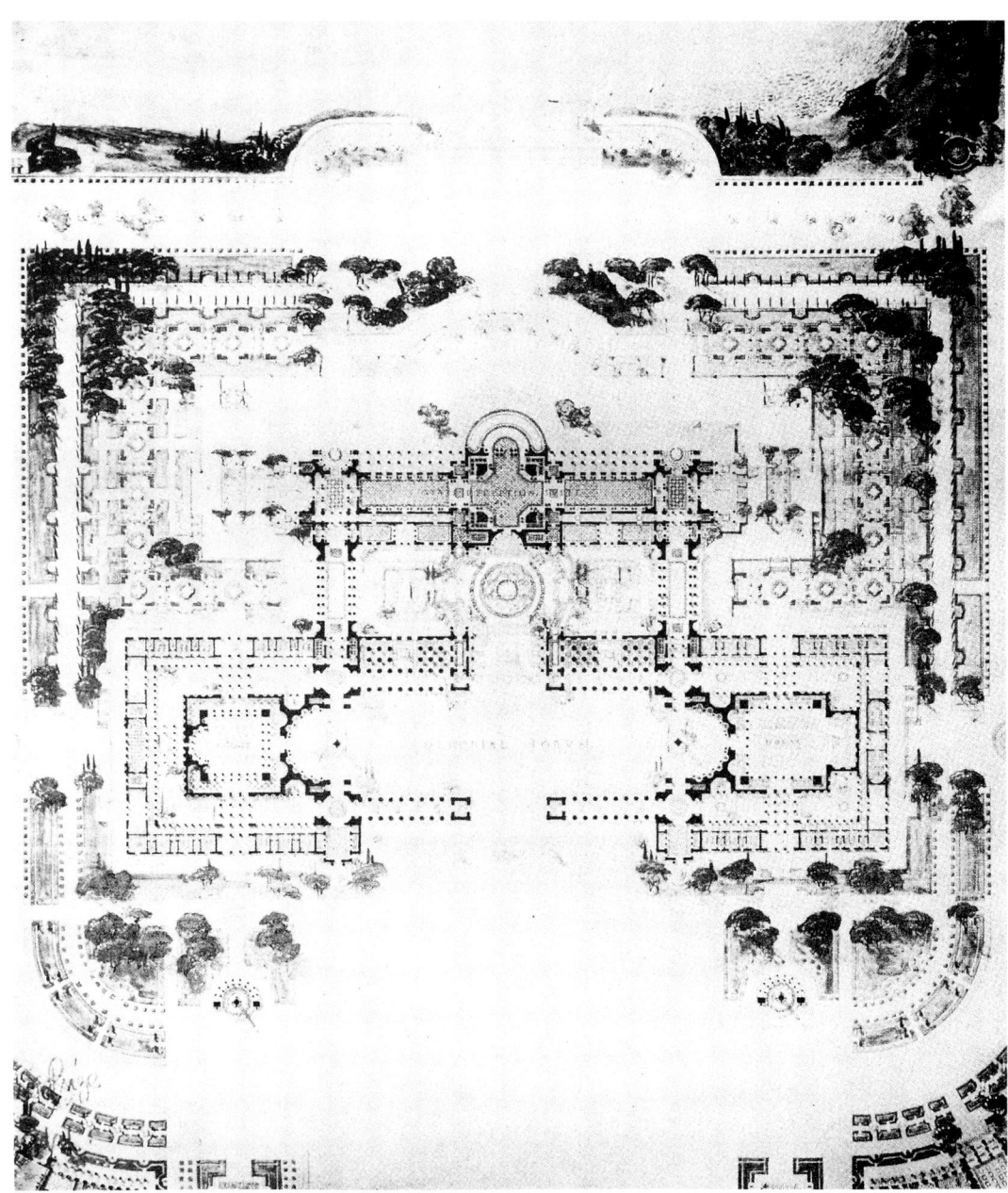

Fig. 152 A Summer Capitol for the United States, winning project for the Paris Prize in 1925: plan (from *Winning Designs, 1904–1963: Paris Prize in Architecture,* New York: National Institute for Architectural Education, 1964)

Fig. 153 A Summer Capitol for the United States: elevation. The Metropolitan Museum of Art, Gift of the National Institute for Architectural Education, 1980 (cat. 1)

Fig. 154 A Summer Capitol for the United States: section

Emmanuel Pontremoli. Although Percy had been interested in attending Perret's atelier, Raymond Hood had recommended Pontremoli, the only Jewish architect at the École; since French anti-Semitism was well known, Hood thought that Percy might be better off with a Jewish critic. The system was quite informal, often requiring no more than two hours a day at the atelier and thus allowing time for travel. Percy enjoyed Paris and the École greatly but did not attempt to get a degree, which would have required a series of examinations on many aspects of architecture, including mathematics, in which he was still poorly prepared and not very interested.

Whitman came to Paris and they shared an apartment. After Whit married, the three of them shared living quarters (fig. 155), near the artist S. W. Hayter, who became a lifelong friend, and next door to Alexander Calder. They had a wide acquaintance with other architects, artists, writers, musicians. Percy met his first wife, Mildred Evans, in Fontainebleau, where she was a music student. He may have continued to work at the school in some capacity as he and Mildred lived there for a time. Some summers he earned his tuition as a guide at the castle, later recalling that, when he did not know the answer to a tourist's question, he made up some story about Francis I or whoever, which never was doubted.

While in France, Percy took up fencing, one of his few athletic interests, and even joined a fencing club. With fewer left-handed fencers than right-handed ones, he was in great demand and quickly improved his skills by fencing against more experienced opponents. At the fencing club, and at the École, some thought he was Turkish, but later he felt that the marked animosity of some of his opponents had to do with his being a Jew.

Fig. 155 Percy with his partner Franklin Whitman and Whitman's wife in Paris, late 1920s (cat. 62)

Whitman, who had gone back to the United States in 1928, cabled Percy that he had an architectural job for the two of them. Percy decided that the time was right for his return and came back to New York City with Mildred. The firm Whitman and Goodman continued for several years, until 1933, designing store interiors, apartments and such. Percy's marriage ended after a year or two in this country. Shortly after their separation, their son, George Ridge, was born. His maternal grandfather took custody, and after Mildred's early death George was brought up and adopted by Mildred's sister. He was an adult before he and Percy made contact.

One of the firm's commissions was to redesign the ground floor of a women's specialty store on 50th Street between Fifth and Sixth Avenues called Jay Thorpe. Their design called for two freestanding columns each with a sculpture on top. The partners arranged for Sandy Calder, also back in the U.S., to make a wood sculpture for each column; they liked Sandy's work and knew that he could use a commission. When the finished sculptures were presented to the clients, they were shocked. One said that he never wanted to see these objects again. Percy was concerned that Calder be paid. The clients agreed to honor their contract but didn't want the sculptures, so Percy kept one and Whitman kept the other. Percy's is still in the family but the whereabouts of Whitman's is unknown.

Around the same time, in the early 1930's, Calder made a double portrait of Percy and Whitman, with Percy's head in black wire and Whitman's in copper wire — Percy had dark hair and Whitman was very fair. When they dissolved their partnership, they cut the wire that held the portrait heads together, each keeping his own likeness. Percy moved to his own office shortly after and, following the move, could not locate the wire portrait. When he called the mover to inquire, he was told that some twisted wire had been included among his effects but had been thrown away (fig. 156).

The problems of finding work during the Depression may have led to the breakup of their partnership. Whitman went back to illustration and moved with his wife to a farm in the Pennsylvania Dutch area. We saw him on the rare occasions when he came to New York City and, in the fifties, visited him once in Pennsylvania. A charcoal drawing of Percy as a young man that

Fig. 156 Percy with wire portrait sculpture by Alexander Calder (cat. 63)

Fig. 157 Apartment building at 25 West 54th Street, New York, 1939

Whitman made in Paris and a sketch of our daughter, Rachel, that he drew during our visit remain in our family.

Percy had become very close to his brother Paul. After meeting again in New York City as adults, they discovered their compatibility, became good friends, and in 1930 began to collaborate. Although they moved in very different circles, they met each other's friends. Percy was able to help Paul, a struggling writer, which was important for both of them.

From 1933 Percy had his own office, while also doing some work in partnership with another architect, Meyer Katzman, an association that lasted until World War II. Percy continued with commercial work, apartment design, and a number of private homes, including one in Westchester for Katzman. The effort was to create a total modern environment: house, furniture, accessories, et cetera. Meyer approached Percy after the war about renewing their association, but Percy's interests in architecture had changed.

During this same period, Percy designed a large apartment for Jack and Edith Straus. Responsible for designing the layout, furniture, rugs, he also selected the paintings, including one of his own; the elegant modern furniture included a grand piano in light mahogany which was cantilevered from a pedestal base (fig. 8). The Strauses became friends, especially Edith, who for a time did interior design work for some projects of Percy's office and for her own clients, sometimes in partnership with him. He designed an unusual modern country house for them which, unfortunately, because of the Depression was never built.

Percy's built architecture, both with Whitman and after, consisted of houses, apartments, store interiors, industrial design — especially furniture — and other special projects. Two of his buildings were the Saint Thomas Church Choir School and the apartment building at 25 West 54th Street (fig. 157), where he lived for a while (he had designed the smaller apartments to suit his own tastes). But his actual architectural practice was only one of his major interests. He de-

Fig. 158 Jefferson National Expansion Memorial, Saint Louis (competition), 1947: bird's-eye view

Fig. 159 Jefferson National Expansion Memorial, Saint Louis (competition), 1947: view of tower

signed housing for low-income families, experimental modern buildings, a prototype city of the future for the 1939 New York World's Fair, and other such projects. For various reasons, in particular the lack of capital during the Great Depression, some of these projects were never built; some, of course, were purely theoretical. Much of this work was an expression of his concern for social conditions in a society fraught with problems.

In this time of great ferment, Percy was part of a group of designers, planners, architects, and art historians who were calling for a "New Day." The group included Meyer Schapiro. They put much effort into reevaluating the capitalist system to try to find out what had gone wrong and how society could be better organized. Sympathetic to socialism, interested in communism, and prolabor, they were interested in projects to improve living and working conditions, through modern design as well as the reduction of hours of work and the payment of fair wages. Percy became disillusioned with communism fairly early, perhaps in part because Paul's anarchist opposition to such an organized society helped him to see the problems.

Percy was involved in trying to found an architects' union, which was to include related professions, called the Federation of Architects, Engineers, Chemists and Technicians. The people to be organized for better wages, however, considered themselves professionals and were not interested in a union. His own office was one of the few that were unionized, although as the boss he himself could not join the union.

Fig. 160 Percy and Bill Hayter at the house in Springs, Long Island, early 1980s

Other architects faced the same dichotomy: work for wealthy clients versus concern for bettering the lot of working people. Design improvements, such as those being developed by Buckminster Fuller, were only part of their interests. In addition to their local involvements, they were deeply concerned about the rise of dictatorships in Europe and about the Spanish Civil War. These New York leftists were on the side of the Spanish Loyalists, as were other liberals. Percy considered going to Spain but was advised that he could be much more useful addressing meetings and raising money in New York for the Loyalists.

In 1937, Buckminster Fuller had started his Structural Study Associates and asked Percy to join the group which consisted of three or four architects and engineers. Fuller was then working on the conservation of water. Despite his own office projects, Percy worked with them when he could. Bucky had developed a fog spray shower which used less water than a conventional one and was hoped to be as effective. Late one winter afternoon, when testing the device, Percy stepped into the shower cubicle. The water turned cold, as the heat went off in the building at six o'clock. Percy developed a very bad cold afterward, possibly pneumonia, and gave up working with Fuller.

Percy was not a licensed architect and had to have his drawings signed by an architect who had a license, which he disliked. He had made a number of efforts to be accepted for the architectural examination but was rebuffed each time. Only graduates of recognized architectural schools or those who had worked in architectural offices for twelve years were qualified to take the examination for the license without special permission. Finally, he contacted a number of well-known architects who certified that, because of his time at the École des Beaux-Arts, he had the equivalent of an architectural school degree. Frank Lloyd Wright was one of the architects who vouched for him and requested that he be permitted to take the exam. Percy was finally allowed to take the examination, passed, and received his license in 1936.

New York University had started an architecture program in which Percy taught as an adjunct professor for several years, starting in 1930. He liked teaching very much and was appreciated by his students, some of whom came to work for him and remained friends for many years.

He also had an atelier in his office and then helped found the Design Laboratory, which lasted for a few years. On the recommendation of John C. B. Moore, whom he had known at the Beaux-Arts, in 1943 Percy began to teach at Columbia as critic for a six-week senior project each year.

Both during these years and later on, Percy frequently entered competitions; he enjoyed the challenges, liked to work on interesting projects, and believed competitions were an important way for architects to obtain recognition (figs. 158–159, pl. IX). He told me about two: the national competition for a new Smithsonian museum (figs. 9–10), where his design placed second, and the international competition for a Palace of the Soviets (fig. 17), in which he placed fourth.

Percy said that Hitler made him a Jew. When the United States entered World War II in December 1941, Percy, who had long been opposed to fascism and had identified with the persecution of Jews in Europe, wanted to be involved. He applied for a commission but was turned down, since his references stated that he was too antiauthoritarian to fit into military life. He later applied to the Air Force, but at age thirty-seven, five feet eight inches tall, and about 135 pounds he was not accepted. So he turned to camouflage, a necessary part of the war effort in which he could help. He formed the Camouflage Engineering Company with S. W. (Bill) Hayter, the printmaker and teacher whom he had known first in Paris (fig. 160); David Reeves, a mathematician and furniture builder whom they had known in Paris; Hector Hoppin, a Jungian analyst with excellent government connections (perhaps also a Paris connection); Milton Gendel, an art historian; Jack Straus, the former client who was a stockbroker and thus believed to be helpful on business matters; plus Kate Abbot, an artist, who was Percy's girlfriend at the time. (During these years, Percy had a number of long-term love affairs, after which he continued to be friendly with the women involved.)

The company bid successfully and completed a number of projects for the U. S. Military, including camouflaging Fort Belvoir in Virginia. Percy and Bill Hayter worked out theories and methods of camouflage based on their knowledge of visual effects, and the group then went on location to supervise the actual work. One objective of camouflage involves the view from the air. On their own, Percy, Hayter, and Reeves worked out a device that enabled pilots to see their targets more clearly. Through Hector's connections, they were able to present their device to upper echelon aviation officers, who were quite impressed but explained that the group had reinvented the top-secret Norden Bombsight and must never discuss their project.

The company bid on a contract that included planting a large dune area with beach grass. None of the partners had any experience with beach grass and assumed that it was similar to grass seed for a lawn, not knowing that beach grass has to be planted in individual pre-started strands. The army engineers involved later admitted that they had all burst out laughing when they opened the bid because the price was so low. They accepted the bid, however, which caused the company to go out of business.

Fig. 161 Welfare Island Service Buildings, designed in 1944 (cat. 19b)

Percy came back to New York City in 1943, arranged for office space with Emery Roth, as did Pomerance and Breines, and worked on minor projects such as remodeling town houses in the city. His first large project was the design of a building commissioned by the New York City government in its effort to prepare for postwar needs (Moore and Hutchins were responsible for the working drawings). The site was on Welfare Island, near Uncle Benny's upside-down building and included three elements — a large laundry, a garage, and a firehouse — which Percy made into a unified complex. It was built after the war (fig. 161).

Not having a full-time practice, Percy used much of his time to read and think about planning and about community as well as about Judaism, discussing ideas with his brother Paul and continuing to develop his own interests in social betterment. Percy and Paul shared areas of common concern and found out how well they could work together. They would talk out the ideas and problems, find their common approach, and work out the schemes. *Communitas* was the result of their discussions and represented a totally joint project: Percy developed the basic ideas; Paul wrote the first drafts, which Percy worked over and they completed together; and Percy drew the illustrations, which were conceived as integral to the text. They wrote articles together as well.

Percy had been made far more aware of his Jewishness because of Hitler and the events of that time; religion had previously not been important to him. He read and thought about Judaism and its relation to him personally, to others, and to architecture. Believing that the world had changed because of the Holocaust, he no longer wanted to spend his time and talents on commercial work or on living arrangements for the rich. Percy decided that he should design for the Jewish community, both as an expression of his Judaism and because of the losses suffered by Jews. At that time, early 1944, this commitment was still in the realm of theory.

Part 2

Percy and I met on the 8th of May in 1944 at a Sculptors' Guild opening. We felt an immediate attraction and talked together all evening. He gave me a fairly complete history of his life, while I told him about mine, which was both shorter and less dramatic. As I was to find out, Percy usually spoke very little about his earlier years. He had discovered his own method of surviving by a determined effort not to look back and by repressing the events of his childhood. But he did refer to his leaving home at age thirteen, a crucial event for him.

During that summer, we saw each other steadily, despite my parents' opposition to our relationship. Percy, who always seemed younger than his years, was forty, while I was twenty-four, a distinct age gap. Percy kept to his standard schedule: he went to his office every weekday around eight o'clock, though his architectural practice was very limited, and often spent the time on theoretical projects; on writing, including book reviews; or on reading both theory and architecture. At home he continued to paint and sketch (pls. VI–VII). He and Paul were completing *Communitas* (which was first published in 1947 by the University of Chicago Press). I was working for a liberal political organization, having graduated from college two years earlier.

Percy wanted to design for the Jewish community; so when he learned that the Warburg house on Fifth Avenue and 92nd Street had been given to the Jewish Theological Seminary to be made into a Jewish museum, he went to one of the trustees whom he knew quite well and told him of his strong interest in this project. He was appointed architect for the museum during the summer. This appointment helped us to marry: it was Percy's first important commission at that time and offered a promising new beginning to his architectural practice. So, notwithstanding my parents' concerns, we were married on September 28th in a small ceremony with my immediate family and Percy's siblings present. This was the beginning of a very interesting life. Percy taught me to cook and presented me with his collections of recipes. He taught me to look at the world with greater discernment since he was always interested in the reasons why, as well the outcome, and believed that the means influenced the end. His creativity and encouragement of mine was an important part of our life. And I was deeply interested in his work, which we discussed often.

With the museum commission, Percy moved out of Emery Roth's offices and rented space at 18 East 48th Street. This would be his third architectural practice — his first was ended by the Depression, his second by World War II — and he wanted it to be his last.

An uncompromising modernist, Percy's first plan was to gut the interior of the Warburg house and construct a modern museum inside its walls. But construction prices had started their postwar rise, and the bids came in far higher than had been anticipated. So Percy had to make a new set of drawings with the minimal alterations required to make the museum conform to the building code and to have suitable exhibition space. That plan became the original museum,

Fig. 162 Untitled plaster sculpture (cat. 54) Fig. 163 Mother and child, plaster sculpture (cat. 50)

which has had two additions since. Percy said later that he was glad that much of the original interior had been preserved since he had grown to appreciate earlier architectural styles, although he did not consider them appropriate for today.

We had moved into Percy's small apartment on West 20th Street, which had his paintings on the walls. It was difficult to find apartments then, as now. I continued my job until the fall election then, because I wanted to begin painting again, attended the Art Students League, working under the abstractionist George L. K. Morris. Percy had advised me to study with Morris or Hans Hoffmann. Despite the limitations of space, we entertained a great deal, as I began to meet Percy's friends and acquaintances and to introduce him to mine. Since we could only do small projects at home, we both worked directly in plaster, making table-size sculptures (figs. 162–163). Percy discovered the possibilities of aluminum foil, strengthened with glue and colored with oil paint, which he used for small sculptures (fig. 139).

When we married, Percy was ready to settle down and was delighted with my pregnancy and the birth of our daughter, Rachel (fig. 164). Our living space was small, so we moved to my parents' apartment temporarily and then were able to exchange 20th Street for a top-floor apartment at Marble House at 8th Street and Fifth Avenue, former servants' quarters, renovated with many skylights. We had to climb eighty-one steps (I counted), but the space was well proportioned and pleasant. When some of the plaster fell from underneath the main skylight, Percy attached a paint brush to a long curtain rod, so that he could reach the area and paint a mural to disguise the damage. He designed wood-backed floor cushions, covered in off-white Naugahyde, which made a floor-level couch. He had studied seating in connection with his furniture design and was convinced that chairs were neither natural nor good for posture. Most of the world sat on the floor, he said, and chairs had been developed only because of cold and the dirt on the floors of earlier Western houses; with modern cleaning and heating, there should be no

Fig. 164 Naomi with her mother, Helen; her daughter, Rachel, and Rachel's son, Bear, circa 1975

Fig. 165 Chiu-Hwa Wang in the office

problem. We did keep his two low chairs with pony skins on the backs.

Percy began to write about synagogue architecture in collaboration with Paul. They had a series of articles in *Commentary*, then a new liberal Jewish magazine. Percy and Paul discussed the meaning of the synagogue in the community, the need for directness and honesty in ritual objects, and the reasons why modern architecture was most appropriate. They explained that, as Jews, we had never had an architectural style of our own but had built in the style of the country in which we were living. Percy believed that modern architecture was for Jews: it did not aspire to heaven, but embraced the earth; it let in light, important in a service based on reading; and it stressed honesty and directness in the use of materials. This was the architectural style of our country and time, and far more related to Jewish beliefs than Roman, Christian, or Islamic building styles which, in addition, came from periods in which Jews had been persecuted.

Percy wanted to develop his ideas into a model synagogue, with modern art made by Marc Chagall and Jacques Lipchitz, who had both come to New York from Europe. He discussed the possible project with them. Also, Chagall offered to paint murals on the walls of the library of the Warburg house in exchange for the cost of the paint; he was not well known in this country and was eager to have his work in a notable public space. Both Percy and Meyer Schapiro — who had been working with Percy on colors for the museum, at the suggestion of the trustees — strongly endorsed Chagall's offer. But the trustees of the Jewish Theological Seminary, not knowing much about Chagall and dubious about taking a chance on the work of a little-known artist, rejected the plan. (Percy later made another effort to use Chagall's work. He had designed Temple Beth El in Providence, Rhode Island, and suggested to the building committee that they commission Chagall to design tapestries for which the artist would charge a low fee in order to have his work on view. The committee members refused the offer, saying, "Who is Chagall?" Chagall said, "What is Providence? I should be in New York!")

The model synagogue never was developed, but Percy found a different opportunity to express his approach to synagogue design. The Union of American Hebrew Congregations (the Reform Jewish group) knew that new synagogues would be built when the war ended, since there had been none constructed for so long and many families had moved to the suburbs or other areas. The U.A.H.C., wanting to help improve the quality of the new buildings, in 1947, organized a conference for interested rabbis, congregational staff and board members, and architects. Because of his writing on synagogues and involvement with the Jewish Museum, Percy was invited to participate. He spoke about his reasons for recommending modern architecture, about the essential requirements for a synagogue, and gave his interpretations, which were based on the Hebrew Scriptures. Percy's first synagogue commissions were a direct outcome of the conference: the Baltimore Hebrew Congregation (figs. 60–67), Temple Beth El in Providence (figs. 70–76), and Temple Beth Israel in Lima, Ohio. He moved to larger offices on 49th Street and Madison Avenue and increased his small staff.

Percy was convinced of the need to incorporate contemporary art as part of the architecture. For many centuries. the greatest art and architecture had been religious, a tradition he believed should be revived. Many of the best contemporary artists were abstract expressionists, which meant that their nonfigurative art was particularly well suited to the biblical commandment forbidding the making of graven images. He convinced many of his clients of the need for modern art in their synagogues and influenced them to commission contemporary artists, local artists in the community as well as major figures such as Motherwell, Frankenthaler, Ferber, Gottlieb, Lassaw, and Rattner.

Chiu-Hwa Wang, who had been Percy's student in the Masters' class at Columbia, had come to work for him in 1950 after graduating, eventually becoming his associate in 1960 (fig. 165). Since Percy was basically a designer and Chiu-Hwa an excellent planner, their abilities were complementary. She became a friend of the family and worked with Percy until he closed his office in 1979. Then she joined her family in Taiwan, taught architecture, and now has a thriving practice in partnership with another Columbia architectural graduate and P. G. student, Joshua Pan.

There always seemed to be housing shortages in New York City. By 1948, we wanted to have another child but realized that 8 Fifth Avenue would present too many difficulties, with all the stairs and only one bedroom. Through the connections of one of my uncles, and a bribe that my father paid, we moved to five rooms at 108 East 86th Street. Our son, Joel, was born while we lived there. We had said that, if we couldn't stay in the Village, we would move to the school district of P.S. 6, considered one of the best public schools in the city. P.S. 6 turned out to have many problems, so, in 1954, both children began to attend the Ethical Culture School on Central Park West, and later Fieldston, schools that I had attended.

We continued to entertain frequently, including architects with whom Percy was friendly (he found many architects too conservative for him); artists, among whom we had many friends;

his Columbia colleagues and students; clients and rabbis; psychoanalysts and therapists, of whom we seemed to know many; and other friends. Percy had been giving a Christmas Eve party in his office for many years. The first December 24th that we were together, we did not send out invitations; but Percy mentioned, casually, that I should have some food and drink on hand as people might drop in. Indeed, they did, and we continued the tradition, giving the party at his office until we had enough space at home. The party became an institution in some circles. We sent out blueprinted invitations to friends and clients, and used them as a holiday greeting for those who were not in New York. The party lasted past its fiftieth anniversary, until Percy died. Even then, some people called to ask if the party would take place. I had no heart to continue.

By then, the family was spending a lot of time on the crosstown bus, so we moved to 40 West 77th Street, where we finally had enough space. Percy moved his office to the West Side (1860 Broadway) and then, in 1968, to 2114 Broadway, where he had ground floor space in a bank building. My father took office space in Percy's quarters; they had long since become good friends. Percy was able to have a small workroom at home, where he painted on Sundays and many evenings. The freedom of creating his own art was an antidote to the restrictions of architecture. Percy discovered new possibilities with spray paint in containers, which he combined with more conventional methods, including painting with acrylic. He continued to make objects of found material, which he called A Use for Unwanted Things. He believed that, in our throwaway society, the container was often more interesting than what it contained. Starting with cardboard egg cartons and apple crates, he went on to Styrofoam, which he carved, painted, and deformed with spray paint (pl. XVI). He heated plastic objects, such as green berry boxes, over the gas stove to make them into jewelry. I still wear a "jade" and gold paint pendant from this period. He named a series of constructions made out of painted and glued Benson and Hedges cigarette boxes Monuments to My Vice (pl. XVII).

Versions of our floor cushions had moved with us, until, in the sixties, we began to notice that our guests preferred the few chairs. When we realized that we, too, kept trying to occupy the chairs, it became clear that we were all getting a little older and finding it uncomfortable to have to bend down and rise up from those elegant cushions. Percy designed benches with back and seat cushions, which provided seating about thirteen inches high; later we raised the height to fifteen inches. Our children and their friends had liked to build houses with the heavy cushions; later, young grandchildren used the long cushions to make bridges between furniture.

Percy and Paul continued to discuss ideas together and to write articles on topics such as banning private cars from Manhattan and on opening up the city's waterfront. Also, they wrote criticizing the grandiose highways and other schemes of Robert Moses, then a powerful figure controlling much of New York City's public construction. While thinking and writing about community, they lived in New York City and were not themselves part of the small communities that they advocated. Both were probably too individualistic to fit into any such group but understood the

Fig. 166 Percy and Naomi in Greece, 1951 (cat. 60)

need and the benefits of such sustainable communities, which they had advocated much earlier in *Communitas*. Later, Percy developed these ideas further in *The Double E* (ecology and economy).

One evening in the spring of 1951 Percy came home and said that he had been invited to go to Israel in July as the American representative on a competition jury for a monument to Theodore Herzl, the founder of Zionism, but had responded that he was too busy. That evening, I convinced him that we should go and arranged with my mother for her to take care of our young children; in a few weeks we departed. It was an interesting trip, but Percy found the Western orientation of the architects and the government inappropriate to the Middle East. He felt that Israelis had much to learn from indigenous architecture and customs. We were both very concerned about the lack of peace between Palestinians and Israelis, so we went to Israel only once more. Percy approved of my work with the Jewish Peace Fellowship and with the Fellowship of Reconciliation. In the early seventies, Percy was invited to be part of a dialogue on Israeli society with an interesting group of Israeli and foreign participants; and, at his suggestion, my mother accompanied us.

On our first trip to Israel, we had stopped in Paris en route and in Greece during our return journey, which made us aware that we could travel even with the responsibilities of children and career (fig. 166). Percy realized that he could leave his practice for a few weeks. We spent time abroad every few years, going back to Paris, which Percy had always loved; visiting his son George and his family in Devon; seeing other friends and former students; looking at architecture, new and old. A number of times Rachel and Joel traveled with us.

Percy cared deeply for our son and daughter and was proud of their abilities, although in my view his many professional interests left too little time with them. Yet our children remembered eating dinner together as a family on most evenings where they exchanged stories of the day's events with him. Percy was impressed with Joel's mechanical and structural skills and felt that schools did not do enough to develop such abilities. We were also close to Paul's children, who often visited our family, both with their parents and on their own: Susan spent many summers with us; Daisy, her younger sister, was a great favorite of Percy's. The tragic death of Paul and Sally's son, Mathew Ready, in 1967, was a blow to all of us.

As I noted earlier, George, Percy's older son, had lived with his mother's family after her death. George had tried to learn more about his father for a long time but his adoptive mother, his aunt Eleanor Evans Ridge, and her husband, Billy Ridge, would not give him any information. As a grown man, he finally saw family documents, which gave his father's full name and profession. Locating Percy's address and other facts about him in *Who's Who,* he wrote to Percy from

England, where he had settled. We all urged him to visit us, so George and his wife met us for the first time in New York in 1964. George and his family have been part of ours ever since (fig. 167).

None of Percy's children followed him into architecture, although he felt that Joel, with his strong aesthetic sense and structural abilities, could have been a very good architect. George had gone into farming, raising beef cattle in Devon. When George and his wife gave up farming and began to turn their farm buildings into rental cottages, Percy planned some of the conversions for them. Rachel decided not to start college after graduating from Fieldston. Percy sympathized with her wish to learn on her own, although he was pleased when she decided later to go to Columbia. In the late sixties, when she went to Oregon to live on the land, Percy and I were as disturbed as other parents of young people who tried to live in communes. Percy believed that communal living required a stronger basis of common beliefs than environmental concerns. Rachel has continued to live in Oregon, where her children, Bear and Iris, were brought up. In the summer she would visit us with her children. Bear, whose model-making skills delighted Percy, would stay with us longer, until he reached adolescence. Percy found adolescent boys difficult, including Joel and Mathew. He was fond of Iris and impressed with Rachel's adaptation to a very different life style; she later became a massage therapist.

When Joel left college before receiving a degree and went to work in film, Percy was concerned because he felt that proper credentials were much more needed than in his own youth. He could understand Joel's interest in motion pictures, which he considered to be the art form of

Fig. 167 George Ridge with Rachel and Joel Goodman, 1989

Fig. 168 Percy with his grandson Amos, late 1970s

our time, and was proud of Joel's self-made career as a film editor, going to see all of his films. Later, Joel and his family were in New York and East Hampton for some time, so we were able to see them more frequently. Joel, his wife Mary Marcus, and their young son Amos lived with us for more than a year. During that time, Percy was retired and working at home so he was able to spend time with Amos, and they made a strong bond, which was very meaningful for both of them (fig. 168). Later, Joel and his family moved to Santa Monica.

Percy knew many architects and much about New York City architecture. To walk down a city street with him was to learn who had designed many of the buildings and when; he would explain how that architect's work compared to other related buildings. Frank Lloyd Wright was occasionally in New York City, and we would see him, generally at some architectural function. For a while, Percy would introduce me as his new wife and Wright would inevitably reply, "Yes, Perce, I had a red-headed wife once, too."

Percy was extremely busy during these years, designing and building more than fifty synagogues in different parts of the country. Each synagogue had its own character, as Percy wanted

Fig. 169 Congregation Beth Israel, Lebanon, Pennsylvania, 1952–59

Fig. 170 Rothschild Residence, Baltimore, 1948–50: exterior view (cat. 21c)

Fig. 171 Rothschild Residence, Baltimore, 1948–50: interior view (cat. 21b)

Fig. 172 Rothschild Residence, Baltimore, 1948–50: interior view (cat. 21a)

to express in the most direct way the particular needs of the congregation and the place in which it was built. One style and approach could not fit every group and circumstance. For instance, he built in steel in Gary, Indiana (figs. 59, 93–96), a steel town, and in wood and brick in New England; he created a barn-style white building with Hebrew lettering on the façade in Lebanon, Pennsylvania, fundamentalist Pennsylvania Dutch country (fig. 169). He believed that the sanctuary should have a central reading platform (bema) instead of a conventional stage at one end of an auditorium, which most congregations preferred. He considered the bema the only Jewish architectural invention, which was the precursor of the theater in the round.

Other buildings related to religious groups included a Y.M.H.A., a Unitarian meeting house, and a Roman Catholic rectory. In 1950, Percy won a competition for a Jewish memorial for New York City (figs. 42–45); the project was exhibited but not built, probably because of the opposition of Robert Moses. Moses' objections also prevented the construction of a housing development in Long Island City, designed in collaboration with Pomerance and Breines, and Andrew Thomas, which would have utilized underdeveloped waterfront (figs. 39–40). Percy designed a few private houses (figs. 170–172), but most of his work was for community projects, including

Fig. 173 Public School 92, New York, 1962–66: interior courtyard with mosaics (cat. 27a)

Fig. 174 Public School 92, New York, 1962–66: exterior view (cat. 27b)

several public schools (figs. 173–174); later he was the campus planner for the expansion of Queensborough Community College.

Three afternoons a week at Columbia Percy was teaching design and planning to graduate students, many of them from other countries (figs. 175–176). He was deeply interested in his students. In helping them to develop their own styles, he encouraged foreign students to keep their own traditions even as they learned and adapted American techniques. One year, he taught a course on utopias, part of his interest in a better society. During the student strikes of 1968, he was on the students' side and, in sympathy with them, held classes in our home. Rachel was among the students who occupied university buildings. Occasionally, Percy would complain about the amount of time that he spent teaching and the difficulties that it caused in his practice. When I would suggest that he stop teaching if it caused so many problems, he would reply in a shocked tone, "Of course not, I love teaching."

From 1955 to 1970, I worked on interiors in Percy's office, selecting furniture, fabrics, and so on. As I have mentioned, I was very involved in his work and discussed it with him frequently. I had been called into the office previously to help in various minor crises concerning interiors and enjoyed working on these projects. But during the Vietnam War, I began to find that my office responsibilities interfered with my work for peace organizations, so my work for Goodman Interiors came to an end, although we did continue to discuss his projects. A little earlier, he had made a series of paintings of heads he called The Waiting Ones, portraits of people waiting for the atomic bomb to fall; they made an impressive exhibition at the Waverly Gallery in 1962. Rachel and Joel had decided on their own (as had Mathew) to protest against the drills held at schools to prepare students for nuclear attacks, knowing that sitting under their desks would not insure safety.

We spent many summers at Fire Island; we all loved the beach and Fire Island was fine for children as no cars were allowed. The lack of cars solved another problem, since Percy had stopped driving with the gas shortage of the war and found that it was a great relief to him not

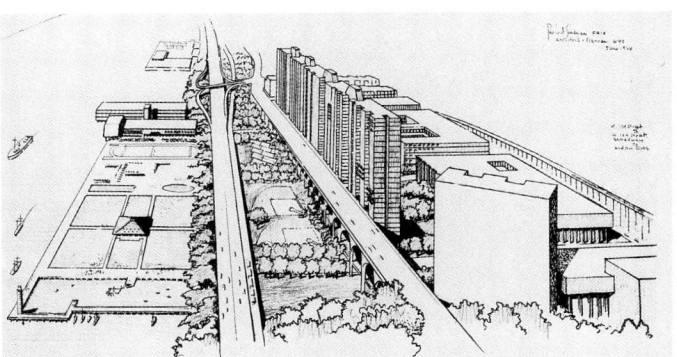

Fig. 175 Manhattanville-on-Hudson (urban redevelopment proposal designed together with students), 1964: early study (cat. 29a)

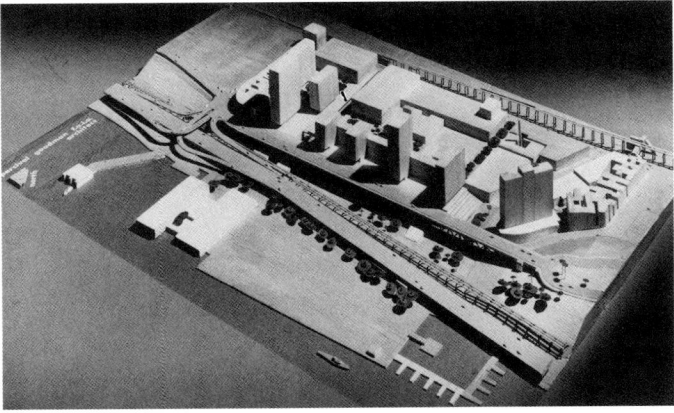

Fig. 176 Manhattanville-on-Hudson (urban redevelopment proposal designed together with students), 1964: model (cat. 29f)

to drive. He would come out on a Thursday evening, with a roll of drawings to work on, and return to the city on Sunday night. His sister, Alice, spent her vacations with us. She had become close to us after our children were born and became a wonderful aunt to her nieces and nephews. Paul, his wife, Sally, and their children were frequent visitors until Paul bought a house in northern New Hampshire.

Growing up in New York City, I had never driven a car, but I did learn so that I could drive in France, where we all spent the summer of '62. We had begun to be dissatisfied with Fire Island's limitations and realized that we missed the trees. Earlier we had tried Amagansett, but it had seemed too far away. After I began to drive, we went back to the East Hampton area again and liked it very much. Attitudes to distance, including ours, had changed.

It was a great irony, much like the story of the shoemaker's children, that we ended up in a house that Percy hadn't designed. I was tired of renting and wanted us to have a place of our own. Percy didn't want to design and build, saying that he didn't have time. He also felt that a house out of the city would encourage weekends there, thus threatening his long workweek, and would make our traveling in the summer less likely. He wasn't pleased with any house that could be bought at a reasonable price. I bought land in Springs, and Percy agreed to design a house for us; but local builders found the construction with cement blocks unusual and wouldn't even bid. We saw a so-called prefab on the roof of Abercrombie and Fitch, the sporting goods store. The house seemed adequate in size, style, and estimated price, so we bought it. Since it was to be used solely in the summer, Percy needed to make only a few changes. In time, he became very fond of the area and liked to go out for weekends, so we added insulation, double-glazed windows, and heat (fig. 177). Also, he began to paint long narrow landscapes to express the flat Long Island countryside, which he felt could not be conveyed in the standard rectangular proportion (pl. XV).

Nineteen seventy-two was a difficult year for Percy. His brother died in August, of a second heart attack. As Percy was older, he had always assumed that Paul would outlive him. Also, he had turned sixty-eight, which was the compulsory retirement age at Columbia. He would have preferred to continue teaching. His retirement party became famous in the annals of the school. The dean decided that a champagne party for the faculty would be an appropriate festivity and called me to ask if a gift of pottery from the current Teachers College exhibit of student work would be a good gift. Although surprised at the choice, I commented that Percy would appreciate something made by a student, not a mass-produced product, adding that he liked to arrange flowers in our house in Springs. At the party, after the usual speeches, Dean Kenneth Smith brought out a box from George Jensen. My heart sank as Percy unwrapped an unattractive, heavy glass vase of squat shape, with a brown rim on top. Horrified, he made a short speech in which he characterized the vase as looking like a chamber pot, said that it exemplified all that was wrong with the school in its lack of taste, and proclaimed it an insult to him to offer him

Fig. 177 *Percy in East Hampton, 1989* (cat. 65)

something so ugly and commercial. At the end of his diatribe, he threw the object on the floor. Since the floor was carpeted, the vase bounced. Everyone followed us out.

After Percy's retirement from Columbia, Raymond Lifchez, a former student and friend who was teaching at Berkeley, arranged for him to give a series of lectures there. He was working on his book *The Double E*, which he had hoped to write with Paul, so he lectured about environmental problems. He kept his office until 1979, when he retired from architectural practice as well. Luckily, we were still living in the large apartment in which our children had been brought up and were able to make him a studio and office in a big corner room with north light. Percy did some consulting, designed a second temple for a New Jersey congregation; wrote articles, book reviews, and poetry; and drew a great deal. Suzanne O'Keefe, an architect who had taken his course on utopias, recorded a series of oral interviews on his architectural experiences, including his early days. Percy adjusted to a new way of living and working at home. Recognizing my other involvements, both with religious peace groups and with writing, he made lunch for us daily, while I made dinner. We traveled often, visiting George in England, Bill Hayter in France, and also a number of former students.

Percy went back to his translation of Auguste Choissy's *Histoire de l'architecture*, an important work that has never been translated into English. He shortened, rearranged, and wrote introductions to the main chapters. He also wrote and illustrated *An Architect's Guide to Utopias*, an account of the narrator's voyage to the great utopias, drawing an imagined architecture for these utopias, with plans and renderings in the architectural style of the time each utopia was written, from Plato to William Morris — something that had never been done before. Percy found postmodern architecture very unsatisfactory and made a series of parodies in the form of elegant drawings (pls. XIX–XXI). Every time that he was finishing a project, and I worried about

 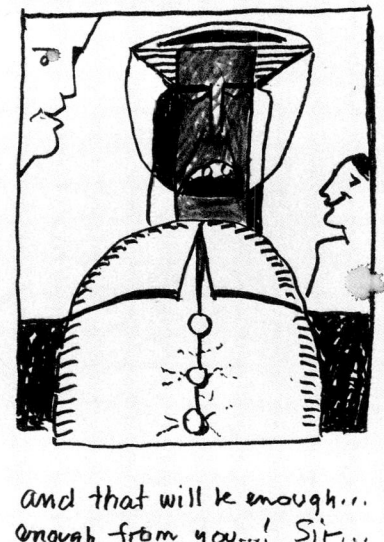

Fig. 178 *The Great Doric Column: Headquarters for a Greek Shipping Company,* 1981, (cat. 46c)

Fig. 179 Magic-marker drawing, 1989. This is the last drawing that Percy made.

what he would do when he didn't have work that he liked, something else would come up or be invented by him. Always interested in mythology, especially Greek, Percy wrote a group of poems about Greek mythology and history, which he illustrated with line drawings. He drew up a satirical series of Greek monuments, which he suggested that the British government should fund as reparations for the Elgin Marbles (fig. 178). Much of this work is unpublished, although many of his paintings and drawings have been exhibited.

Percy did not stop smoking until he was sixty-five, despite several attempts and a cough that did not clear up. In 1969, he was part of a live television panel that he interrupted with a long bout of coughing. He was so embarrassed that he vowed to quit smoking and did. In the fall of 1988, however, a routine X ray showed a tumor in one lung. In January, we received the bad news that the tumor was slightly larger. Percy had always seemed younger than his calendar years, and the doctors discussed "physical age" and "chronological age," assuring us that, although his actual age was eighty-five, he was in the condition of a man twenty years younger and should have no serious problems with an operation to remove the tumor.

Percy never recovered from the lung operation that took place in February 1989. Most of the cancerous tumor was removed, but he was never well enough for further treatment. He became weaker, more miserable, and developed related symptoms. He wasn't even able to draw. We went out to our house in Springs for the summer; but by the end of August, he was much worse and was readmitted to Mount Sinai Hospital, where the doctors told Joel and me that his illness was terminal. Although I had really known this, hearing it officially was devastating. We were advised that Percy should be part of a hospice program. He agreed with the hospice approach — to make the final days easier and not to try to prolong life — and was able to live at home during this period. Joel and his family were still in New York; George came from England; Rachel and Iris visited. George's daughter Gale and her three young children, his great-grandchildren, came to see him. Percy looked at many of his drawings and paintings with George and began to draw again, using magic markers in a blank notebook (fig. 179), since he could only draw for a limited time when sitting down. Percy's condition became worse in early October, and he died at the Beth Israel Hospice on October 11th, 1989.

His funeral was attended by many people: family, friends, architects, students, and others. Our niece Tamar Beach played music that Percy had liked on the oboe. Rabbi Martin Freedman, a close friend and client for whom he had built two synagogues, conducted the service and delivered a moving eulogy. George spoke about his father; and Michael McKinnell, a former student and friend, talked about Percy's influence as a teacher. Percy was buried in the family plot at Salem Fields Cemetery, next to my parents.

Fig. 180 Percy in his study with rolled drawings and model, circa 1960 © Arnold Newman/Liaison Agency

List of Projects, 1925–1989

Completion date, when known, is shown in parentheses.

1925   18th Paris Prize in Architecture, Society of Beaux-Arts Architects; winning prize: A Summer Capitol for the United States

1928   Reconstruction of a portion of Paris under Phillipe Le-Lel, prepared for the Society of Beaux-Arts Architects
Stewart & Co., 56th Street and 5th Avenue, New York *unbuilt*

1929   Department store building for I. Magnin, San Francisco
Jay-Thorpe Inc., New York (Whitman & Goodman)

1929–30   Saks & Co., New York, Salon Moderne (Whitman & Goodman)

1930s   Apartment for Adam Gimbel, New York
Apartment for Emil Schwarzhaupt at the Pierre Hotel, New York
Bar for Schenley Distillery Co., New York
Department store, New York *unbuilt*
Dr. Rosen's study, New York
55 Park Place, New York (probably designed while working with another architect)
New York State Journal of Medicine's permanent technical exposition, 33 West 42nd Street, New York
Reception room for shoe manufacturer, New York (Whitman and Goodman)

Roger Kent store, unidentified location (number 1607)
Unidentified hat shop, possibly Miller's in San Francisco
Unidentified interior (photograph labeled "Apartment House, 139 East 35th Street")

1930   Design for natatorium, hotel-apartment house, and garage, New York   *unbuilt*
Offices of Lennen and Mitchell; Straus and Company, New York
Palace of the Soviets, Moscow, competition, fourth-prize winner   *unbuilt*
Proposal for "Revising the Teaching of Architecture in the Colleges," submitted to New York University
Sample house for a group of 21 houses to be erected at Fox Meadows Estate, Westchester County, NY   *unbuilt*
Saks Department Store, White Plains, NY   *unbuilt*
Unidentified house (proposed house in Bermuda)   *unbuilt*
Unidentified store interior (photograph labeled "Sports")

1931   Apartment for David Tishman, New York
Bonwit Teller shop, Palm Beach
Building in Wellesley, MA, for E.T. Slattery Co.   *unbuilt*
House for Philip Batchker, Long Beach, Long Island   *unbuilt*
Proposals to City Planning Commission of New York for municipal planning
Proposals for town planning at Pennsylvania Building Congress
Shoe shop for Sommers, Inc., 2 West 57th Street, New York
Standard Sanitary Manufacturing Co., bathroom competition   *unbuilt*
Working City   *unbuilt*

1931–32   Community Service Homes, proposal for "high-low" housing   *unbuilt*

1932   Apartment for Edith and Jack Straus, 1111 Park Avenue, New York
Design for movie sets   *unbuilt*
Apartment house, possibly part of the Community Service Homes (rendering is labeled "Shelter–Salvation Army," although this note may have been added later) *unbuilt*
Illustrations for "The Golden Ass of Apuleius" (Limited Edition Club)
Moscow Philharmonic Concert Hall and Hotel (prepared for Albert Coates, conductor, Moscow Philharmonic)   *unbuilt*
Patents on 11 types of special furniture construction
"Week-end" aluminum beach house, Montauk, Long Island   *unbuilt*

1933   Exhibition building for the Kellogg Company, Century of Progress International Exposition, Chicago   *unbuilt*

Exhibition building for Standard Oil Company (Indiana), Century of Progress International Exposition, Chicago *unbuilt*
Fashions Building, Century of Progress International Exposition, Chicago *unbuilt*
Finlay Strauss (jewelry store), New York
Florida Tropical Home, Century of Progress International Exposition, Chicago
Residence for Edith G. Straus, Mount Kisco, NY *unbuilt*

1934 Residential development for H. Arthur Colen, Hempstead, Long Island *unbuilt*
Unidentified interior (library/guest room)

1935 Unidentified fabric shop or showroom (possibly Saks Fifth Avenue, Chicago, or a shop in New York)

1935–38 Residences for Westmanton Realty Co., Croton, NY

1936 Apartment House for Ely Culbertson *unbuilt*
Central Terminal Building alteration, 415 Lexington Avenue, New York
Unidentified flower shop, New York

1937 Apartment for Norman K. Winston, 270 Park Avenue, New York
Collective Design for Labor Pavilion, 1939 New York World's Fair
Design for residence, commissioned for publication in *McCall's* magazine

1938 Plan for double-decking 5th Avenue from 34th to 59th Street, New York *unbuilt*
Richards Grape Juice Plant, Brocton, NY

1939 Betty Wales Building, New York City (with Thomas M. Bell)
14-story apartment house, 25 West 54th Street, New York
Lasalle & Koch Co. Department Store, Toledo, OH (1941)
Saint Thomas Choir School, 102 West 58th Street, New York (with Thomas M. Bell)
Saks Fifth Avenue, children's floor, New York City (Goodman, Katzman & Straus)
Smithsonian Gallery of Art, Washington, DC, competition, second-prize winner *unbuilt*
Wheaton College Arts Center, competition, fourth-prize winner *unbuilt*

1940 Ernst Kern Co., Detroit
Orange Drip, proposal for a juicer
Patent on new type of plywood truss floor construction
Proposal "A New Architecture for Cantonments," submitted to the National Advisory Council
Proposals for town planning under the Defense Program *unbuilt*

Residence for J.M. Kaplan, Croton, NY
Suburban store units for R.H. Macy & Co. (with Meyer Katzman) *unbuilt*
Theater for RKO Corp., Brooklyn *unbuilt*

1940–42 Partner in Camouflage Engineering Co., Inc., New York

1941 Dormitory building for the Hessian Hills School, Croton, NY (labeled either 1941 or 1947) *unbuilt*
Illustrations for *Stop Light* (Noh Players) by Paul Goodman, published by 5x8 Press
Precast, prefabricated splinterproof shelters in reinforced concrete *unbuilt*
"Proposal for Camouflage Site Plan for Workers" housing, Bristol, CT
Report "Camouflage of Industrial Buildings"
Residence, Oxford, CT
Studies on the theory of smoke camouflage, started with Camouflage Engineering, Co., Inc., staff
Tiedke's Department Store, Toledo, OH

1942 Designs for Aeroplane Dispersal Pits for Air Fields and Splinterproof Personnel Shelters *unbuilt*
Report on Passive Defense for the Department Store, written for the National Retail Dry Goods Association and published in their bulletin
Report "Site Planning of Defense Housing with a View to Camouflage"
Report "Site Planning of Important Industrial Installations with a View to Camouflage"

1944 Proposal for Treatment of East River Shore, New York
Welfare Island Service Buildings, Welfare Island (Roosevelt Island), NY (1946)

1944–46 Riverview Community Housing Development Proposal, Long Island City (Pomerance & Breines, Andrew J. Thomas & Percival Goodman) *unbuilt*

1946 Bloomingdale's Competition, "A House for the New York Suburbs" *unbuilt*
Club House, Skyline Lakes, New Jersey *unbuilt*
Zilboorg Residence, Bedford Village, NY (1948)

1947 Jefferson National Expansion Memorial, Saint Louis, competition *unbuilt*
Publication of *Communitas*, with brother Paul Goodman
Steinbach Residence, Harrison, NY

1948 Baltimore Hebrew Congregation, Baltimore (1953)
Nassau Community Temple, West Hempstead, NY

           Rothschild Residence, Baltimore (1950)
           Temple Beth El, New London, CT (1953)
           Temple Beth El, Providence (1955)
           Temple Beth Israel, Lima, OH

1949   American Memorial to Six Million Jews of Europe, competition, winning entry *unbuilt*
           Congregation B'nai Israel, Millburn, NJ (1951)
           Jewish Community Center, Wilkes-Barre, PA
           Jewish Museum, 1109 Fifth Avenue, New York (conversion of residence, commissioned by the Jewish Theological Seminary)
           Valentine Residence, Westchester, NY

1950   Canton Hebrew Congregation, Canton, OH *unbuilt*
           Congregation Goel Tzadeck, Toronto (consultant) *unbuilt*
           Fairmount Temple, Cleveland (Beechwood Village) (1955)
           Popkin Residence, Lima, OH
           Proposed museum for Jerusalem *unbuilt*
           Temple Beth El, Springfield, MA (1953)
           Temple Emanuel, Davenport, IA
           Warburg Playhouse, White Plains, NY
           West End Synagogue, Nashville

1951   East End Synagogue of Long Beach, Congregation Beth Sholom
           Illustrations for *Parents' Day* by Paul Goodman, published by 5x8 Press
           Old Towne Factory and Warehouse, New York
           Temple Israel, Holliswood (Jamaica), New York

1952   Congregation Beth Israel, Lebanon, PA (1959)
           Jewish Center of Jackson Heights (Queens), New York *unbuilt*
           Temple Beth Am, Port Washington, NY (1960)
           Temple Beth El, Gary, IN (1954)
           Temple Israel, Tulsa

1953   Peters Residence, Fire Island, NY
           Temple Beth Am, Chicago (1956)
           Temple Beth Emeth, Albany, NY (1957)
           Temple Beth Sholom, Miami Beach (1954)
           Temple Emanuel, Denver (1960)

          Temple Emanuel, Pittsburgh
          Temple Israel, Miami *unbuilt*

1954   Batchker Office, New York
          Fain Residence, Providence
          Hillel Building, Brooklyn College, New York
          Macy Apartment, New York
          Temple of Aaron, Saint Paul (1956)
          Temple Beth El, Quincy, MA *unbuilt*
          Temple Mishkin Tefila, Newton, MA (1958)

1955   Beth-El Congregation, Durham, NC
          Congregation B'nai Israel, Bridgeport, CT (1957)
          Jewish Community Center, West Hempstead, NY
          Temple Emanuel (addition), Providence
          Temple Israel of Fairfield County, Westport, CT
          United Cerebral Palsy of Queens, New York *unbuilt*

1956   Congregation Sha'arey Zedek, Detroit (Southfield) (1963)
          Crestview Country Club, Agawam, MA (1956)
          Fifth Avenue Synagogue, New York City (1959)
          Jewish Community Center, Paramus, NJ
          St. Jude's Rectory, New York City
          Temple Adath Yeshurun, Manchester, NH (1956)
          Temple Beth Sholom, Roslyn, NY (1956)
          Temple Emeth, Teaneck, NJ
          Temple Israel, Columbus, OH (1959)

1957   Temple Beth Emeth (addition), Albany, NY
          Temple Emanuel (addition), Pittsburgh
          Union Reform Temple, Freeport, NY

1958   Conservative Synagogue of Riverdale, New York (1962)
          Temple Beth Am, Springfield, NJ
          Temple Emanuel (addition), Denver
          Temple Emanuel of South Hills, Pittsburgh

1959   Beth El Synagogue, Highland Park, IL (1964)
          Congregation Beth Shalom, Oak Park, MI

            Congregation Sons of Israel, Palisades Park (Leonia), NJ *unbuilt*
            Katz Residence, Springfield (Longmeadow), MA *unbuilt*
            Temple of Aaron (addition), Saint Paul
            Temple Emanuel (alteration), Englewood, NJ *unbuilt*
            Temple Israel, New Rochelle, NY (1962)
            West End Synagogue (addition), Nashville

1959–60   Franklin Delano Roosevelt Memorial, Washington, DC, competition *unbuilt*

1960   Congregation Adas Kodesch Shel Emeth, Wilmington
            Congregation Adath Israel, Dover, NJ
            Temple Anshe Sholom, Olympia Fields, IL
            Temple Beth El, Rochester, NY (1963)
            Temple Beth Israel, Port Washington, NY
            Temple Beth Sholom (addition), Roslyn, NY
            Temple Israel, Reform Congregation of Staten Island, New York (1963)

1960–61   Welfare Island Redevelopment Proposal (Terrace City), Roosevelt Island, New York
            unbuilt

1961   Cadman Plaza Renewal Proposal
            Congregation Ohev Sholom, Chester, PA
            East End Synagogue of Long Beach, Long Beach, NY
            Valley Jewish Community Center, North Hollywood, CA

1962   Boston City Hall, Boston, competition *unbuilt*
            Congregation B'nai Israel (addition), Millburn, NJ
            Crestmont Country Club, West Orange, NJ *unbuilt*
            Great Neck Synagogue, Great Neck, NY
            Public School 92, 222 West 134th Street, New York (1966)

1962–63   Classical Central Educational Center, Providence, competition *unbuilt*
            Park Avenue North Development, 97th to 132nd Street, New York *unbuilt*

1963   Barnert Temple, Paterson, NJ
            Congregation K.K. Adath Israel, Cincinnati (Amberley Village)
            Public School 126, 80 Catherine Street, New York (1966)
            Reform Jewish Congregation of Merrick, Merrick, NY
            Unitarian Universalist Church of Central Nassau (Fellowship Hall), Garden City, NY

1964 "Break-through to the Hudson," Hudson River Project, Yonkers to Peekskill, developed at the School of Architecture, Columbia University, Percival Goodman and Alexander Kouzmanoff, co-coordinators *unbuilt*

Manhattanville-on-Hudson Proposal, Hudson River to Broadway, 125th to 135th Street, New York City (with Chiu-Hwa Wang) *unbuilt*

Monmouth Reform Temple of Greater Red Bank, Shrewsbury, NJ *unbuilt*

Morningside Heights and West Harlem Proposal, 110th to 125th Street, New York *unbuilt*

Rabbi Sholom Elezer Rogosin High School, Jersey City, NJ

Westchester Reform Temple (alterations and additions), Scarsdale, NY

1964–65 Replanning Manhattan's Shore ("Around Manhattan Proposal") *unbuilt*

1965 Congregation Sons of Israel and Yeshiva of Hudson County, Jersey City, NJ

Monument to the Six Million, "We remember" *unbuilt*

Public School 345, Brooklyn (1967)

Temple Ahavas Israel, Grand Rapids, MI *unbuilt*

Temple Beth El (addition and renovations to 1950 building following a fire), Springfield, MA (1966)

1965–66 Washington Heights and Inwood Master Plan, proposed by the School of Architecture, Columbia University, Percival Goodman, director *unbuilt*

1966 Harlem River Project, prepared by the Institute for Urban Environment & School of Architecture, Columbia University, Percival Goodman, Director *unbuilt*

Temple of Aaron (addition), Saint Paul (with Val Michelson)

Temple Adath Yeshurun, Syracuse, NY (1968)

Temple Beth Joseph, Kings Point, NY *unbuilt*

Temple Emeth (addition), Teaneck, NJ

1966–67 New School for Social Research, proposed expansion of the campus (art center), 66 West 12th Street, New York *unbuilt*

1967 Housing Studies, University of Iowa, Iowa City *unbuilt*

University Arts Center, University of California, Berkeley, competition *unbuilt*

1968 Chinese Information Service, Republic of China, alteration of 157–159 Lexington Avenue, New York (with Chia-Hwa Wang)

1969 Agudas Israel Congregation, Hazelton, PA *unbuilt*

Beth Israel Synagogue, Norwalk, CT

Congregation Ohev Sholom, Chester, PA

                Fairmount Temple (addition), Cleveland (Beechwood Village)
                Jacksonville Jewish Center, Jacksonville *unbuilt*
                Jewish Home for the Aged, Providence *unbuilt*
                Madison Avenue Temple, Scranton, PA
                Public School 57, Staten Island, New York (1976)
                Queensborough Community College Master Plan 1970–1975, Bayside, New York
                Temple of Aaron, Saint Paul, Capp Lounge furnishings
                Temple Israel (phase II addition), New Rochelle, NY

1970   Temple Israel (phase III addition), New Rochelle, NY

1971   Center for American Studies, Taipei (Nankang)

                Queensborough Community College, administration/business building, Bayside, New York (1976)

                Queensborough Community College, feasibility study/parking area, Bayside, New York

                Queensborough Community College, interiors (Humanities and Cafeteria Building), Bayside, New York

1972   Dix Hills Jewish Center, Dix Hills, NY *unbuilt*

                Temple Israel, Memphis, TN (consultant)

1973   Har Zion Temple, Merion, PA *unbuilt*

1974   Miami Beach Housing, Miami Beach, competition *unbuilt*

                Temple Beth El, Gary (Schererville), IN *unbuilt*

1975   Memorial to Walter Burley Griffin, Canberra *unbuilt*

1976   Braude Residence, East Hampton (Amagansett), NY

                Embassy of the Republic of China (alterations to 2311 Massachusetts Avenue), Washington, DC (with Chia-Hwa Wang)

                69th Regiment Armory (alteration and conversion for proposed botanical garden and aquarium), Lexington Avenue between 25th and 26th Streets, New York *unbuilt*

1977   Publication of *The Double E*

1978   Pahlavi National Library, Tehran, competition (with Chia-Hwa Wang & Medhat Salam) *unbuilt*

                Springs Lane Housing Development, East Hampton, NY *unbuilt*

1979   Congregation Adath Yeshurun (alteration of bema after a fire), Manchester, NH

Illustrations for *The Good Book Cookbook* by N. Goodman, R. Marcus, and S. Woolhandler

Regional/Urban Design Assistance Team of the American Institute of Architecture Study of the Impact of International Energy Exposition of 1982 on Knoxville, Tennessee.

Temple Anshe Chesed (Madison Avenue Temple), Scranton, PA (consultant)

1980s   Kent State Memorial Competition *unbuilt*

Design for an Urban Synagogue *unbuilt*

1980   "An Illustrated Guide to Utopia: An Architect's Diary," drawings and text

Garibaldi-Meucci Memorial Museum, A Cultural Center Addition, Staten Island, New York, competition *unbuilt*

Karlin Residence (alteration of existing house by architect Carl Anthony), East Hampton, NY

1981–83   "A Direction for Post-Modern Revivalism," drawings

1982   Temple Israel of Great Neck, NY (consultant to Robert M. Nervig & Associates) *unbuilt*

1982–83   "Road to Parnassus," drawings

1983   "Houses 1–10," drawings

Congregation B'nai Jeshurun (Barnert Memorial Temple), Franklin Lakes, NJ (design architect; Wells Associates, project architect) (1987)

1984   Braddon Farm Buildings and Development, Ashwater (Devon), England *unbuilt*

East Hampton Housing for the Elderly, East Hampton, NY *unbuilt*

Residence for Michael Zweig, Schererville, IN (architectural design services)

1985–88   Congregation Emanuel, Denver (consultant for temple expansion; Barker, Rinker, Seacat & Partners, architects)

1987–89   Suffolk County Vietnam Veterans Memorial *unbuilt*

1989   "Herodium," drawings

Contributors

Costa N. Decavalla Born in Athens in 1925, Costa Decavalla received the M.Arch. from Columbia University in 1953 and in 1956 was awarded a certificate in town and country planning from University College, London University. From 1952 to 1954 he was an associate of Goodman's, and from 1956 to 1960 he served as chief architect and planner with the Greek Ministry of Public Works for the reconstruction of Santorini following the 1956 earthquake. Since 1960 he has maintained his own architectural practice, teaching at the National Technical University of Athens from 1980 to 1993. He was elected an honorary fellow of the American Institute of Architects in 1984.

Peter Eisenman Peter Eisenman is an architect and educator. Since establishing his professional practice in 1980, he has designed a wide range of works including large-scale housing and urban design projects, innovative facilities for educational institutions, and a series of inventive private houses. He was the founder and former director of the Institute of Architecture and Urban Studies, an international think-tank for architectural criticism. Having taught at Cambridge, Princeton, Yale, and the Ohio State University, he is currently the Irwin S. Chanin Distinguished Professor of Architecture at the Cooper Union in New York City and a visiting professor at Princeton. Among his publications are *House X, Moving Arrows, Eros and Other Errors*, and *Chora L Works*, co-authored with Jacques Derrida.

Kimberly J. Elman A Ph.D. candidate in the architecture school at Columbia University, Kimberly Elman is currently researching architecture in Czechoslovakia from 1918 to 1938. Her article "Garden Cities and Company Towns: Tomas Bat'a and the Formation of Zlin, Czechoslovakia" recently appeared in *The Harriman Review* (Fall 2000). Born in Longmeadow, Massachusetts, she and her family are longtime members of Temple Beth El in Springfield, Massachusetts, designed by Percival Goodman.

Robert Fishman Robert Fishman is a professor at the A. Alfred Taubman College of Architecture and Planning of the University of Michigan, Ann Arbor. He is the author of *Urban Utopias in the Twentieth Century: Ebenezer Howard, Frank Lloyd Wright, and Le Corbusier* (1977) and *Bourgeois Utopias: The Rise and Fall of Suburbia* (1987). In 1999 he was a Public Policy Fellow at the Woodrow Wilson International Center for Scholars, Washington, D. C.

Kenneth Frampton Kenneth Frampton is the Ware Professor of Architecture at the Graduate School of Architecture, Planning and Preservation at Columbia University. He has taught at a number of leading institutions in the field, including the Royal College of Art in London, the ETH in Zurich, the Berlage Institute in Amsterdam, the EPFL in Lausanne, and currently, the Accademia di Architettura in Mendrisio. He is currently a member of the international jury for the Carlsberg Prize and the Alvar Aalto medal. His books include *Modern Architecture: A Critical History* (1980), *Modern Architecture and the Critical Present* (1980), *Studies in Tectonic Culture* (1995) and *American Masterworks* (1995).

Martin Freedman Martin Freedman is rabbi emeritus of the Barnert Temple, the oldest synagogue in New Jersey, originally located in Paterson and now, for the past eleven years, in Franklin Lakes. Goodman designed two temples for his congregation, twenty-six years apart. The Temple in Franklin Lakes was Goodman's last architectural design.

Angela Giral Angela Giral is the director of the Avery Architectural and Fine Arts Library at Columbia University. She co-edited *Linking Art Objects and Art Information,* a special issue of *Library Trends* (1988) and *Avery's Choice: Five Hundred Years of Architectural Publications, One Hundred Years of an Architectural Library* (1995) and is the author of numerous articles on information in art and architecture.

Romaldo Giurgola Born in Rome in 1920, Romaldo Giurgola studied at Columbia University as a Fulbright Fellow, receiving his M.Arch. in 1951. In 1958 he started his own firm with Ehrman B. Mitchell, Jr., in Philadelphia, and in 1969 opened an office in New York. In that same year, he was appointed the Ware Professor of Architecture at Columbia University, where he also served as the chairman of the School of Architecture. His firm of Mitchell/Giurgola & Thorp designed Australia's Parliament House. Now residing permanently in Canberra, he is a consultant to the firm as well as a professorial fellow at the University of Melbourne and an adjunct professor at the University of Sydney.

Naomi Goodman The widow of Percival Goodman, Naomi Goodman is a peace activist, a past president of the Jewish Peace Fellowship, and an honorary vice-chairperson of the Fellowship of Reconciliation. She is co-author of *The Good Book Cookbook: Recipes from Biblical Times*, co-editor of *The Challenge of Shalom: The Jewish Tradition of Peace and Justice* (1994), and author of articles on the biblical Eve, about whom she is writing a book.

Rudolf Guyer Born in 1929 in Switzerland, Rudolf Guyer worked as a painter in France, Italy, and North Africa before studying architecture at the Institute of Technology in Zurich. After working for nine months in Percival Goodman's office in New York (1958–59), he returned to Zurich and opened his own firm, together with his wife, Esther, in 1960. They won more than forty architectural competitions and built many schools, churches, community centers, and housing developments, as well as several projects in historical surroundings. They retired in 1999, with their firm being carried on by two of their partners.

Raymond Lifchez A professor of architecture at UC Berkeley since 1970, Raymond Lifchez has had a varied career as a practicing architect and as a writer about architecture, pursuing the theme of architecture as a social art. His publications include *Design for Independent Living: The Environment and Physically Disabled People* (1981), a nominee for the American Book Award; *Rethinking Architecture: Design Students and Physically Disabled People* (1987), which received the San Francisco Bay Area Review Award; and *The Dervish Lodge: Architecture, Art and Sufism in Ottoman Turkey* (1992), all published by the University of California Press.

N. Michael McKinnell Born in Salford, England in 1935, Michael McKinnell came to the United States as a Fulbright Traveling Scholar, receiving the M.Arch. from Columbia in 1960. A fellow of the American Institute of Architects and of the American Academy of Arts and Sciences, McKinnell has maintained a dual career as architect and educator. In 1962 he co-founded Kallmann, McKinnell & Wood, Architects, and for twenty-five years taught at Harvard University's Graduate School of Design. Currently he is Professor of the Practice of Architecture at the Massachusetts Institute of Technology.

Val Michelson Born in Saint Petersburg in 1916, Val Michelson immigrated to the United States in 1949. After receiving his architecture degree from Columbia in 1953, he joined the office of Marcel Breuer, where he worked for seven years. Relocating to Minnesota, he opened Val Michelson & Associates (1961–91), designing a number of notable projects in the Midwest. From 1964 until 1985, he combined his professional practice with a teaching career at the University of Minnesota.

Suzanne O'Keefe The architect Suzanne O'Keefe has held various positions in New York City government and has taught urban planning at Columbia. She is now overseeing streetscape development in downtown Manhattan for the Alliance for Downtown New York.

Joshua Jih Pan From 1967 to 1976 Joshua J. Pan worked with the firms of Philip Johnson & Richard Foster; Davis, Brody & Associates; and CUHA. He returned to Taiwan, where he has practiced and taught architecture since 1976, designing and completing more than three hundred projects, many of which have received awards. In 1994 he was elected a fellow of the American Institute of Architects and in 1996 was named Outstanding Architect of the Republic of China.

Taylor Stoehr Taylor Stoehr is a professor in the English Department at the University of Massachusetts, Boston. He has written numerous books on various literary and cultural subjects, among them *Hawthorne's Mad Scientists* (1978), *Nay-Saying in Concord: Emerson, Alcott, and Thoreau* (1979), *Words and Deeds: Essays on the Realistic Imagination* (1986), and *Here Now Next: Paul Goodman and the Origins of Gestalt Therapy* (1994). The literary executor for Paul Goodman, he has edited many volumes of his work, including *Decentralizing Power: Paul Goodman's Social Criticism* and *Crazy Hope and Finite Experience: Paul Goodman's Final Essays,* and is currently working on an authorized biography of him.

Patrick Ping-tze Too Born in 1945 in Chungking, China, Patrick Ping-tze Too received his M.Arch. from Syracuse University in 1971 before coming to Columbia to study urban planning. He began working for the Department of City Planning in New York in 1973 and since 1982 has been principal urban designer there. He served as urban designer for the Tri-State Regional Planning Commission from 1975 to 1979, taught at the School of Architecture of the City University of New York, and has been advisor to the Department of Urban Development of Taipei City since 1989. His many publications include *Privately Owned Public Spaces* (New York, 2000), co-authored by J. Kayden and MAS.

Chiu-Hwa Wang Chiu-Hwa Wang started working part-time for Percival Goodman while still his student and continued full-time for nearly thirty years, becoming an associate in 1960 and later a partner. Completed projects include more than fifty synagogues and community centers and a number of public schools and college buildings. Moving to Taiwan in 1979, she established her own firm four years later in partnership with Joshua J. Pan, Architects and Planners, and built a number of university libraries and medical and biological research centers.

Pl. I Sample House for a group of 21 houses to be erected in Westchester County, 1930: perspective with garden (cat. 6a)

Pl. II   Sample House for a group of 21 houses to be erected in Westchester County, 1930: perspective (cat. 6b)

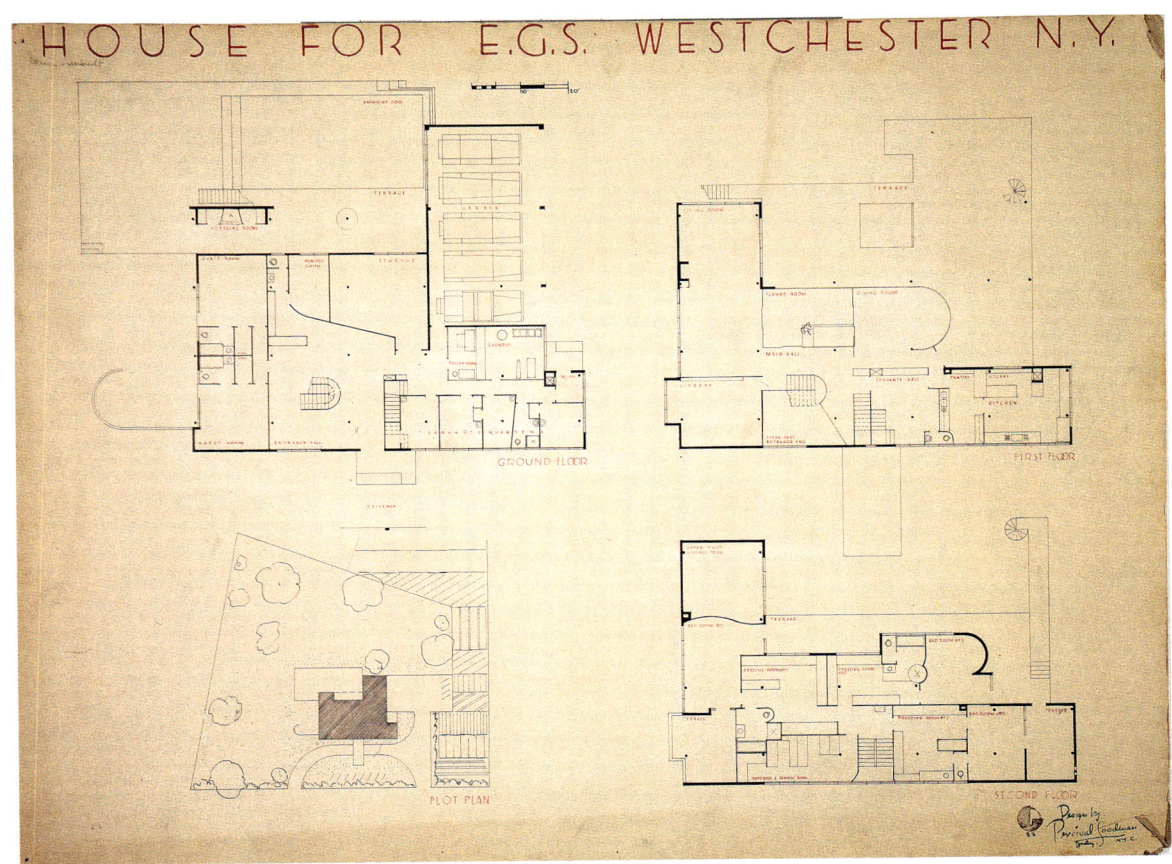

Pl. III   Residence for Edith G. Straus, Mount Kisco, NY, 1933: plans

Pl. IV   Community Service Homes, 1932: perspective rendering of housing units (cat. 9d)

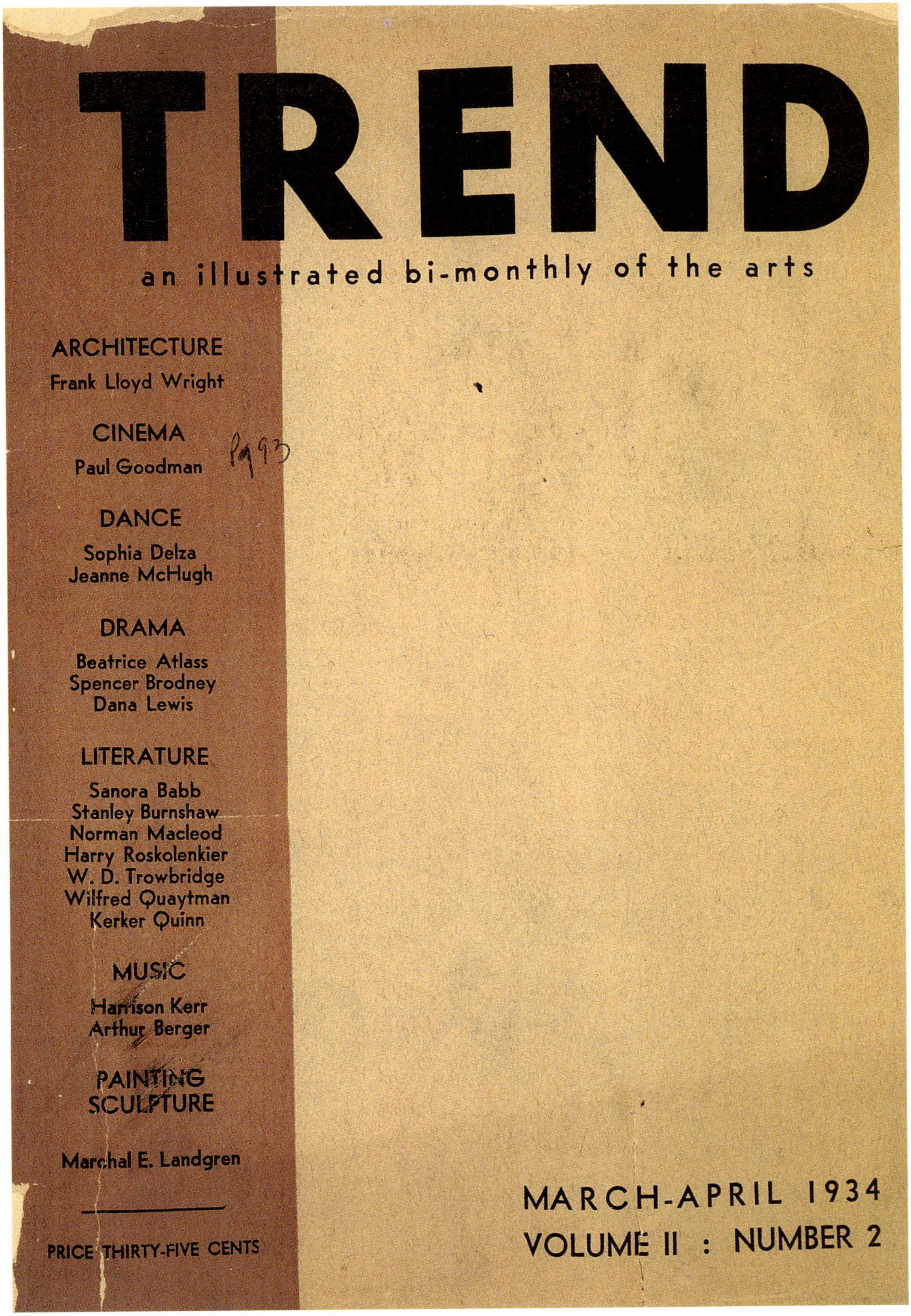

TREND

an illustrated bi-monthly of the arts

ARCHITECTURE
Frank Lloyd Wright

CINEMA
Paul Goodman

DANCE
Sophia Delza
Jeanne McHugh

DRAMA
Beatrice Atlass
Spencer Brodney
Dana Lewis

LITERATURE
Sanora Babb
Stanley Burnshaw
Norman Macleod
Harry Roskolenkier
W. D. Trowbridge
Wilfred Quaytman
Kerker Quinn

MUSIC
Harrison Kerr
Arthur Berger

**PAINTING
SCULPTURE**

Marchal E. Landgren

PRICE THIRTY-FIVE CENTS

MARCH-APRIL 1934
VOLUME II : NUMBER 2

Pl. V   Cover design for *Trend*, 1934 (cat. 33)

Pl. VI *Cat's Cradle,* 1932, Conté crayon on paper (cat. 38)

Pl. VII *Men at War*, 1944, pencil, watercolor, and gouache on paper (cat. 39)

Pl. VIII   Cover and inside pages of promotional leaflet for first edition of *Communitas*, 1947

Pl. IX Jefferson National Expansion Memorial Competition, Saint Louis, 1947: aerial view (top), view along walkway (middle), view from the garden (bottom)

Pl. X   Temple Beth El, Providence, 1948–55: interior perspective (cat. 20e)

Pl. XI   Baltimore Hebrew Congregation, 1948–53: view of sanctuary

Pl. XII Congregation B'nai Israel, Millburn, NJ. 1949–51: sketch by Robert Motherwell for lobby mural (cat. 23a)

Pl. XIII Congregation B'nai Israel, Millburn, NJ, 1949–51: children gathered at the ark (cat. 23e)

Pl. XIV Temple Beth Emeth, Albany, NY, 1953–57: interior view with hangings designed by Samuel Wiener

Pl. XV *Long Landscape*, circa 1970, acrylic on plywood (cat. 42)

Pl. XVI Untitled
Styrofoam constructions (cat. 51)

Pl. XVII *Monument to My Vice*, circa 1970, construction with cigarette boxes and acrylic paint (cat. 43)

Pl. XVIII
A Summer Capital for the United States, from the series A Direction for Postmodern Revivalism, 1981–83 (cat. 46a)

Pl. XIX
Law Courts and Prison, from the series A Direction for Postmodern Revivalism, 1981–83

Pl. XX *Looking to the Future*, from the series A Direction for Postmodern Revivalism, 1981–83 (cat. 46d)

Checklist of the Exhibition

Unless otherwise indicated, all works are by Percival Goodman and are from the Percival Goodman Collection at the Avery Architectural and Fine Arts Library, Columbia University. Dimensions are in inches, height before width before depth.

PROJECTS

1. Paris Prize in Architecture, 1925
A Summer Capital for the United States: elevation
pen, colored inks, black ink, watercolor, and gouache,
36 1/2 x 85 1/2 in.
The Metropolitan Museum of Art, Gift of the National Institute for Architectural Education, 1980
fig. 153

2. Saks & Co., New York, 1929–30 (Whitman and Goodman)
a. Salon Moderne: room with circular mirror
photograph, 6 x 8 in.
fig. 3
b. Salon Moderne: main hall with glass partition wall
photograph, 6 1/2 x 8 1/8 in.
fig. 2

3. Apartment for Emil Schwarzhaupt at the Pierre Hotel, New York, 1930s
a. Chaise longue
photograph, 9 1/2 x 7 1/2 in.
fig. 1
b. Bedroom
photograph, 7 5/8 x 9 5/8 in.
fig. 6
c. Bar with 4 stools
photograph, 7 1/2 x 9 1/2 in.
fig. 7

4. Natatorium, Hotel-Apartment, and Garage, Riverside Drive, New York, 1930
Exterior perspective
ink on board, 22 x 22 3/4 in.
fig. 151

5. Palace of the Soviets, Moscow (competition), 1930
a. Presentation board
photostat mounted on board, 30 x 22 in.
fig. 17
b. Plan, section, site plan
ink on paper (computer generated drawing by Brian Loughlin), 36 x 24 in.
c. Perspective
ink on paper (computer generated drawing by Brian Loughlin), 36 x 24 in.
d. New model, by Brian Loughlin and Andrea Schroeder-Jaenecke

6. Sample House for a group of 21 houses to be erected in Westchester County, NY, 1930
a. Perspective with garden
watercolor and ink on board, 16 1/16 in. x 15 1/2 in.
pl. I
b. Perspective
watercolor and ink on board, 22 x 29 5/8 in.
pl. II

7. Saks Department Store, White Plains, NY, 1930
pencil on paper, 8 x 8 3/4 in.

8. Working City, 1931
a. Comparison chart between New York City in 1890, 1930, and Working City, XX Century (A)
ink on tracing paper, 13 1/2 x 8 in.
fig. 18
b. Diagram showing development of New York City in 1890 (B)
ink on tracing paper, 13 1/2 x 8 in.
fig. 19
c. Diagram showing maximum development possible in New York City (C)
ink on tracing paper, 13 1/2 x 8 in.
fig. 20
d. Map showing comparative size of Working City in relation to Manhattan Island (D)
ink on tracing paper, 13 1/2 x 8 in.
e. Diagram showing development of thousand-by-thousand-foot section of Working City (E)
ink on tracing paper, 13 1/2 x 8 in.

9. Community Service Homes, 1931–32
a. Development for housing of 112 families and 128 bachelors: perspective, plan, and excerpts from prospectus
black and red ink, colored wash, and pencil on board, 23 x 39 1/2 in.
b. General plan and typical apartment (AH¹)
ink on board, 24 1/2 x 30 in.
fig. 11
c. Typical floor plan, typical apartment, plot diagram (AH²)
ink on board, 16 1/2 x 30 in.
fig. 12
d. Perspective rendering of housing units (AH³)
gouache over pencil on board, 18 7/16 x 29 7/8 in.
pl. IV
e. Foundation plan, first-floor plan, second-floor plan, roof plan (RH³)
ink and Conté crayon and pencil on board, 12 9/16 x 29 1/2 in.
fig. 13
f. Perspective (RH³)
Conté crayon and ink on board, 18 1/2 x 26 1/2 in.
fig. 14

10. Apartment for Edith and Jack Straus, 1111 Park Avenue, New York, 1932
Interior
photograph, 9 1/2 x 11 1/2 in.
fig. 8

11. Apartment House (?), possibly part of the Community Service Homes, 1932
Perspective rendering, labeled "Shelter–Salvation Army"
black crayon on illustration board, 13 1/2 x 20 1/2 in.
fig. 15

12. Movie Sets, 1932
a. Interior perspective
Conté crayon and graphite pencil on board, 20 x 15 in.
b. Interior perspective
Conté crayon and graphite pencil on board, 20 x 15 in.

13. Moscow Philharmonic Concert Hall and Hotel, 1932
exterior perspective
Conté crayon on board, 22 x 29 7/8 in.
fig. 16

14. "Week-end" Aluminum Beach House, Montauk, Long Island, 1932
photograph of model with text mounted on Fomecor, 15 1/2 x 10 7/8 in.

15. Florida Tropical Home, Century of Progress International Exposition, Chicago, 1933
a. Chair, metal frame and back painted white, with leather seat
photograph, 7 1/2 x 5 3/8 in.
fig. 29
b. Chair, chrome frame with leather cushions
photograph, 6 x 7 1/8 in.
fig. 30
c. Chaise longue
photograph, 7 1/2 x 9 1/2 in.
fig. 28
d. Interior
photograph, 9 1/2 x 7 1/2 in.
fig. 31
e. Rear façade
photograph, 7 3/8 x 9 1/2 in.
fig. 27
f. Promotional brochure, 11 x 8 1/2 in.

16. A Plan for Double-Decking 5th Avenue from 34th to 59th Street, New York, 1938
a. Perspective at corner 33rd Street and Fifth Avenue, plan at 34th Street: entrance and typical transverse section
ink on board, 20 x 30 in.
b. Plan at Fifth Avenue, promenade level
ink on board, 20 x 36 1/2 in.
c. Perspective at Saint Patrick's
ink on board, 20 x 30 in.

17. Smithsonian Gallery of Art, Washington (competition), 1939
a. Floor plan
ink on paper (computer-generated drawing by Brian Loughlin), 11 x 17 in.
fig. 10
b. Elevation
ink on paper (computer-generated drawing by Brian Loughlin), 11 x 17 in.
fig. 9

18. Riverview Community Housing Development Proposal, Long Island City, 1944–46

a. Perspective rendering
ink on board, 15 x 20 in.
fig. 39
b. Model
photograph, 7 x 9 1/2 in.
fig. 40

19. Welfare Island Service Buildings, New York, 1944–46

a. Perspective drawing
photograph, 5 1/2 x 9 3/8 in.
b. View from Manhattan
photograph, 7 3/8 x 9 1/2 in.
fig. 161
c. View toward laundry building from the street
photograph, 6 7/16 x 9 1/2 in.

20. Temple Beth El, Providence, 1948–55

a. Exterior perspective: entrance
pencil and Conté crayon on board, 17 1/2 x 23 in.
fig. 72
b. Exterior perspective
pencil and Conté crayon on board, 22 x 30 in.
fig. 70
c. Elevations
pencil on tracing paper, 30 1/2 x 54 1/2 in.
fig. 71
d. Longitudinal and transverse sections
pencil on vellum, 30 3/8 x 54 1/2 in.
e. Interior perspective
crayon, pencil, Conté crayon, and gouache on board, 20 x 24 1/8 in.
pl. X
f. Entrance
photograph, 8 x 10 in.
fig. 73
g. View from street
photograph, 8 x 10 in.
h. Chapel with domed roof
photograph, 7 1/2 x 9 3/8 in.
fig. 74
i. Sanctuary
photograph, 8 x 10 in.
fig. 75
j. Lobby looking toward sanctuary
photograph, 7 3/8 x 9 3/8 in.
fig. 76

21. Rothschild Residence, Baltimore, 1948–50

a. Living room looking toward backyard
photograph, 7 1/2 x 9 1/2 in.
fig. 172
b. Living room with fireplace
photograph, 7 1/2 x 9 1/2 in.
fig. 171
c. Exterior view
photograph, 7 5/8 x 9 1/2 in.
fig. 170

22. American Memorial to Six Million Jews of Europe (competition), 1949

a. Site from above
photograph, 8 x 10 in.
fig. 44
b. Site looking toward Riverside Drive
photograph, 8 x 10 in.
fig. 45
c. Shadowed plan
Conté crayon and pencil on tracing paper, 19 1/8 x 33 1/2 in.
fig. 42
d. Main memorial wall, north side: elevation
pencil on tracing paper, 15 1/2 x 41 1/2 in.
fig. 43

23. Congregation B'nai Israel, Millburn, NJ, 1949–51

a. Sketch by Robert Motherwell for lobby mural
gouache on paper, mounted on board, 11 x 22 in.
courtesy Joel Goodman and Rachel Goodman
pl. XII
b. Lobby, with mural by Robert Motherwell
photograph, 8 x 10 in.
fig. 56
c. Exterior perspective
photograph, 7 1/2 x 9 1/2 in.
fig. 57
d. Sanctuary
photograph, 10 x 8 in.
fig. 69
e. Children gathered at the ark
color photograph, 9 1/2 x 7 1/2 in.
pl. XIII

24. Temple Beth El, Springfield, MA, 1950–53, 1965–66

a. Main Floor Plan, 1952
pencil on tracing paper, 23 1/2 x 48 1/2 in.
b. Exterior elevations, 1952
pencil on tracing paper, 24 1/2 X 48 1/2 in.
c. View from street, 1953
photograph, 7 1/2 x 9 1/2 in.
d. Main sanctuary, 1953
photograph, 8 x 10 in.
fig. 85
e. View from sanctuary into social hall, 1953
photograph, 7 1/2 x 7 1/2 in.
fig. 54
f. Front façade with Ibram Lassaw sculpture *Pillar of Fire*, at night, 1953
photograph, 7 1/2 x 7 3/8 in.
fig. 86
g. Eternal light by Ibram Lassaw
photograph, 5 x 7 in.
fig. 87
h. Tapestry panels by Adolph Gottlieb, 1953
photograph, 5 1/2 x 9 1/2 in.
fig. 89
i. Ark rug in chapel by Robert Motherwell, 1953
photograph, 9 5/8 x 7 5/8 in.
fig. 88
j. Ground floor plan south (rebuilt after fire) 1966
pencil on tracing paper, 30 x 48 1/2 in.

k. Plan of synagogue complex: main floor, 1966
ink on vellum, 36 x 58 1/2 in.
l. Elevations and sections, 1966
pencil on tracing paper, 30 x 42 in.
m. Sanctuary and bema, 1966
photograph, 8 x 10 in.
fig. 92
n. View down center aisle of main sanctuary, 1966
photograph, 8 x 10 in.
fig. 91
o. Front façade (west elevation) with Ibram Lassaw sculpture, 1966
photograph, 7 1/2 x 9 1/2 in.
fig. 90

25. Congregation Sha'arey Zedek, Detroit (Southfield), 1956–63

a. Exterior perspective
pencil on tracing paper, 21 x 31 1/2 in.
b. Main hall sections and elevations
pencil on vellum, 30 x 42 in.
c. Wood ark design, sanctuary interior
pencil and Conté crayon, colored pencil, and colored marker on tracing paper, 16 1/2 x 12 in.
d. Main floor plan
pencil and colored pencil on tracing paper, 36 x 53 in.
fig. 103
e. Plan of main floor of sanctuary showing holiday and regular seating
pencil on tracing paper, 30 x 41 7/8 in.
fig. 106
f. Chapel: exterior perspective
pencil on tracing paper, 21 x 31 1/2 in.
g. Exterior view of sanctuary
photograph, 8 x 9 5/8 in.
fig. 102
h. Early study model
photograph, 8 x 9 5/8 in.
fig. 53
i. Exterior view of sanctuary: detail
photograph, 10 x 8 in.
fig. 47
j. Detail of concrete forms from the exterior
photograph, 10 x 8 in.
fig. 104
k. View of main sanctuary
photograph, 10 x 8 in.
fig. 108
l. Interior view of main sanctuary from the ark
photograph, 8 1/8 x 10 in.
fig. 107
m. View from ark toward social hall
photograph, 8 x 10 in.
n. View of ark area under construction
photograph, 8 x 10 in.
fig. 109
o. New model, by Brian Loughlin and Andrea Schroeder-Jaenecke

26. Temple Beth El, Rochester, NY, 1960–63

a. Exterior perspective, early study
pencil on tracing paper, 18 1/2 x 22 1/2 in.
fig. 116
b. Exterior perspective, early study
black ink on paper, 18 x 34 in.
c. Main sanctuary façade, early study
pencil on tracing paper, 15 x 18 1/2 in.
fig. 118
d. Plan of main floor, early study, 1960
pencil on tracing paper, 30 x 41 1/2 in.
fig. 115
e. Aerial perspective
pencil on paper, 18 1/8 x 23 in.
fig. 117
f. Elevation of sanctuary end wall
pencil on tracing paper, 16 x 29 1/2 in
fig. 119
g. Plan of bema end of sanctuary, 1961
pencil on tracing paper, 16 x 29 1/2 in.
fig. 121
i. Exterior perspective
pencil on tracing paper, 29 1/2 x 22 1/2 in.
h. View of main façade
photograph, 9 1/8 x 7 1/2 in.
fig. 112
i. Exterior perspective
photograph, 8 1/8 x 10 in.
j. Sanctuary
photograph, 8 x 10 in.
fig. 120
k. Bema and ark in main sanctuary
photograph, 10 x 8 in.
fig. 122

27. Public School 92, 222 West 134th Street, New York, 1962–66

a. Interior courtyard with mosaics
photograph, 8 x 10 in.
fig. 173
b. Exterior view
photograph, 10 x 8 in.
fig. 174

28. "Breakthrough to the Hudson," Hudson River Project, Yonkers to Peekskill, 1964

a. Sketch for a shoreline by using fill to create new parks and promenades
black ink on paper, 10 x 14 in.
b. Aerial view of Peekskill to Ansville Creek
black ink and gouache on card stock, 25 x 19 in.

29. Manhattanville-on-Hudson Proposal, New York, 1964

a. Early proposal
ink and crayon on tracing paper, 18 x 30 1/2 in.
fig. 175
b. Site plan
ink on tracing paper, 25 1/2 x 18 in.
c. Sections
ink on tracing paper, 18 x 25 in.
d. Aerial perspective
pencil on vellum, 23 1/2 x 30 1/8 in.
e. Early proposal
photograph, 8 1/2 x 10 in.
f. Model
photograph, 6 1/2 x 10 in.
fig. 176

30. Harlem River Project, 1966

a. Sedgwick site: aerial view
photostat of ink drawing, 11 x 18 in.
fig. 144
b. Bronx Market site: view along the river
ink on vellum, 13 7/8 x 21 1/2 in.
fig. 142
c. Bronx Market site: roadway
ink on card stock, 15 x 22 1/16 in.
fig. 143

31. Queensborough Community College, Bayside, New York, 1971–76

a. New buildings
pencil on vellum with press-apply lettering, 24 1/2 x 20 in.
b. Administration/Business Building
pencil on vellum with press-apply lettering, 19 x 29 1/2 in.
c. Model, 6 1/2 x 28 x 28 in.

PUBLICATIONS

32. "Notes on Community Planning"

Architectural Progress 6:2 (February 1932)
see fig. 32

33. Cover design for *Trend: An Illustrated Bimonthly of the Arts* 2:2 (March–April 1934)

pl. V

34. "Frank Lloyd Wright on Architecture"

by Paul Goodman and Percival Goodman, *Kenyon Review* (Winter 1942)
fig. 34

35. *Communitas, Means of Livelihood and Ways of Life,* with Paul Goodman

a. first edition (Chicago: University of Chicago Press, 1947), 8 5/8 x 11 1/8 in.
b. second edition, revised (New York: Vintage Books, 1960), 7 1/2 x 4 3/8 in.
c. second edition, revised (New York: Vintage Books, 1960), 7 1/2 x 4 3/8 in. (subtitle on cover *"Ways of Livelihood and Means of Life"*)
d. second edition, with preface by Paul Goldberger (New York: Columbia University Press, Morningside edition, 1990), 8 x 4 7/8 in. (subtitle on cover *"Ways of Livelihood and Means of Life"*)
e. Spanish edition: *Tres ciudades para el hombre: medios de subsistencia y formas de vida*, translated by Emilio y Jorge Colombo (Buenos Aires: Editorial Proyeccion, 1964), 7 7/8 x 5 7/8 in.
f. Japanese edition: *Komyunitasu: Risō Shakai e no Shisaku to hōhō*, translated by Fumihiko Maki and Hiroshi Matsumoto (Tokyo: Shōkokusha, 1968), 7 1/2 x 5 in.
g. Italian edition, with introduction by Carlo Doglio: *Communitas: mezzi di sostentamento e modi di vivere* (Bologna: Il Mulino, 1970), 8 1/2 x 5 1/2 in.
h. German edition, with introduction by Hartmut von Henlit: *Communitas: Lebensformen und Lebensmöglichkeiten Menschlicher Gemeinschaften* (Cologne: EHP, 1994)

36. "The New Synagogue"

Brooklyn Jewish Center Review (October 1953)
fig. 50

37. *The Double E*

(Garden City, NY: Anchor Press/Doubleday, 1977), 7 x 4 in.

PAINTINGS AND OTHER ART WORK

38. *Cat's Cradle,* 1932

Conté crayon on paper, 27 1/2 x 21 1/2 in.
Courtesy Joel Goodman and Rachel Goodman
pl. VI

39. *Men at War,* 1944

pencil, watercolor, and gouache on paper, 25 1/2 x 19 1/2 in.
Courtesy Joel Goodman and Rachel Goodman
pl. VII

40. *The Waiting Ones,* 1962

acrylic on Masonite, 22 x 30 in.

41. *Long Landscape,* circa 1970

acrylic on wood, 11 x 60 in.
Courtesy Naomi Goodman

42. *Long Landscape,* circa 1970

acrylic on plywood, 11 x 60 in.
Courtesy Naomi Goodman
pl. XV

43. *Monument to My Vice,* circa 1970

construction with Benson and Hedges cigarette boxes and acrylic paint, 30 x 10 x 5 in.
Courtesy Naomi Goodman
pl. XVII

44. *The Prison: In Memory of Piranesi,* 1974

acrylic on Masonite, 22 x 30 in.
fig. 146

45. *Monument for a Hero of a South American State (Readily Demountable),* circa 1980

watercolor on paper, 18 x 23 1/2 in

46. A Direction for Postmodern Revivalism, 1981–83

a. *A Summer Capital for the United States*
ink and wash on paper, 18 x 24 in.
Pl. XVIII
b. *Monument to the Cloaca Maxima (Rome)*
ink and wash on paper, 18 x 24 in.
c. *The Great Doric Column: Headquarters for a Greek Shipping Company*
ink and wash on paper, 18 x 24 in.
Courtesy Amos Goodman
fig. 178

d. *Looking to the Future*: conceptual sketch showing ambience in Los Angeles after the earthquake
ink and wash on paper, 18 x 24 in.
pl. XX

47. *Another Painting Himself* (on a sonnet by Richard Elman)
Styrofoam construction, 13 1/2 x 15 x 14 in.
Courtesy Naomi Goodman

48. *Bronze-Colored Face*
plastic container with spray paint, 8 1/2 x 6 1/2 x 3 1/2 in.
Courtesy Naomi Goodman

49. "Jade and gold" pendant
melted plastic container and gold paint
Courtesy Naomi Goodman

50. *Mother and Child*
plaster, 13 x 5 x 5 in.
Courtesy Naomi Goodman
fig. 163

51. Pair of untitled constructions
Styrofoam and acrylic paint, 33 x 5 1/2 x 3 in.
Courtesy Naomi Goodman
pl. XVI

52. The Parthenon Project
ink drawing and poem on paper, framed together, 25 1/2 x 31 in.
Courtesy Bear Goodman

53. Untitled
acrylic on Masonite, 22 x 30 in.
Courtesy Naomi Goodman

54. Untitled (humanoid figure?)
plaster, 11 x 6 1/2 x 4 1/2 in.
Courtesy Naomi Goodman
fig. 162

55. Untitled construction
aluminum foil and spray paint, 16 1/2 x 5 1/2 x 2 1/2 in.
Courtesy Naomi Goodman
fig. 139

PERSONAL PHOTOGRAPHS

56. Goodman with a cigarette at drawing board, circa 1945
20 x 16 in.
frontispiece

57. Sidonia and Benjamin Levitan (Aunt Sadie and Uncle Ben) with Augusta Goodman, circa 1911
6 7/8 x 5 in.
Courtesy Naomi Goodman
fig. 150

58. Percival, Alice, and Arnold Goodman, 1911
5 x 7 in.
Courtesy Naomi Goodman
fig. 149

59. Percival with Uncle Benny at the Beach, 1917
5 x 3 1/2 in.
Courtesy Naomi Goodman
fig. 25

60. Naomi and Percy in front of the Parthenon, 1951
3 1/2 x 5 1/2 in.
Courtesy Naomi Goodman
fig. 166

61. Portrait in honor of Paris Prize victory, 1925
10 x 8 in.
fig. 26

62. Goodman with his partner, Franklin Whitman and Whitman's wife in Paris, late 1920s
10 x 8
fig. 155

63. Goodman with portrait of himself by Alexander Calder, circa 1940
15 7/8 x 10 in.
fig. 156

64. Paul and Percival Goodman, circa 1960
10 x 8 in.
fig. 24

65. Portrait, taken by his son Joel Goodman, East Hampton, Long Island, 1974
10 x 8 in.
Courtesy Naomi Goodman
fig. 177

WORKS BY OTHERS

66. *Seated Woman* by Alexander Calder
(done for top of column in the interior of Jay-Thorpe, a women's specialty store redesigned by Whitman and Goodman)
Wood sculpture, 15 x 18 1/2 x 10 in.

67. Portrait of Percival Goodman by Franklin Whitman, circa 1925
Brown pencil on paper, 13 x 9 in.

Photograph and other credits

All photographs are courtesy Avery Architectural and Fine Arts Library, Columbia University, unless otherwise noted; when known, photographers are indicated. Arabic numerals refer to figures, roman numerals to color plates.

Architectural Forum: 55
Architectural Progress: 32
Associated News Photographic Service, Inc.: 156
Brooklyn Jewish Center Review: 50
Cosmopolitan Studios, NY: 6
Emelie Danielson: 2–3
Alexandre Georges: 51–52, 54, 68, 73–75, 84b, 86, 123–124, 140, 169–172, XIV
Joel Goodman: 177
Courtesy Naomi Goodman: 25, 149–150, 166, 177
Paul L. and Sally L. Gordon: 112–114
Shorwin Greenberg Studio: 110–111
Jewish Publication Society (*Synagogue Architecture in the United States*): 49
Kenyon Review: 34
Kootz Gallery: 88–89
Baltazar Korab: 47, 105, 108
Nathaniel Lieberman and Todd Watts: 90–92
Martin Linsey: 79, 81–82
Norman McGrath: 173–174
Courtesy Metropolitan Museum of Art: 153
New Republic: 38
Arnold Newman: 180
Photo Arts: 100
Dwight Primiano: 137–139, 146, 162–163, 178, VI–VII, XVI–XX
Ruth Standinger Schaffner: frontispiece, 24
Courtesy Taylor Stoehr: 25, 149–150

Set in Frutiger Sans type

Printed by The Studley Press, Dalton, Massachusetts

Designed by Jerry Kelly